Life Is Yours to Win

LESSONS FORGED *from the* PURPOSE, PASSION, *and* MAGIC *of* BASEBALL

━━━━━━━━━━━━■━━━━━━━━━━━━

AUGIE GARRIDO

INTRODUCTION BY KEVIN COSTNER

A TOUCHSTONE BOOK
Published by Simon & Schuster
New York London Toronto Sydney

Touchstone
A Division of Simon & Schuster, Inc.
1230 Avenue of the Americas
New York, NY 10020

First Touchstone hardcover edition May 2011

TOUCHSTONE and colophon are registered trademarks
of Simon & Schuster, Inc.

For information about special discounts for bulk purchases, please contact Simon & Schuster Special Sales at 1-866-506-1949 or business@simonandschuster.com.

The Simon & Schuster Speakers Bureau can bring authors to your live event. For more information or to book an event contact the Simon & Schuster Speakers Bureau at 1-866-248-3049 or visit our website at www.simonspeakers.com.

Designed by Joy O'Meara

Manufactured in the United States of America

10   9   8   7   6   5   4   3   2   1

Library of Congress Cataloging-in-Publication Data

Garrido, Augie.
Life is yours to win : lessons forged from the purpose, passion, and magic of
baseball / by Augie Garrido ; introduction by Kevin Costner
p. cm
"A Touchstone Book."
1. Garrido, Augie. 2. Baseball coaches—United States—Biography.
3. Baseball—Anecdotes. 4. Conduct of life. I. Title.
GV865.G32 2011
796.357092—dc22
[B]
2010050145
ISBN 978-1-4391-8693-0
ISBN 978-1-4391-8695-4 (ebook)

This book is dedicated to all of the teachers and coaches who impart upon their students not just the facts they need to know, but the principles and values they need to thrive in a challenging environment. Your work changes lives and creates a better world. I know for certain you've changed my life and you've bettered my world. Bless your hearts.

Finally, I dedicate this book also to Jeannie Grass, my beloved, without whom there would be no stories worth telling.

Contents

Introduction *by Kevin Costner*   ix

CHAPTER ONE: For Love of the Game   1

CHAPTER TWO: A Chickenshit, Dooflopper, and Curb Cryer   14

CHAPTER THREE: The Fearless Field   40

CHAPTER FOUR: The Game of Failure   89

CHAPTER FIVE: Be a Player, Not a Prospect   114

CHAPTER SIX: Small Ball/Big Game   131

CHAPTER SEVEN: Step Up, Superman   149

CHAPTER EIGHT: The Tao of Teamwork   169

CHAPTER NINE: The Reward Is Not on the Scoreboard   198

CHAPTER TEN: Five Things I Think I Know about Baseball   221

CHAPTER ELEVEN: Be Your Own Best Friend   247

Introduction

by Kevin Costner

I was invited back to my alma mater, California State University at Fullerton, in 1992 to help dedicate the school's new baseball stadium. I didn't play baseball in college, but by that time I'd made a couple of movies, *Bull Durham* and *Field of Dreams,* in which I apparently faked it pretty well.

I did learn a great deal about baseball and life at Cal State Fullerton. Most of it from one man in particular. I saw the invitation to the stadium dedication as an opportunity not only to thank that man but to introduce myself to him. You see, even though he had a big impact on my life, we'd never met.

Augie Garrido was the baseball coach at Fullerton while I was there, but he wasn't my coach. I was a short, skinny guy who couldn't make the team. Still, Coach Garrido was a source of enlightenment and inspiration for me in my college days. I can honestly say that he inspired me to do much more with my life than anyone else, including me, had thought possible.

My response to the university president when he invited me to the CSUF stadium dedication was this: "I'll come if you'll give me thirty minutes alone with Augie Garrido."

I'm told that my request threw the president and other school administrators for something of a loop. They agreed to my terms, but then they went to Augie and demanded to know why Kevin Costner wanted to meet with him—of all people.

Augie, bless him, was dumbfounded by the whole deal.

"I don't know Kevin Costner. I've never met the guy. I have no idea why he would want to talk to me," he said.

He was telling it straight, as always. Augie did not know me then. But I knew him, and that is where this story and this book begin. It is the story of one man's ability to positively influence the lives of others. Even people he does not know.

Initially, I went to baseball games at Fullerton because the best athlete from my high school, Jim Irvin, was on the team. After the first few games, I kept going so I could listen to his coach, Augie Garrido.

Thirty years later, I'm still listening to Augie. I still seek him out for advice, inspiration, insights, and camaraderie. Coach Garrido created a dramatic turnaround for the baseball team at Fullerton in my years there. He did the same thing for me. Augie simply changed my life.

Cal State Fullerton was not a glamour school like UCLA or USC. It offered an education for kids from working-class families like mine. We didn't have many resources and neither did the school.

Augie was hired to coach a Fullerton baseball team that had only won 35 percent of its games in the previous eight years. He built it into a national powerhouse, turning blue-collar grinders—players no one else wanted—into champions. He had no scholarships to offer them. He barely had enough baseballs, bats, and uniforms to go around. There were no lights on the field and no locker rooms. The guys changed out of their street clothes in the parking lot.

The team's annual budget was $4,000 when Augie got there. They raised it to $6,000 when they moved to Division I—still the lowest budget of any team at that level. When Augie started at Fullerton, the gray felt Titan baseball uniforms were so wretched that he ordered his equipment manager to burn them. It was the only way the school would buy new uniforms.

In his second season, his team made it to the regionals but the school couldn't afford to send them, so Augie took out a second mortgage on his house to pay for the trip. Four seasons later, Fullerton won its first national championship. Under Augie's leadership, my blue-collar alma mater won three College World Series championships, beating teams from the biggest schools in the country—teams with legendary baseball programs and budgets in the millions of dollars.

Obviously, Augie is a great coach, one of those who can always figure out a way to win, but even watching from the stands as a college kid, I could tell there was something more unusual about him. He didn't just coach baseball. He taught his players how to be better men. He was a student of the game, but even more, he studied each of his players to determine what motivated them and what they needed from him. He worked to bring out the best in each of them. He helped those young guys figure out who they were, where they were going, and how they could get there.

Most coaches have one speech. Augie has a hundred of them, and each is custom-designed to inspire his young charges; not just the stars, but every kid who needs guidance and encouragement. From my seat behind the dugout, I listened to Augie teach his players, and I learned along with them. I learned some baseball, but I picked up even more about being a man and chasing my dreams. The things Augie said resonated with me. I'd had similar thoughts but wasn't sure how to apply them. I wasn't sure if they were even realistic. I saw that Augie's players succeeded as a baseball team because of the people they became under his guidance. I came to understand that their growth and success as individuals meant more to their coach than all the trophies they took home—and Augie's teams have picked up a lot of glass and brass.

Augie has a take on that too, and it offers insight into why so many people admire and appreciate him as a mentor and role model. He says, "The real trophies in life are the relationships we have with others."

I've been friends with Augie for nearly twenty years now, and I know that he believes that and he lives it. Thanks to him, so do I. He sometimes jokes that he is "magical." By that, he is not claiming any supernatural powers. What Augie means is that pure magic is the only possible explanation for the blessings that have come to him, the humble son of migrant field and factory workers.

Those blessings include more victories than any other coach in the history of college baseball. They also include a rewarding career at the top of his field, the love of a beautiful woman and loyal family members, legions of friends, and hundreds of coaches and athletes who respect him even when his team whips up on them time after time.

I have my own theories about the source of Augie's influence and success. I think both are due to his humility, his decency, his insights into the human condition, and his genuine desire to keep growing while helping other imperfect men and women create lives that fulfill them. I trust him. He has value. Augie is clearly someone who makes a difference in this world.

Augie also is fond of saying that he has no hobbies. That's a little misleading. He is not a one-dimensional person. He is engaged in the world and he's not a bad cook either. Yet, it's true that Augie's thoughts always drift back to young men playing baseball. Neither his mind nor his spirits are ever far from his sport. That's why I had to cast him in *For Love of the Game,* which is one of my favorite films because of his presence on the set. I didn't want another actor in the role of the New York Yankees manager. I had to have Augie because he is absolutely authentic. He also is a romantic guy in the way that he loves the game; he loves the poetry of it. Yet, he understands the viciousness of the baseball gods and how cruel they can be.

Augie is always in the moment. He finds a way to reach each young man on his team. He understands their individual personalities. He loves molding them into a team with a shared goal. He revels in their accomplishments. Yet, Augie is ready to be wrong and to change when necessary. Not long ago, he tore into one of his young stars for not showing up to participate in summer workouts.

"You can't just show up," Augie chastised him. "You have to work if you want to be a ballplayer."

The kid told Augie, "I worked hard. It just wasn't at baseball. I had a job."

Augie later learned that this talented young man, who had beat out several scholarship athletes for his position, had spent the summer on a garbage-truck crew so he could afford to return for another semester.

My friend Augie saw the poetry in that revelation.

"I worked on a garbage truck once," Augie told his player. "I know how hard it is. You have my respect, so please accept my apology."

There is another thing I admire in Augie. Like many men, he had a loving but sometimes complex relationship with his father. Yet, Augie wisely notes that as we grow into imperfect men ourselves, we appreciate our fathers even more because we better understand them and the challenges they faced.

In reading this book, you may come up with your own theories about what makes Augie Garrido tick and why so many people credit him as a positive influence. I'm willing to bet that you will learn a little about yourself too, and after turning the final page, you will share my gratitude for the opportunity to have met him and learned from him.

It's been said that several of my movies, particularly *Field of Dreams*, inspired and touched audiences because they explored father-son relationships and the male perspective. I think this book will touch people in much the same way. I've learned a lot from Augie just talking with him late into the night. I feel blessed to have him in my life, and I am sure you will feel the same way.

Life Is Yours to Win

CHAPTER ONE

For Love of the Game

My favorite thing to do as a boy was to open the living room window on summer days and place our round-top Philco radio on the sill so in the driveway outside I could hear the New York Yankees broadcast. Then, as I took my position on the concrete drive, baseball mitt in one hand and a tennis ball in the other, my imagination carried me to center field at Yankee Stadium.

The Yanks' radio broadcast provided the sound track to my driveway fantasy games, and the music of baseball is what I've danced to ever since. Nearly all my blessed life, I've tried to hang on to the joy of that kid caught up in his game; losing track of time and place, bouncing that tennis ball off the stucco wall for hour upon hour.

Pitch by pitch. Hit by hit. Out by out. Inning by inning. That's how I first played baseball as a boy, and it is how I coach it today; staying in the moment, focusing on the fundamentals, letting the score take care of itself.

For most of my seven decades, baseball has been at the center of my life. This game both beautiful and cruel has taken me all over this world and even into the alternative universe of the movies, strange as that may be. Baseball is so much a part of my life, I joke that my heartbeat sounds like a ball smacking a glove. I have no doubt my obituary will read like a box score, tallied up in wins and losses—not to mention strikeouts, foul balls, and errors in the field.

They'll want to bury me in a baseball uniform, and there will be plenty to choose from given all the teams I've played for and coached. As a player I've worn the colors of Leo's Louisiana Laundry, the Benicia Mud Hens, the New Pisa Restaurant, the Fresno State Bulldogs, the Alamance Indians, the Portland Beavers, and the Humboldt Crabs to name just a few. As a coach, I've suited up with Sierra High School Chieftans (1966–69), the San Francisco State University Gators (1969), the California Polytechnic State University Mustangs (1970–72), the Cal State Fullerton University Titans (1973–87/1991–96), the University of Illinois Fighting Illini (1988–90), and the University of Texas Longhorns (1996–present).

My love of the game began on those solitary afternoons I spent lost to the world in the driveway of our apartment building in Vallejo, California. Federal Terrace, our public housing project, was built in 1939, the same year I was born. World War II drove a boom period for Vallejo. The working-class town's population tripled from thirty thousand to ninety thousand in my first five years as wave after wave of eager workers, many of them poor immigrants like my father's family, rushed in to grab coveted government jobs in the massive Mare Island Shipyards nearby.

Vallejo and central California were far removed from Yankee Stadium in the Bronx, but the Bronx Bombers were my favorite major-league team because of Joe DiMaggio, the Yankee Clipper, out of San Francisco. My dad, an absolute fanatic about baseball in particular and sports in general, often drove up to see the San Francisco Seals minor-league games before I was born. He became a devoted fan of Joe DiMaggio and his older brother Vince when they were with the Seals early in their careers. My dad was a DiMaggio guy and a Yankees guy for the rest of his life. I inherited his player and team as well as his competitive drive.

GOLDEN GAME

Joe DiMaggio's 56-game hitting streak with the Yankees was my father's favorite topic of conversation, and I welcomed it because his second and third favorite topics were my shortcomings and screwups. Dad, who often practiced tough love to the extreme, finally took me to see our shared baseball idol in 1948, late in DiMaggio's career.

The Yankees were playing their own Triple A team, the Oakland Oaks in Emeryville. This rare trip to a game featuring big leaguers was one of those magical days, a peaceful interlude in our father-son wars. That he bought me a ticket was itself a big deal. Most games, my father treated me like a third wheel. If he had two tickets, he'd take a friend. I was allowed to tag along, but only with the understanding that if I wanted to see the game, I'd have to sneak in on my own.

I rose to the challenge and became an expert gate-crasher. In those days they didn't have turnstiles or heavy security so it wasn't all that difficult. I'd bide my time near a gate, wait for a group of preferably large and distracted adults to come along, and then I'd just squeeze my scrawny body into a forest of thick thighs and steal a seat.

On the rare occasion when I was caught and thrown out, I'd earnestly apologize and immediately head to another gate to await another opportunity for a stealth entrance. One way or another I'd make it. Gate-crashing became part of the sport for me, sort of a pregame warm-up.

Somewhere, though, I still have a ticket stub to the New York Yankees and Oakland Oaks game my dad took me to. It's golden in my memory and well regarded in history too because Joe DiMaggio wasn't the only Yankee legend present. Two other men destined to follow him in Yanks lore were there, but they were in the Oaks dugout that day. By the start of the very next season, Casey Stengel would be the Yankees manager, but for this game in 1948, he was leading an Oaks team nicknamed the Nine Old Men because so many of the players were aging veterans down from the majors. The second baseman was an exception, a fresh-faced rookie by the name of Billy "the Kid" Martin, who also became a Yankee manager and something of a legend himself.

I can still recall every moment of that game with the clarity of a kid experiencing rapture. The sights, the sounds, the smells, I was a boy walking among the gods in pinstripes. I felt a sense of belonging because I'd been Joe DiMaggio in the driveway hundreds of times by then. I'd embraced my father's sport and his hero as my own.

THE GAME PLAN

Baseball has been fairly beaten to death as a metaphor for life so I'll try not to add to the carnage. Still, I'll share a few lessons if you don't mind, most of them gleaned from my sport and my life in it. It's not that I want to impress you with my wisdom. There is no false modesty in play when I say I'm still living on a learner's permit. There is substantial evidence to support that claim, including a well-publicized stay in the Travis County jail a couple years back. More on that later.

After many years of working on my mental game, observing my college players, and doing what I can to guide them to their destinies not only as athletes but as men, I am compelled to share some thoughts on baseball, character, and life. I hope you will find it of value. I've come to consider myself a teacher because first and foremost that is what a good coach is. I try to coach the person as well as the player by helping young men see the lessons offered within the game.

Those lessons are many, but probably the greatest thing the game teaches you is how to deal with adversity and distracting emotions while continuing to pursue your goals and dreams.

When I first started coaching, I'd begin each season laying down the law. I had a long list of rules about hair length, facial hair, how to wear your uniform—all these regulations. I don't do that anymore. Now, in my first team meeting each season I have just a simple set of four rules.

No. 1: Do what's right.

No. 2: Do your best.

Then I tell our players that they don't know what their best is—yet. I tell them they have potential that has not yet been tapped and that unleashing that potential will be an ongoing process.

"We will strive for perfection, but you will fail. It takes courage to keep striving after you fail," I tell them.

Then I give them rule No. 3: When you fail, recognize the message that's in that failure and be motivated to get better. And then to do your best again and again until you find the solution.

The final rule I give them, No. 4, is this: If you've followed the first three rules, then you've accomplished something of value so give yourself credit for that. Treat yourself like you would your best friend, and give your best to your team.

These four rules are the tools I give our young guys to help them deal with the challenges of the game, but they apply to life too. Whenever fear strikes, and it always does, the emotion takes you out of the moment and into your own head. Whether you are hitting or pitching, it throws you off and destroys your focus on the task at hand. Then fear takes you even further out of the moment and away from your mission, whether it's in the batter's box or on the mound. The typical reaction is to realize something is wrong and to try to "fix" it, which usually results in trying harder, and when you do that, you keep failing. The cycle continues and the spiral is downward. The baseball player caught up in that spiral kicks the dirt, throws his bat down, and stomps it. The golfer in the same mode throws his club in the pond.

Players break the downward spiral only when they quit trying and return to playing. I think that's why baseball is important. It creates these challenges and lets us fail. It's a cruel game in the same way that life can be cruel. To love baseball is to have it break your heart time and again. But if you take the right approach and understand that there are ways to manage your emotions and to move past failure, you become a different person, a better person. If you learn that self-mastery on the baseball field, then the game is more than a game; it's an educational tool, a force for positive change. That's why I think baseball's important. It provides opportunity to learn valuable life skills and to better yourself.

I asked Kevin Costner to write the introduction to this book not because he is a celebrity but because he was the first person to tell me that my coaching and teaching had value beyond baseball. He also helped me understand the far-reaching power of a teacher, coach, parent, or any authority figure who is truly invested in the success of those around him.

Kevin described for you the lessons he drew from my coaching and my relationship with the players at Fullerton, even from his seat in the stands. As he noted, I had no idea he was listening, or that he was even there. Of course at the time he was just a student, another young guy struggling to figure it all out.

This book will offer chapters that impart some of those same lessons Kevin picked up on, hopefully to inspire or help you wherever you are right now to find your purpose, whether on the field or in the stands, parent or child, teacher or coach. The chapters look at the importance of:

- Finding your purpose and pursuing it with passion
- Recognizing your fears and managing them
- Learning from failures and moving forward
- Committing to mastery of the skills you need to succeed
- Sacrificing and doing whatever it takes to achieve realistic goals

- Creating and seizing opportunities and acting upon them
- Being a team player willing to play whatever role is needed
- Enjoying the spiritual rewards of each moment and each day
- Being as good a friend to yourself as you are to others

MENTAL MASTERY

When everyone on the field has superior athletic ability, knowledge of a game's strategy, and mastery of its skills, success is usually claimed by those in command over the mental aspects of baseball. The mental skills of the game are essential, and they are applicable to most other pursuits in business and in life. At times in baseball, for example, you simply step up to the plate and swing away, but perhaps even more often you dig into the batter's box and work the pitcher and the game itself. Fans cheer the home runs, the no-hitters, and spectacular fielding, but serious students and teachers of the game know that the elements of "small ball," such as getting ahead on the count, taking a walk, sacrifice bunting, making productive outs, and choosing the proper pitch for the proper moment, are every bit as critical in a season.

Those baseball and life skills also will be a focus of this book. Those aspects examined will include:

- Staying in the moment by clearing the mind of past failures and future rewards
- Filtering out distractions
- Breaking down the game to the basics of throw and catch and hit
- Taking what the game gives you
- The undeniable importance of winning
- The undeniable importance of losing
- Putting yourself in position to score
- Striving for quality at bats and productive outs

- Building and keeping momentum
- Approaching each inning as a game in itself
- Being aware of your role within the team
- Always expanding your boundaries and living without limitations

PLAYING WITH CHARACTER

Character is yet another vital aspect of sports and life. I am far more interested in how a young man responds to pressure or disappointment than I am in how far he can hit a fastball. I coach for character. Few things thrill me as much as watching a young man step up and discover something about himself that will stay with him and serve him for a lifetime.

I've had to work on the development of character throughout my life. I've had many good teachers who tried to get through to me. Few of them struck a spark in my younger years because I was a hardheaded kid who didn't care a lot about learning. As I grew older, it hit me that I soaked up more of their lessons and kindnesses than I realized. After the Texas Longhorns baseball team won the national championship series in 2002, I received a handwritten note in graceful cursive writing from a ninety-two-year-old woman who had been my kindergarten teacher in Vallejo.

"I think you might be the same Augie Garrido I had in kindergarten," she wrote. "I taught my students to be trustworthy, to study hard, and to have good character and good manners. Somewhere along the line, you must have gotten that."

Yes, I hope somewhere along the line those principles did sink in. I certainly learned to be grateful to caring teachers who never gave up on their students, not even after more than fifty years. Now, my staff and I have the opportunity to be a positive influence. It's not just about baseball, it's about life. The mental game is the same. Emotional intelligence is just as important in one realm as the other.

I want our players to have the critical ability to self-correct and to always be aware of what is most valuable to them. Is it a bat or a ball or a glove or the ability to use those things? No. It's our minds and the ability to use them. My job is to help our players find balance in their lives. By teaching them the fundamentals of baseball and seeing that they receive an education that includes life skills, I am helping them help themselves seek and fulfill their destinies. I want them to become whom they are meant to be.

I don't have heroes like Joe DiMaggio any longer. My heroes walk around my locker room and in and out, and back into my life. It's interesting because my former players usually come back to me in more reflective moods after they've earned degrees or become parents and taken on family responsibilities. That's when they often begin to see how the lessons of baseball apply to the real world. Many of them have become major leaguers, professional ballplayers with astounding salaries, but most have become fine men, good husbands, caring fathers, and productive citizens; and of that I am most proud.

Jeremy Carr is among the former players I've coached who say they apply lessons learned in baseball to their daily lives. Now thirty-nine and the owner of a $10 million medical supplies business in San Antonio, Jeremy was a five-foot-nine-inch speedster who came to Cal State Fullerton out of junior college. He was not drafted out of high school or junior college but proved himself invaluable to our 1992 and 1993 seasons at Fullerton. He was a scrappy, hard-nosed ballplayer totally committed to everything he did. His determined spirit inspired his teammates. Jeremy was one of the important spirits of the team.

To give you an idea of just how determined he was, Jeremy was one of the top ten base stealers in Fullerton history, and he did it on chronically bad knees that caused him almost constant pain. He could hit too. In his junior year, I had him batting third in the lineup with Phil Nevin at cleanup because I knew Jeremy would get on base and Phil would bring him home.

Jeremy lived and breathed baseball and desperately wanted to be drafted by a major-league team. That expectation weighed heavily on him at the start of his senior year and it showed. He struggled at the plate and in the field. He was striking out three times in a game, and that just wasn't like him at all. He had always made good contact before.

I pulled him aside one day and told him that he needed to get out of his own head, clear his mind of all expectations about the major leagues and just play the game he was capable of playing. I told him that he didn't need to "try," all he had to do was play because he was one of the most talented hitters on the team. I told him to trust himself and take it pitch by pitch and let the ball show him what to do.

"You will do just fine. This team needs you, so just go out there and do your best because I'm telling you that your best is better than most of the guys out there day in and day out."

Jeremy took that to heart and played so well that he was drafted at the end of the season by the Kansas City Royals. He played seven years in their minor-league system, and I have no doubt that he would have made it to the major leagues if his knees hadn't given out on him. He had more than 50 stolen bases in one minor-league season, but he needed four operations to keep his knees working.

At thirty, he left baseball with no business experience and no job prospects. One of his former teammates, Jason Moler, helped him find an entry level position in the health care field, and as he always had on the baseball diamond, Jeremy took that opportunity and ran with it. Today, Jeremy has about a hundred employees working at his medical supply company.

"Everyday I preach the same things to my business team that

Coach Garrido told our baseball team," he says. "I tell them to do their best every day to move the business forward, just like Augie telling us to take productive at bats and to win the game inning by inning. I also catch myself telling my employees to stay focused and concentrate on the little things because if we do them right, they will bring us the big scores eventually.

"When we were in the College World Series in 1992 and headed into the final game, Coach Garrido told us, 'Don't hold anything back. Leave everything you have on that field. If you give everything you have and you still come up short, at least you won't have any regrets. This time will go by faster than you can imagine, and when you look back, you don't want to have regrets.'

"I still get chills when I think about that speech, and those words are part of my life and part of what I try to teach my employees and also my kids," Jeremy says. "I'll be telling my son to stay focused and to stay with the process and not to worry about the outcome and I'll think, 'Jeez, I got that from Augie too.'"

Jeremy says that although he is a business owner, he follows my coaching model and thinks of himself as "a teacher and the person who empowers his team so they can go out and be their best."

When I decided to become a baseball coach, I didn't even ask how much it paid or whether there was job security. I just went for it because I loved baseball. After doing it for a while, I still loved the job but I realized it wasn't so much the game I loved as the people in it, the quality of the relationships and the experience of helping young people such as Jeremy Carr figure out who they are and what they are capable of doing.

The real reward for me is to hear our former players say they've benefited from our experiences together—that they learned something that can be of value to their lives. Teaching is the profession that I most respect because if it were not for my best teachers and my best coaches . . . well, I might have had more than one fleeting experience as a county jail inmate. My goal in writing this book is the same as my goal as a teacher-coach, and it is rooted in many lessons I learned the hard way. I had some issues to overcome due to a loving father who lacked parenting skills. I realized not long ago that I've spent most of my life trying to become the man I wanted my father to be and the hard-nosed but caring coach I'd always yearned to have on my team.

> [Augie] taught you the right way to play the game. He's changed a ton. I think he has more patience now, is more caring for the players. Back then, it was a tough love.
>
> TIM WALLACH
> *Cal State Fullerton*
> *Montreal Expos*
> *L.A. Dodgers Triple A manager*

If I've learned nothing else, it is that you must demonstrate that you care about young people before they will begin to care about what you say to them. You can only be the teacher when the student is ready to learn. I want each of them to succeed as human beings, with my help or in spite of it. However, don't get the impression that I coddle our players. They'll tell you that I am not always a warm and fuzzy guy in the dugout or in the locker room. I'll always find a way to break through any resistance to my "gentle encouragement," and it's usually not a pleasant experience for the obstinate or the defiant. I'm determined to make a difference in their lives.

Coaching isn't a hobby for me and it's more than a profession. It's who I am. I coach baseball to its core because it is in my core. I coach every minute motion, every angle of the field, and every aspect of the game: the physical, the mental, and the spiritual. I've been successful beyond any dream I ever dared to conjure. The only thing that carried me from 210 Benson Avenue in the public housing projects of Vallejo to the grand life I've experienced is my passion for doing what I do and my desire to be the best at whatever I am engaged in. That's my story and I'm sticking to it.

Given my humble background, I feel there is something magical in my success, something beyond my skill as a teacher and my knowledge of the sport. I do not claim responsibility for that magic, nor do I claim to know how it works. It just works. That said, I'll try not to take myself too seriously in this book. I'll keep in mind the words of my mother, who considered it her duty to keep me humble.

Years ago after I'd signed a five-year professional baseball contract for more money than my parents had ever seen, I came home over the Christmas holiday for a visit. Family and friends were there, and though many of them were older and wiser, I was feeling full of myself. I was making very good money for the first time in my life. I had a college degree and I'd been through boot camp and military service. So, of course, I knew all there was to know and I was eager to share my wisdom with all those assembled.

After listening to her cocky young son carry on for a half hour or so, my mother offered this observation from her West Texas font of true wisdom:

"Boy, you know that philosophy you got going on there? There's a mighty fine line between that philosophy and bullshit."

CHAPTER TWO

---◼---

A Chickenshit, Dooflopper,
and Curb Cryer

Somewhere on this book's jacket there is a description of me as
the "winningest baseball coach in the history of Division I athletics." You can read that as "luckiest baseball coach in the history
of Division I athletics," and you won't receive any argument from
my late mother, or me. The assistant coaches and young athletes
I've coached have compiled the wins and losses and five College
World Series championships credited to my account. I prefer to
keep score according to their performance as men both on the field
and long after they've left it.

I credit my father with motivating me to become a pretty
good ballplayer and a successful coach. I resented his controlling
my life as a boy, but in the end I am who I am because of him,
and I take full responsibility for my choices after I became independent. A big part of deciding what we want to be is realizing
what we want to avoid becoming. My dad gave me that, and he
gave me the gift of baseball, the sport that has defined my life.
We have choices, and in the end we are responsible for who we
become.

Kevin Costner's baseball movie *Field of Dreams* ends with a father and a son playing catch, and it's the rare man who doesn't get

a lump in his throat or a tear in his eye at that moment. The movie captures the spirituality of baseball and the connections forged by those playing the game together. For me, the spiritual element is the shared experience and the bond of picking each other up, working together, wanting each other to succeed.

Over a career, it can't be just about winning because you can't possibly win every time. The important thing is that you do your best, learn from failures, and strive to be better and to be a true friend to your teammates and, most of all, to yourself.

> Sometimes when you set goals and get result-oriented and you don't attain those goals, you feel like a failure. Augie always talked about setting attainable goals, not hitting .400 in college but taking every at bat like your last or playing every game like your last. Give it everything you have, and if you fall short, that's okay as long as you left it all on the field. I love that philosophy. It teaches you to give 100 percent in everything you do, and win or lose, you will feel good about yourself.
>
> MARK KOTSAY
> *Cal State Fullerton*
> *Chicago White Sox*

TAKING MEASURE

This book is steeped in baseball because that's my expertise; it's where I hang my hat. But ultimately I'm writing about relationships, how we should treat each other, what we should expect of ourselves. I know young men. I take their measure every day. I study them on the practice field, in the dugout, at bat, in the field, and on campus. I am always assessing our players, probing their minds, reading their body language, deciphering their wisecracks and comments, calculating their motivations. I'm a coach. That's what I do.

My biggest challenge with student-athletes coming out of high school or junior college has been to release fear's hold on them. Sometimes they aren't aware of it. Often, they won't acknowledge the source. My job is to free them of that burden and to show them better, healthier sources of motivation. If fear is a problem for you, I'll offer that same guidance to you in these pages.

I want my players and you the reader to understand that while it is possible to achieve considerable outward success with fear as a driving force, that particular driver will eventually bring most people to their knees—as it once did me. Fulfillment and happiness come only when you are pursuing your passion and are totally engaged because of your love of the game, whatever your game might be.

MAN UNDER CONSTRUCTION

I found success in coaching not right away but quickly enough. From the outside it probably looked as if I were having a ball. Yet, on the inside, I was cowering and miserable, and eventually my emotional fragility was revealed in the volatility of my relationships. Eventually the lights came on and it hit me that just maybe the problem wasn't *them*, it was me. So, I undertook a journey through therapy, religion, and introspection to fix me as best I could. Through trial and error, and more error, I learned how to hold up my end of a stable relationship. Jeannie, who has been with me for more than nineteen years, may have her own opinions on just how successful I've been. One thing is certain: Her sainthood is assured.

The first part of my life I didn't know how to overcome my fear. I didn't know I had a choice. In this, the second part of my life, I am running toward what I love. That's a key coaching point, one good for a lifetime. When you are driven by fear, you may win but you have no peace. When you pursue your passions, you find fulfillment in every moment, every day, every swing of the bat, every pitch thrown.

Once I stepped onto a fearless field, I realized that life is about having the courage to act on your ideas, to keep stretching and growing and to pursue your destiny and fulfillment. What a privilege that is!

THE FATHER-SON GAME

I'd like to share a little more of my background to help you understand how I formed the coaching and life philosophies offered in this book. My journey began under the strict guidance of my dad, August Edmun Garrido Sr., who worked through his own childhood with his Spanish immigrant parents in the produce fields of Northern California. In those fields my father met my mother, Lois, a Lubbock sharecropper's daughter with an eighth-grade education, seven brothers and sisters, and a mixed heritage she described simply as "Texan."

Dad made it through high school in Vacaville, California, so he had that on her. Mom was bighearted but brooked no nonsense. Neither of them knew how to be a parent. They had few nurturing skills and minimal relationship skills. They were a pair of perpetual teenagers who loved each other but had no idea how to be married. My parents' relationship was a never-ending cycle of being together, breaking up, marrying, fighting, separating, getting back together, then frequently ripping at each other in passion or rage, often both.

As soon as I was old enough, I worked alongside my parents picking cherries, apricots, peaches, and plums for twenty-five cents a box. Now you can understand why at that time in my life I didn't share the romantic notions of the Napa Valley region. It was Death Valley as far as I was concerned; hot, dusty, and home to back-breaking work. I was in grade school by the time my father and mother moved from toiling in the fields to more steady year-round work at the shipyards in Vallejo.

Dad worked and willed his way up the ladder to become supervisor of an eight-acre warehouse packed with nuclear-submarine parts. He made no effort to hide his hatred of that job and most other aspects of his hardscrabble life. Sports were his escape. He loved all sports, but softball was the game he played when I was growing up. His night job allowed him to pursue that passion. Dad was director of the community recreation center in our housing project, which meant that he organized, coached, and played in the night leagues.

My dad was a big personality in a small package. Someone once said that he could strike up a conversation with the wind. Aggressively gregarious, he was a leader in our little blue-collar community, the mayor of every meeting, the feisty little guy who would do whatever he could to beat you whether it was softball, Ping-Pong, or a jog around the park.

Athletic, compactly built, and competitive in the extreme, he lived to win. Dad also enjoyed being right. When his playing days ended, he became an umpire, and you can bet that once he made a call, there was no overturning it. I'm fairly certain that my father was the only umpire in history who never missed a call, at least by his accounting.

Dad was coach, captain, and catcher on the rec center's fast-pitch softball team. I began as his batboy, a bad omen given his penchant for swatting me. Still, I did learn the fundamentals of the game early on, and I continued to soak up baseball basics as I moved into playing in the youth leagues. My father was usually my coach, but the only favoritism I received was as his favorite target. He was harder on me than anyone else. He wanted me to be the best only because my performance reflected on him. It wasn't about me. It was about him. Everything I did on the field belonged to him. If I didn't play well, he yelled at me and told me I embarrassed him. If my performance was not up to his standards, he made me walk home. It was not an easy walk, ever.

THE NO-PARKING ZONE

Like most kids, I learned the skills needed to survive in my environment, for better or worse. My father's methods left me with a mistrust of adults and their rules. I felt he was unreasonable. So, for many years I had a rebellious attitude toward authority. It's not that I was robbing banks or vandalizing churches, though I did become a fairly notorious parking scofflaw at CSUF.

At Fullerton my office was about five hundred yards from the baseball field and its parking lot. Coaches and faculty had no assigned spaces so we had to battle the students for parking spots. I grew sick of that so I created my own parking space by driving onto a practice field and leaving my car on the grass next to my office. I did that every day for a year and a half or so. The campus parking enforcers rewarded me with a ticket, every day; sometimes twice a day. I didn't pay them.

Two days before Christmas I was hosting a party for our coaches and friends in my condo near the ball field. Two cops showed up without invitations, but they did have a warrant for my arrest, based on 430 unpaid parking tickets. With my guests looking on in a mixture of great amusement and horror, the cops cuffed me and hauled me off to the county jail.

Fortunately, the judge who heard my case was a baseball fan. He chastised the Fullerton athletic department for forcing its baseball coach to park so far from the workplace. He fined me just $25. I kept parking my car illegally but somehow avoided incarceration.

PLAYING THE GAME INSIDE OUT

My minor rebellion against parking rules was an example of Augie Jr. still thumbing his nose at Augie Sr. Silly as it was, I carried around this conflict and the fear that still simmered inside. I mention this only because it is important that we know ourselves, that we are aware of what drives us, the good and the bad. As a coach I see many young men who struggle when they get to the college level because, like me, they are carrying conflicts and fears that they've never confronted. You can't fix it if you don't recognize it, acknowledge it, and take responsibility for overcoming it.

When I coach our players to "stay in the moment" and block out all fears and expectations at the plate, I'm giving them advice I sorely needed early in my baseball days. In my Little League days, they weren't so strict about organizing teams and leagues according to age. That's how I ended up as a nine-year-old batting against a sixteen-year-old pitcher who put fear in my heart. Joe Piccolo had more than a few years on me. I was barely five feet tall and still shopping in the boys' department. He was six foot three inches tall with a full beard. He looked like a grown man. Worse yet, Joe was more intimidating than any adult I knew.

Standing at the plate waiting for him to throw at me, I couldn't feel my feet on the ground or the bat in my hands. I was numb. He threw, I flinched. He threw, I flinched. He threw, I flinched. The umpire called the third strike but I never heard it. I just felt a nudge directing me toward our dugout from where my father offered his usual words of encouragement.

"If you're gonna be a chickenshit, don't play the game!" he yelled across the field.

I tried to tune him out but his words burned. My temporary paralysis at the plate against Joe Piccolo left me to ponder, *What just happened?*

My father provided the answer in his postgame summary: "You

were scared shitless out there! I can't believe I raised such a chickenshit kid!"

On the long walk home that day, I knew he'd be waiting to jump on my ass when I walked in the door. I vowed that he wouldn't make me cry. I vowed that fear would never again conquer me. Instead, I would use it, channel it, thrive on it. *Screw you, Dad. I'm not afraid of you. I'm not afraid of anything.*

SURVIVAL MODE

Initially, I conquered my fears by becoming fear-driven. I turned it into defiant determination. "I'll show him!" For many years that approach worked for me, though ultimately it might have destroyed me. I was naturally athletic, and once I became focused on the playing field, I excelled. Then I hit high school and size became a factor. I'd had an early growth spurt in grade school, but suddenly the other guys were passing me by. I didn't catch up until my senior year. Then the baseball coach, Bob Patterson, gave me a shot at second base, with a warning: "I'll play you in the first game, but I don't think you can hit, and if you can't hit, you won't be playing much."

I responded by striking out my first time at the plate. To my shock, Coach Patterson didn't yank me. I was so tense and pale when I came up for a second at bat, I looked like death at the plate. For the record, if ever I've claimed to have seen the pitcher throw that first pitch, I was lying. All I know was that suddenly the ball was there and I flinched to avoid getting hit.

The baseball gods intervened. Somehow, the ball hit the bat, and a hit was what I claimed. Miraculously, the baseball soared over the first baseman's head. It may have been divine intervention, El Niño, or a downdraft caused by a passing Budweiser delivery truck, we'll never know.

If a hit could be an error on the batter, that's what the scorecard should have said, but it was hit enough for me. The next time up, I had a legitimate single, and after that it was fire up the marching band. I was on my way to a .420 batting average for my senior season. Even with those big numbers, I was just the seventh-best hitter on a team overstuffed with ripe athletic talent. My baseball skills drew only a little attention amid the wealth of prospects on my team. Both Stanford and the University of Southern California sent letters inviting me to visit their campuses as a possible baseball recruit, but I lacked both the grades and the vision at that point.

THE YO-YO OPTION

My dad grew up during the Depression and put little stock in education. Early on, he informed me that he didn't have the money to send me to college. Then, at the end of my senior year, we had a classic father-son clash, a defining moment in my life.

"I have a job for you in the shipyard once school is out," he said.

"I'm not doing that," I replied. "I want to be a coach."

"Everybody wants to be a coach. You can't make a living doing that."

"Well, I know something you don't know."

It was a poor choice of words.

The conversation ended then and there.

To his credit, Dad placed a high premium on steady work. He thought he was setting up his shiftless son with a guaranteed-for-life job on the government payroll.

My scoffing at his effort no doubt hurt his feelings. What I'd meant to tell him was that I'd seen something on television that had made me think it was possible to do what I truly loved and also earn a living. I'd seen the young National Yo-Yo Champion performing on *The Ed Sullivan Show*. I watched his act in amazement with my face pressed close to our tiny ten-inch black-and-white television set. His tricks weren't anything special. I could do most of them better. I'd won a bunch of ribbons in yo-yo competitions at the rec center when I was ten years old. I knew I could beat that guy so I felt like I could succeed at whatever I did. Those blue ribbons gave me confidence in myself.

What fascinated me was that this guy was making a living as a performer rather than a worker. He appeared to love it. Even Ed Sullivan was impressed. I realized in that moment that if I became the best at something I loved to do, I might be able to make a living at it too.

I'd already had one factory job like my dad's and I was miserable in it. My dad knew the union boss in an onion and garlic processing factory. He'd hooked me up with a summer job scouring and hosing out steel drums that reeked of onions and garlic and so did I. No one sat next to me on the bench during games in the nightly softball league. To make it even more fun, I had to wear a rubber work suit. The only good part was that my dad bought me a battered Chevy sedan for $50 so he didn't have to drive me to work. The bad news was that I couldn't drive it anywhere else, and it broke down nearly every other day.

By the end of that summer, I never wanted to see the inside of another factory. I wasn't sure if I could make a living as a coach, but I knew I didn't want to end up like my dad. He was convinced that I was a dreamer. But I was determined to carve out my own life. I signed up for classes at Vallejo Junior College, hoping to raise my grades and maybe play a little ball. The one financial aid program I qualified for was the Army Reserve program. I signed up for one year of A, which meant six months of active duty and six years in the reserves.

I made the basketball team and the baseball team the first season at Vallejo. Things were looking up, but then I had to drop out of school to do my six-month active-duty hitch in the U.S. Army

Reserve. I thought I was putting my education on hold, but I learned some valuable lessons in those six months of 1956.

PRIVATE GARRIDO

After basic training at Fort Ord in California, I was assigned to Fort Huachuca in a cactus patch somewhere in southeastern Arizona, just fifteen miles from the Mexican border. The strange thing was that my Reserve unit was supposed to be training in underwater rescues, in a post set high and dry in the desert.

I respect what today's men and women in the military are doing around the world. My outfit was not what you'd call an elite military unit. We were more like the "Dirty Dozen." Most of the guys were draftees without any direction in their lives other than avoiding hard duty. I must have seemed more ambitious, or at least more talkative than most, because my superiors made me the troop information and education private. The desk job provided an office tucked in the back of the barracks, so the conversations of some of the least enthusiastic draftees were the background noise of my day. They didn't vary much. Mostly they talked about getting out of the army, getting a woman, drinking, buying a trailer, finding a job that left plenty of time for hunting and fishing and drinking, and retiring someday to do more hunting and fishing, and drinking of course.

I wasn't much with math, but the formula for their lives seemed to me to be zero plus zero equals zero. I found their lack of ambition pretty sad, especially when I compared them to the officer training candidates. My duties included reviewing the educational records and test results for soldiers at the base. As I looked at those records and the recommendations on them, the two distinct career tracks became clear to me. The soldiers with college degrees gave orders. Those without degrees took them.

FINDING A PATH

My other assignment during my tour in the Reserves was not exactly hazard duty, but it felt like it. I was chosen to be the fort's morning news anchorman, for reasons that escaped me. It wasn't because I had anchorman hair. I wore a crew cut the like everyone else. Still, every Friday, I'd stand before the entire company and read the military version of the news.

This wasn't a network anchor job, but I had to overcome my fear of standing in front of people and delivering the news. The other soldiers listened to me because they had to; still, people recognized me and my confidence got a boost. I became the Al Roker of Fort Huachuca.

This slow awakening and a lot of spare time left me pondering my future, which was rare for me. I've always been so intensely in the moment that the past and the future usually aren't on my radar. The good news is that I live in the moment. The bad news is that I often can't remember where I parked my car.

Still, at that time I was forced to look ahead. I knew I didn't want my father's factory life, and I sure didn't want the feckless lives being mapped out by the soldiers in my barracks. Given my lifelong involvement in sports, coaching still seemed a natural path, and then teaching too, since they went hand in hand. I was eighteen years old and I had the nagging sense that I needed direction. I wanted to be doing something more satisfying than just collecting a paycheck.

When my six-month Reserve duty ended, I returned to Vallejo Junior College determined to revise my whole approach to studying. I never considered myself college material and my counselors had picked up on that. Now, I had a goal, a purpose, and a mission. Thanks to my military experience serving my country, I was a better man.

COACHING CZAR

I returned to the baseball team at Vallejo JC and managed to make the All Conference team with my new dedication and focus. One of my high school coaches who was also coaching at Vallejo JC, and an old friend of my dad's, told me that I was playing well enough to move up to a bigger school if my grades improved. He'd gone to Fresno State University and he recommended that I contact the coach there, Pete Beiden, who was known as "the Casey Stengel of college baseball."

I had a few friends who'd gone to Fresno State, and my parents also had friends who lived nearby. Fresno was just 166 miles from Vallejo. It seemed like a natural move, and a positive move. Or so I thought until I met Coach Beiden, a Russian immigrant with a chiseled jaw, a voice like a rake over gravel, and a czar's iron-fisted rule. He was a great coach, a baseball genius, and beloved by his former players. But in many ways, Coach Beiden was just like my father. He tended to dwell on the negative and motivated his players not with pats on the back but kicks in the ass. For the next three years, he took me under his wing, which closely resembled being in a headlock. That's okay, I was used to it.

Dad accompanied me on my first meeting with Coach Beiden. Naturally, they hit it off. They cut a deal that provided me a $50-a-month scholarship and living wages from a grunt's job on Coach Beiden's five-acre weed ranch disguised as an orange grove. I'd run away to college to get an education and play baseball, and there I was back hacking at the ground with a hoe. Every now and then I wondered if my destiny was to return to migrant labor for the rest of my life.

Coach Beiden was gruff and rarely bothered to learn our names, or at least he never used them. Instead, he hailed us by the "Beidenese" nicknames he invented for us. If you were short,

Coach Beiden called you a "sandblower." In general, we were hailed in his haphazard manner as "Whitney," "Albert," "Ivanhoe," "Clem," or "dooflopper." A cross between Dr. Seuss and a drill sergeant, Coach Beiden knew his baseball. He'd turned down offers to coach the Yankees' minor-league team and other bigger jobs.

Today the field at Fresno State is named in his honor, and a seven-foot statute of him keeps an eye on modern doofloppers and sandblowers. He is still considered to be one of the best baseball minds of his era, a guy whose teams won 600 games in twenty-one seasons. Many respected coaches were either on his teams or his coaching staffs at one time. I know now that I was lucky to have Pete as a coach, though at the time I found him to be a tough task-master.

When I arrived for the 1959 season, he'd already assembled the best team in Fresno State's history. I came in as a second baseman just hoping to crack the lineup. Coach Beiden's practices were the most organized workouts I'd ever experienced. He made the army drill sergeants seem like slackers. He was the man with a plan, written on the ripped-off lids of baseball boxes and posted before each practice. We followed his regimen to the minute.

Coach Beiden assigned each player to go through a series of stations, much like military drills, so we were in constant motion. There was no standing around with your thumb up your butt at his practices. Coach prowled the field ready to pounce on anyone who wasn't going all out. In one of my first practices I was on the main baseball diamond at second base, taking ground balls from another player hitting with a long, skinny fungo bat, which I'd never before seen.

I thought I looked pretty sharp out there, but Coach Beiden seemed to have another perspective.

"Hey, dooflopper, what position are you playing?" he asked.

"Second base, Coach."

"Where exactly is second base?"

I locked up. With Coach Beiden there were never any easy answers. He might have been looking for the longitude and latitude for all I knew.

"Well, second base is right here, I guess," I said.

"Why?"

I was headed down the rabbit hole and I knew it.

"I don't know Coach. Because it's between first and third?"

Coach Beiden then set me straight. "If a right-hander is at bat, you should be ten steps off the base and twelve steps back."

"I'm sorry, Coach, could you repeat that?"

"You are a good player, Albert, but you have no knowledge or control of your game."

And so began my real education in the game of baseball.

Coach Beiden had a map for each position in each situation, and his players were expected to learn that map and follow it without fail. I had ample opportunity to learn it because I played every position but catcher and pitcher in my first season with Beiden's Bulldogs. He tried to keep me in the lineup anywhere he could because I'd developed into a strong hitter, with a .397 average that season. Nothing was handed to me though. Coach Beiden made his players earn it every game. Our budget was tight so he took only thirteen players on each road trip. We had play-off scrimmages between teammates to determine who stayed home and who joined the traveling squad.

I made the first road trip thanks to my hitting. Coach Beiden put pressure on his players, but I'd grown up with my dad riding my back and I'd learned to use the adrenaline rush of fear to pump myself up. We were playing the University of California at Berkeley, which is just twenty miles south of Vallejo, so my father could drive to the game. This was a big game and I quickly realized I wasn't ready for it.

BEHIND THE CURVE

I was a junior, but as a transfer student I wasn't as familiar with Coach Beiden's system as most of the other starters. I'd also failed to pick up on one of the coach's quirks: He actually expected his players to prepare for games on their own.

"We're using the same signs as the last year," he told us just before the game.

What signs? I thought. *I wasn't here last year. How am I supposed to know the signs he's talking about?*

Panicked, I asked an older teammate how I was supposed to know the signals.

"Coach expects you to talk to the other guys on the way up here and ask those questions," said the veteran player. "You were supposed to be thinking about the game and what you needed to know going into it. So figure it out."

Great! I was clueless about the coach's signs for the game, the hand and body signals that told us when to bunt, steal, swing away, and other strategic moves. My nerves were shot anyway since my dad was in the stands. As the game progressed, I tried to fake it, picking up what I could along the way. Naturally, Coach Beiden's system wasn't simple. The signs he gave had different meanings depending on the sequence in which he gave them and the game situation. He'd also devised all sorts of tricks to keep other coaches from stealing his signs.

The realization sank in that I was way behind the curve, so to speak, in my baseball knowledge. To that point, I'd pretty much cruised along thinking that if you could throw, hit, and run, you were a baseball player. My ignorance was put on full display late in the game when Cal Berkeley was up 4–0. We had a runner on first and nobody out. I was the batter.

I'd been milking our teammates for information on the signs, and I'd picked up just enough to be dangerous. Basically, I'd learned that if Coach Beiden swiped his hand up his shirt I was supposed to bunt. If he swiped his hand down his shirt, I was supposed to hit away. As the pitcher went into his windup, my eyes went to the stoic coach. I saw him swipe his hand up his shirt, so I prepared to bunt if the pitch was decent. The pitcher delivered. I laid down the sacrifice bunt and advanced our teammate to second base. I thought I'd done exactly as ordered, but when I looked at Coach Beiden on my way back to the dugout, he glared at me as if I'd just backed my car over his favorite hunting dog.

Uh-oh, somehow I screwed up.

The inning ended without our guys scoring. As I grabbed my glove and started to head out for the field, Coach Beiden issued a command that froze me on the bench:

"Sit down, dooflopper!"

I retreated to a corner of the dugout where my dad couldn't see me, but Coach Beiden found me easily enough. He walked up and placed his hand in a vise grip on my forehead.

"Lad, did you see me swipe up?"

"Yes, Coach, and I thought that meant to bunt."

"And, lad, did you then see me swipe my hand down my shirt?"

"No, Coach, I didn't see that."

He studied me as if trying to decide whether to put the bullet between my eyes or behind my ear.

"I did not know that they let such jackasses into our fine college," my coach said before walking away in disgust.

Later, I learned that we were supposed to follow the last sign Coach gave, but in my ignorance I'd responded to the first sign instead. Coach Beiden was a rough guy who used threats and insults to motivate his players. It didn't feel like tough love. It was just tough.

As my senior baseball season began, Coach Beiden announced that the members of the team would choose their team captain by popular vote. I'd worked hard to learn Beiden's way and I'd tried to be a good teammate. I was maturing as a person and as a ballplayer, realizing that it wasn't all about me and my stats and my expectations. I'd taken some big steps toward being a well-rounded player and person.

We voted by ballot during a team meeting. Coach stood at the front of the room tallying the votes on his chalkboard. When he realized that I was way out in front, Coach Beiden contorted his face with the pained expression of a man passing a kidney stone. He smacked his forehead and said:

"Oh, no, not that hot dog!"

He was dead serious. I honestly don't know why he acted that way. My relationship with him was as good as that of anyone else on the team, but Coach Beiden, bless his soul, was not a guy to pat you on the back unless he knew you had sunburn.

At the end of my senior year, we gathered for a big team barbecue. Coach Beiden stood up after the meal to announce the annual awards.

"Well, we have a Most Valuable Player award again this year, and the winner, you chose, well, you know it's the guy who played in the outfield, and you can't really tell me that any gol-danged outfielder is more valuable than a pitcher who wins ten games, but whatever. You made your choice. It's that dark-haired kid from Vallejo. Where is he?"

Since I'd grown up with that sort of treatment, I knew how to respond to it. Those players who took his harangues and wicked teasing personally did not last long. I reverted to my "I'll show you" attitude. That's not to say I wasn't uptight when I played for him. Every trip to the plate was life or death for me because Coach Beiden was always whipping the flames of fear. If I struck out, I'd throw my bat over the stadium wall, kick the ground, curse the batboy, and contemplate suicide. Every pitch was absolute war. Striking out, making an error, or losing a game triggered the old fears of abandonment and disapproval. Death might have been easier.

If I had a bad game, you didn't want to be around me. For better or worse—and it eventually became much for the worse—I responded by becoming a good baseball player. I certainly became much savvier about the game thanks to the old Russian, even if he was more Stalin than Chekhov.

I managed to have a great time in college, despite my hotheaded temper and resentment of authority. On the outside I was a confident, determined, and fun-loving guy living like a baseball Bohemian in a shack tucked into an old almond grove. I had a big group of friends but I didn't know who I was, or maybe I did and I just didn't like myself.

It would take me a long time to figure it out, but I was a classic case of someone whose whole life was built around the approval of others. Instead of loving myself and being comfortable with pursuing my own goals and objectives, I let others define me. My fear of disapproval and abandonment drove almost everything I did, both my successes and my failures.

This is a lesson I try to teach our players. So many young people fall into the same trap that I did. If you spend your life seeking approval or rewards from others—whether it's their love or their acceptance—you will never find the sort of fulfillment that comes from accepting and loving yourself. It's only then that you can truly trust and reach out to others and let them be a part of your life.

OMAHA SWEET OMAHA

While I only grudgingly admired the fearsome Coach Beiden when I played for him, we became friends as I matured into a head baseball coach myself. I finally seemed to impress him in 1975 when our Cal State Fullerton team became just the second California state school to go to the College World Series, held each year in Omaha, Nebraska.

The first California state school to go to the College World Series was Coach Beiden's 1959 Fresno State team, and I was his left fielder; not that I like to bring up what was a personal debacle. As a coach, I've taken five teams at two different schools to the championship of the College World Series (CWS) in Omaha, and believe me, every one of them has been sweet revenge.

You see, each time we make it back to Omaha, it's like returning to the scene of the crime for me. In my first and only appearance as a player in that series, I failed miserably. My performance in that game marked a disastrous introduction to an event and a city and a home away from home that have been good to me over the years.

Before I tell you that humbling story, I'd like to share some of my history with Omaha sweet Omaha and the College World Series, fondly known as the Greatest Show on Dirt. By the time I first stepped foot in Rosenblatt Stadium in 1959, the NCAA championship series at season's end had been around for twelve years. Omaha was in its ninth year as host and well on its way to becoming to college baseball what Augusta is to professional golf and Daytona is to NASCAR. I know at least one college baseball coach, Paul Mainieri at Lousiana State University, who motivates his players through each season by keeping an entire locker-room wall painted with just one word—OMAHA.

Yet, I'd gone through my college baseball career and even most of that 1959 season having no clue that there was even a College World Series. The only West Coast college baseball team that had made it to Omaha consistently at that point was the University of Southern California. Fresno State had come close just once before. The CWS just wasn't on my radar or on our team's radar until late in the season, when suddenly the coaches were buzzing that we might have a shot to "make it to Omaha."

Omaha? I thought back then. *What's in Omaha?*

I had no idea even where Omaha was located on the map. I wasn't a real worldly young man. The farthest I'd been from home was Yellowstone National Park. My first trip aboard an airplane was to Omaha and the College World Series of 1959. Since then, of course, Omaha has become my home away from home in many ways. The CWS is the ultimate goal of each baseball season for every Division I college team. As a coach at a school with the athletic resources and dedicated fans of the University of Texas, I am expected to guide the Longhorns team to Omaha each season and to bring home the trophy.

That doesn't always happen, as witnessed by the 2010 season, when we failed to make it to Omaha despite having an excellent Longhorns team. Losing our bid for the CWS was particularly painful in that season because it was the last year for Rosenblatt Stadium, nicknamed the 'Blatt, which will be replaced by a new and bigger downtown stadium starting in 2011. The old hilltop ballpark has received many face-lifts over its six decades, and even in its final year it remained a bright gem of a place, home to cherished memories for thousands of players, coaches, and fans.

I've journeyed to Omaha and its grand old stadium as a participant fourteen times. Our Cal State Fullerton team won it three times. Our Texas Longhorns have won it twice. I am the only active college baseball coach who has won the CWS as a coach and also appeared in it as a player. So, my history with Omaha and Rosenblatt Stadium is long and rich. The College World Series has given me many opportunities to fulfill my destiny. Omaha helped this fruit picker's son to become more than I ever thought I could be, and for that my gratitude is eternal. Many other athletes, coaches, and their supporters feel the same way about Omaha. They too love the city and the series. It's just a great American event.

Better writers than me have waxed poetic on baseball's timeless allure. Few venues capture that timelessness as well as Rosenblatt Stadium and the College World Series. Norman Rockwell could have turned out a lifetime of great Americana just painting scenes from the 'Blatt and the surrounding neighborhood during this series: Eager kids chasing autographs and foul balls. Young athletes measuring themselves against the competition. Fans hustling to the hot dog stand between innings. The world's oldest stadium organist (Lambert Bartak, age ninety) at the keyboard of his ancient Hammond. Fathers and sons playing catch on the grass outside the stadium. Suntanned mothers and daughters cheering on their boys. Tailgaters grilling burgers and toasting the passing throngs.

Omaha residents open their hearts and their city to the teams, coaches, and fans each year, and we return their favor. I can't think of any other major sporting event where the team buses pull up out front of the stadium before each game and the players, already dressed in their uniforms, walk in through the main entrance, signing autographs, high-fiving fans, and receiving pats on the back from parents and boosters. That tradition alone makes this a unique and wonderful sporting event.

The mutual admiration extends beyond the 'Blatt and into the great neighborhoods throughout this welcoming Midwestern city. Warren Buffett isn't just money smart. He's been in Omaha his entire life for good reason. My waistline and I can testify that his hometown boasts some of the finest family-owned restaurants you'll find anywhere, including my favorite slice of Italy on the prairie, Lo Sole Mio, owned by the Losole family.

For all the love that I have for the College World Series, Omaha, and its people, our relationship did not begin on a good note back in 1959. Rosenblatt Stadium, which was then a dark, sparse, and rickety old ballpark, seemed kind of grim.

I didn't make a good impression on it either.

In my first College World Series I started in left field for Coach Beiden's Fresno State team. We'd made it to the semifinals. To get to the championship game we had to beat Oklahoma State. In the seventh inning a runner was on second. The score was 0–0. Their batter hit a ground ball to me in left field. I picked it up, and in my overzealous attempt to throw the runner out at home, I demonstrated the strongest arm in all of college baseball.

My adrenaline-powered throw sailed over the catcher's head and hit halfway up the backstop. The runner scored. Oklahoma State seized the momentum and rallied. They racked up three more runs and beat us 4–0, knocking us out of the tournament and ending our season. I watched from the bull pen. For most of the year I'd been the starting left fielder and leading hitter on the team. After my error Coach Beiden demoted me from All-Conference outfielder to bull pen catcher, confirming for all that he felt I'd blown the game.

I was heartbroken and traumatized. After that game, I went to a street corner to wait alone for the yellow school bus that would take us to the hotel. I sat there on the curb crying like an abandoned child until we loaded up.

But wait, there's more! This is, after all, a story of redemption. Twenty years later, the Cal State Fullerton baseball team I coached won its first College World Series championship in Omaha. After that victory in 1979, I walked out to that same street corner, jumped over that same curb, and said, "I got you! I got you back."

And for every championship victory since then, I've gone back and jumped over the curb at the front entrance of the 'Blatt to celebrate. That's the stuff of great memories, and that's why I can say that win or lose, like countless others, I am who I am because of my College World Series experiences.

COACH TO COACH

On our way to that 1979 NCAA championship in Omaha, I invited Coach Beiden to sit in our dugout for the regional tournament in Fresno. We had reversed roles and bonded as friends by then. He asked me one question after another about my coaching methods and the drills I had devised to improve hitting and fielding. I had to admit that it was touching to have my former coach, mentor, and tormentor acknowledge my system. Even more gratifying was that he finally remembered my name and no longer called me "dooflopper." He told me then that he'd been harder on me than on other players because I joked around too much for his taste—though his wife enjoyed my humor. He often told me, "If you want to be a clown, join the circus."

I respectfully gave him his due because he was a pioneering strategist and a masterful coach from whom I'd learned a great deal.

"You know, Pete, I've taken all that I learned from you and your philosophy about the game and incorporated it into my own coaching system," I told him. "I learned the fine details of the game from you as well as how to break things down and organize practices. Over the years I've continued to explore other coaching methods, but you gave me the foundation."

Before my old coach could thank me, I added, "But it's also true that I've taken your philosophy on how to motivate and handle players and done just the opposite."

Coach Beiden got a kick out of that. We had our scraps when I was his player, but we ended up loving each other. He loved me because I became one of the most successful coaches who'd ever played for him. I came to love him for what he taught me, both the good and the bad.

PUSHING BUTTONS

My relationship with my father was more complicated, but we eventually came to our own sort of truce. They say that your parents know how to push your buttons because they installed them. That was certainly the case with my father and me.

At eighty-five, he was dying, and he wanted to go home. We moved him back to his three-bedroom tract home in Vallejo. Dad had survived two strokes and five years of kidney dialysis by then.

He was tough as an old shoe. But his mind was fading in and out of consciousness. I sat by his bed, the loyal but still vulnerable son at sixty-one years old, still in the game as a coach at the University of Texas.

"Augie?"

"Yeah, Dad, I'm here."

"I see you've got some relief pitching. You're finally winning some games."

"Yeah, Dad, we're coming around."

Then, an hour or so later he was back.

"Augie?"

"Yeah, Dad. I'm still here."

"I bought a satellite dish two years ago. The only reason I bought it was to watch Texas in the College World Series."

I let that pass. We'd lost 12 of our last 20 games and our hopes for making it to Omaha and the World Series were dimming.

"What's wrong with you, Son?"

Even on his deathbed, my father was on my case. He was teasing, of course. And I had to admire his tenacity. He was always true to himself.

By then, I'd read that DiMaggio clashed with his father while growing up, so I could identify with Joltin' Joe on that front too. We were each from immigrant families, and we each eventually rejected our father's domineering ways and his plans for our life. Joe didn't want to be a fisherman like his dad. I didn't want to work in the shipyards like mine.

Rather than following in our fathers' footsteps, we chased their dreams. DiMaggio and I, we wanted to show our dads. We wanted to rise above them, beat them at their own game, and I guess we did. Of course, DiMaggio became an American icon. His record is part of baseball history. I'm still scratching away to make my mark, but I'm genuinely happy with my life, at peace with who I am (most of the time), and filled with joy that I seem to be a coach who is a good teacher. I'm also surrounded by extraordinary people.

I like to imagine that my life is what my father, who always lived in fear, might have wanted for himself if only he'd had the vision; if only he had believed that you can really build your life around something that gives you joy; something like a sport that never stops teaching you about yourself. What I've learned is that how you feel about yourself is the most important factor in your success.

CHAPTER THREE

The Fearless Field

All-American Dante Powell turned down a signing bonus of $425,000 from the Toronto Blue Jays after his senior year in high school. Instead he joined our Cal State Fullerton baseball team. We felt very lucky to land him. At 6-2 and 180 pounds, Dante was built like a Greek god. On top of that, he was as fast as greased lightning. He was one of the best prospects ever to join our team, just a great kid with a strong work ethic. I was so impressed with Dante I worked with the school to get him a full scholarship, only the second one we'd given up to that point in my coaching career.

Dante made first-team All-Big West Conference as a freshman, hitting .307 and setting new school and conference records with 9 triples. Still, early on I saw that this young man was plagued by fears and doubts that threatened to hinder his development. Many of his friends and advisers were telling Dante that he made a mistake coming to Fullerton instead of taking the major-league money right out of high school. I'm sure they had his best interests at heart, but that question seemed to hang over him throughout most of his college career.

This talented athlete was dogged by concerns that he might have blown his big chance. Professional scouts often came to watch him play in our games, but their presence could intimidate him despite our best efforts to encourage him to be himself. As a result, while he was a good player for us, Dante didn't fully unleash his talents at Fullerton until the final series of his junior year, which was the 1994 College World Series.

Dante had run up a scary streak of 22 at bats without a hit in his previous College World Series appearances. But this time, he produced in a big way. His salvation came just as we were preparing to play in that 1994 tournament in Omaha. The San Francisco Giants drafted Dante in the first round. He later signed for a $507,500 bonus. The security and confidence he gained from making the major leagues and being a first-round pick freed Dante from his demons just in time for the tournament. He was electric in that College World Series. He ran better, swung the bat better, and for the first time in three years, he played out of joy instead of fear. He played with the confidence that is every athlete's best friend.

THE MENTAL GAME

More than any other team sport, I think baseball is a mind game. Basketball, football, and soccer flow more freely with less time for emotions to affect performance. The mental challenges baseball players deal with are similar to those golfers deal with. At high levels of competition in which nearly everyone is a gifted athlete, the ability to manage fears and other emotions is critical.

Coaches and players rarely talked about this in the past, but more and more you read and hear about major-league players, such as Khalil Greene of the St. Louis Cardinals or Detroit pitcher Dontrelle Willis, being treated for anxiety or depression. Even the players' union has recognized this by sponsoring a three-day rookie camp with sports psychologists and therapists to prepare young athletes for the mental side of the game.

Since the late 1970s, I've been working with a sports psychology consultant, Ken Ravizza, to help players overcome fears, deal with anxiety, and manage their emotions. Ken later built upon what we'd done and wrote a book considered a classic coaching guide called *Heads Up Baseball* with the help of a colleague, Tom Hanson, who was a graduate assistant on my team at the University of Illinois.

Ken and I were both at Cal State Fullerton, where he recently retired, when we put our heads together. He had some of our players in his classes who told me about his successful efforts to help members of the school's gymnastics team with the mental aspects of their sport. They told me, for example, that the gymnasts were having trouble on the balance beam, and it was carrying over to their performance on the uneven bars. They came into practice one day and Ken had put the balance beam across the uneven bars to demonstrate to them visually what they were doing mentally; letting one part of their routines interfere with another.

That sort of thing intrigued me because our players often did the same thing. If a batter struck out on offense, he'd often let that affect his play on defense and commit errors in the field. I met with Ken and we had a series of discussions about his approach. He didn't know much about baseball, so I spent some time explaining the game's complexities to him. He jokes that this went on for about a year before I trusted him enough to let him near any of my players. I wanted to give him a deeper understanding of the game and the background he needed.

At first, Ken wasn't sure how his work with the gymnasts would translate to baseball since one is an individual sport and the other is a team sport. I convinced him that baseball really is an individual sport within a team sport. Each player performs individual tasks within the team framework, whether it's standing at the plate to hit, fielding a ball, or throwing and catching. When I laid it out like that, Ken began to see how to apply some of the same exercises and techniques he'd been using with the gymnasts.

Ken had helped Fullerton's gymnasts develop preperformance routines that focused them and prepared them for competitions with higher levels of concentration. To focus our batters in the same way, we had to think about when an "at bat" begins. Does it begin when the player steps into the batter's box, or should focusing the mind begin much earlier? Maybe, we thought, each batter should begin preparing while sitting in the dugout, studying each pitch thrown to his teammates and noting the rhythm and timing of the pitcher's delivery.

As we worked out our approach to coaching the mental aspects of baseball, Ken and I eventually agreed on some key points that applied to baseball players and to just about every aspect of life, whether it's what you do for a living or how you approach your relationships. Those key coaching points for managing the mental and emotional aspects of performance include:

1. Creating a statement of purpose that includes why you play the game, what you hope to accomplish, and what sort of person you hope to become.

This is "the map" that lays out what baseball means to each of our players, what they hope to get out of baseball, and what sort of player and person they want to become. Ken and I ask them to state where they want to go and how they want to get there. Having a statement of purpose like this helps them check their progress and gives them guidelines so they can self-correct if they stray off course.

We begin every season by identifying our final destination—winning the College World Series—and then we plot out our step-by-step journey, figuring out what route we need to take to get there. Our players are encouraged to do the same thing with their personal lives. We want them to decide where they want to go and then to figure out how to get there, step by step, always staying focused on the ultimate destination.

Early in each season, Ken comes to a practice and does an exercise where he lays out the entire season step by step by putting baseballs down to mark each stage of the season. He starts with arriving on campus to start the semester, fall ball, preseason, nonconference games, conference games, conference tournament, regionals, superregionals, the College World Series, the finals of the College World Series. Ken puts baseballs down on the floor across the front of the room. The idea is to give the players a visual image of the season. Ken talks about thunderbolts, the adversity they will encounter at different stages and how different players will take on different roles at each stage. This is to give them an image of the journey, where we are going, and what it is going to feel like. We tell the players that they will need to keep improving at each stage, learning as they go and building their skills.

It's one thing to have a dream, but it means nothing if you don't take determined action by setting goals, committing to them, and moving toward them every day, step by step, always focused on making the dream a reality. Goals without commitment are nothing more than wishes. You have to dedicate yourself to your own success and then do whatever it takes day after day. Begin each day by asking, What can I do today to make it happen? Then at the end of each day, you should reflect on what you did to make progress and what you can do the next day to build on it.

2. Take responsibility for your emotions and thoughts.

This seems elementary but gifted athletes rarely have to give much thought to the mental and emotional aspects of competition until they reach college or the professional ranks. At those levels, nearly everyone on a team has superior size, speed, and coordination. To become an all-star or a Hall of Fame member, athleticism isn't enough. Even the biggest and strongest and fastest must master more than physical conditioning and the strategies of their sport.

Natural athletes often resist talking about controlling their emotions or managing their thoughts until they realize that mastery of the mind game will help them perform at a much more consistent and even higher level of play. I've had players admit that they never realized they had a choice in how they could respond to failures, fears, or even their successes. Yet, every season, I see again and again that the quality of a player's next performance is determined in the split second when he decides how to respond to his last performance. It doesn't matter if he had a great game or a crappy game. What matters is his response, the attitude that he comes away with.

I've seen pitchers throw beautiful games that I thought would give them enough confidence to carry them for a lifetime. All too often though, a pitcher will come off a great performance and decide that he has to match it or surpass it in every subsequent appearance. That "high expectations" response is a recipe for disaster. Keeping it simple and controlling what you can is the best approach.

About midway through our 2010 Texas Longhorns baseball season, our longest and lankiest pitcher, Taylor Jungmann, widely considered one of the top pitchers in the country, went through a rough stretch. The six-foot-six-inch sophomore from Temple, Texas, had begun to pay too much attention to the expectations of others. So many people had told him he was the best pitcher in America that he decided he had to be perfect, which is never a good thing.

In March, he racked up 17 strikeouts in a game we took from the Iowa Hawkeyes. It was a career high for him and fell just two short of a school record. That same day, he'd allowed only 1 run on 5 hits and 1 walk. I was among those who heaped praise on him because it was truly a brilliant performance in which he dominated the game.

Sometimes, though, what you do in the moment isn't as important as your response to it. That beautiful pitching performance could have given Taylor more confidence, but instead, he began walking out to the mound with the demon of expectations on his back. He felt he had to perform at that same level all the time. When the magic didn't happen, Taylor could have had the confidence to work through it, but instead he lost his rhythm and lost his timing because he didn't focus on throwing to the catcher's mitt.

Even throwing fastballs in the 90s and with the same great curveball that had devastated so many hitters, he struggled. Pitching is like real estate. It's all about location, location, location. He wasn't locating his pitches in the strike zone and began walking more batters than usual. Then, they'd become runners on base, which made him more careful and caused him to think and try rather than to throw and play.

Playing well doesn't automatically reward you with unshakable confidence. You can be intimidated by your successes just as you can be motivated by your failures. I tell our players that unless they can walk on top of the water and across Lady Bird Lake in mid-July, perfection is not an expectation.

In the spring of 2010, Taylor had a string of three or four games in which he was pitching out of fear. He didn't want anybody to get a hit because he didn't want to let anyone down. The All-American, who turned down a major-league contract out of high school, was embarrassed if every pitch wasn't perfectly thrown.

Taylor is such a great pitcher that his struggles didn't become obvious to most fans until about two weeks later. We played Texas Tech on their home field in Lubbock with gale-force winds blowing out across the dry South Plains. They handed Taylor his first loss of the season and hit him harder than he'd ever been knocked around, with 7 hits and 4 walks that helped them beat us 12–5.

Our coaches had a talk with him. We told him that he had the power to ignore the expectations of others and to instead do his best pitch to pitch, trusting himself and his abilities. A couple days later Taylor had to face the University of Oklahoma, another big-hitting team, in forty-mile-per-hour winds. This time, he played within himself and was a dominant force in the game. As a result, we had our best team performance of the season. Taylor pitched seven innings against Oklahoma, striking out 6 batters, allowing 4 hits and 2 walks, and helping us to a 5–0 victory.

Like fear, expectations can be crippling. When we buy into them, it is because we are striving to please others. Realistic goals serve you. Expectations serve someone else. Goals motivate you from the inside out. Expectations motivate you from the outside in.

It is difficult to play inside out, to meet your own goals rather than the expectations of others, because from our first days in school we are conditioned to seek the rewards of good grades, gold stars, and blue ribbons. The problem is that as long as you buy into the expectations of others and base your performance on rewards, you are dealing with things you can't control. You can't control things around you but you can control your response to them.

Our coaching team must often retrain players by teaching them to set their own goals for each at bat, or each inning, while block-ing out expectations placed upon them by fans, parents, girlfriends, scouts, or the media. Our coaches encourage players to be aware of the differences between their goals and the expectations of outsid-ers. When an athlete works to achieve his goals, he is in control of his destiny. When he tries to live up to the expectations of others, he gives up control to others.

The best performance in the world can become a monkey on your back if you go into the next game with expectations that it will be as good or better than the last one. On the other hand, a mediocre performance can motivate you to play at a much higher level in the next game if you handle it right. We all know the un-derdog has less pressure than the top seed.

After a great performance, a player can choose to learn from it and to stay with what worked or to play to the higher expectations. But that's much easier coached than done because we grow up playing for the rewards of praise, ribbons, and trophies. But the universe doesn't owe you anything if you do well, and it doesn't want to take anything away from you if you do poorly. So the choice is yours. Do you become distracted by success or more focused because of it? Does failure make you bitter or better? The choice is yours.

The rule of choice doesn't apply just to baseball players, of course. It's part of our human experience. We make these important choices all the time, but in watching sports we can quickly observe the results. I don't play golf but I watch PGA tournaments with great interest because they provide me the opportunity to see these highly trained, skilled, and experienced professional golfers choose their responses and either benefit or suffer as a result.

3. Stay focused on the basics of performance.

We advise our hitters, pitchers, and fielders to clear their minds about what happened in the past or what might happen in the future and to instead stick to the simple basics of the game. For pitchers that means throwing to the catcher's mitt without fear of the batter. For fielders and hitters that means watching the ball and reacting to it.

As simple as it sounds, this is often difficult to pull off because we grow up seeking rewards. You can't focus on doing your best in the moment if your mind is full of thoughts about receiving the rewards when you are done. For example, the rap on our 2010 Texas Longhorns baseball team was that we had great pitchers and weak hitters. The skeptics were half-right. We had great pitching, no doubt about that, but we also had great hitters. Hitting is just much more difficult.

We worked on the basics of hitting every day, and by mid-April we were beginning to see the results. In our three-game series with Texas A&M, we were lucky to win the first by 4–3 after 11 innings. Then our players blew out the Aggies in the next two games, outscoring them 22–0 and outhitting them 28–5. Our next game was against the University of Texas at Arlington team. We talked to our players before that game and encouraged them not to think about their success against A&M, but to instead have quality at bats in each trip to the plate.

"Don't think about the runners on base or the score or how you hit in the last game," we told them. "Instead, stay with the basics. Grind it out by keeping it simple. See the ball and make good choices on whether to swing or not."

In that game, we had 21 hits and 21 runs. We went on a 5-game tear in which we outhit our opponents 70–19 and outscored them 62–3. We succeeded because our players stayed in the moment, approaching each at bat as a fresh experience unaffected by the past (previous performances) or the future (the rewards of winning).

4. Don't try, play.

Once you've done all you can do to prepare yourself, you no longer need to try. You should simply play, trusting in your mastery of the game. We give players tools to take possession of their area of the field. We find players benefit when they have a process for handling challenges and tough situations so that they can mentally access it when needed as a source of confidence and courage. Our staff help them develop routines and phrases and visual images for every situation, and especially for times when they feel their control of their emotions may be slipping or that they are losing focus.

It often helps to have them store a favorite memory of overcoming a challenge so they can summon that feeling of confidence and use it to banish self-doubt and fear of failure. We've also encouraged each player to create his own space on the field. When the pitcher steps on the rubber, he should be thinking, "I'm in my space. Let's go." All the negative stuff is outside the circle.

The same method can be applied by the hitter as he steps in the box. He should think of that area as his sacred place. We coach him to tell himself something like *This is my batter's box and I'm ready to compete.* Fielders have their own "circle of focus." They designate a spot to physically step into, putting themselves into the game mentally as they do it.

The mental image of the circle of focus helps players to relax and clear their minds between pitches and then to refocus for each pitch so they can simply play the game without distractions. We coach them to step out of their circle when there is a break in the game, then to step back into it when play resumes.

Many of my former players have told me that they use the circle-of-focus concept in their careers after baseball. Whether preparing for a job interview, a sales presentation, or a meeting with their office team, they'll mentally take a moment to:

- Visualize themselves stepping into a place of quiet comfort
- Consciously strip away all distractions and fears related to the past or present
- Hone in on the immediate goal
- Call up successes and accomplishments of the past to build confidence
- Offer themselves encouragement
- Express gratitude for the opportunity to use their gifts and talents

THE REAL WORLD

My former player, assistant coach, and friend Joe Martelli is now a successful businessman who says that baseball taught him to:

- Believe in himself
- Be true to himself
- Respect relationships
- Be accountable
- See failures as a normal part of learning and growing

Joe was a catcher and designated hitter on our 1979 national championship team at Cal State Fullerton. He returned to campus in the early 1990s to help me out as Fullerton's hitting and catching coach. He played some ball after college in Italy, but Joe knew he wasn't destined for a long professional baseball career. He was more of a natural in business, even taking real estate classes during college summers. Still, many of the lessons Joe learned from his baseball experiences helped him thrive as the owner of a California real estate and mortgage banking investment company that has many professional baseball players as clients.

"Like Augie often says, the failures in baseball can be cruel, just like business, and life can be brutal on an even higher level, so you'd better have a solid process for dealing with the challenges and failures that come along," Joe said. "Every business has adversity. For example, when I saw in 2006 that the real estate market was about to collapse, I got out of it and I kept my clients out of it too. The recession affected most businesses in negative ways over the next four years, and it brought people down financially and mentally. To get through that successfully, I've applied many things I learned in baseball. I chose to remain positive despite the negative circumstances, and I chose to focus on solutions rather than problems, and as a result we began five new hotel projects. I also learned from Augie to prioritize what is important on the playing field and to eliminate negative distractions, which I've done in both business and my personal life.

"Augie always stressed that when we stepped on the field, we should be intent on becoming the best we can be, always pushing to become better at whatever we do, and that we should let winning or success take care of itself. I've followed that philosophy in business too, and it's served me well."

PRACTICE PERFECT, PLAY FOR FUN

[Coach Garrido] used to tell us all the time, "You don't realize how much fun you are having. This will be the most fun you will ever have playing baseball. The wins and great successes you will have here at UT will be the most rewarding experiences you have in your life. You know why? Because you are doing it just to do it."

I am not saying I don't love playing pro baseball. I consider it a privilege and blessing, but if you want to talk about pure fun—that's the purest form of commitment and dedication I have ever experienced.

HUSTON STREET
University of Texas
Colorado Rockies

Practice is where you strive for perfection. In competition, you should trust yourself to play and have fun. In the 2010 Masters in the final round, Phil Mickelson hit his drive into the trees on the par-five thirteenth hole. He had a two-stroke lead. His ball was in the pine needles but he had a four-foot opening between two trees.

The announcers and just about everyone else thought he would chip out onto the fairway for a lay-up because he was still 209 yards from the hole, which has a creek running right in front of the green. Mickelson chose instead to go for the green because it was a shot he was comfortable taking. "I kept saying that if I trust my swing, I'll pull it off," he said later.

5. Work to be better, always.

Mastery of the emotional game comes with confidence maintained by constant step-by-step improvement. Unfortunately, you can't buy confidence in a can, unless of course you are Popeye. It's something you build over time, pushing yourself to new levels of achievement in small increments so that you can build one success upon another. This requires you to reward yourself rather than to seek the approval of others. It also means that you have to feel worthy of success so that setbacks and failures are merely bumps in the road instead of dead ends.

This process is about "sharpening the saw" by always doing your best and then looking for ways to do it even better. At Texas and on all the teams I've coached, the staff mentors and encourages our Longhorns team members to set daily goals for improvement—even goals for each at bat—and work every day to enhance their physical conditioning as well as their understanding of all aspects of the game.

With few exceptions, the greatest athletes are those who never stop working on their game. The world's best golfers are constantly adjusting their swings, testing new equipment, and working on managing their emotions during competition. The same is true of athletes in other sports. Tim Tebow, the University of Florida quarterback whose teams won two college football national championships, and who won a Heisman Trophy, underwent intense retraining to change his throwing motion in preparation for a professional career. Whether he'll be successful is still to be decided as I write this, but Tebow is committed to continuous improvement.

Learning never ends. Even failures and losses have value if you are open to learning from them and figuring out what you need to know to do better the next time. It is always important to know what you don't know. The real joy in sports and any endeavor is the never-ending acquiring of knowledge and experiences and then building upon them so that you feel your life is moving peak to peak. Know that there will be valleys in between, but that as long as you keep moving forward, you will climb to the top again.

LOOKING WITHIN

I love baseball, but it is a complex and cruel sport dressed up as a child's game. Often fans don't see how hard it is on the players because in games the camera stays with the winner. The observer may sometimes see the outward display of emotions, but rarely do fans understand the inner anguish and turmoil, all of the scatter-shot thoughts and feelings that run through the minds of players before, during, and after a performance. Because of my own experiences as a player who sometimes struggled with the mental aspects, I've always been tuned in to the minds and moods of our athletes. Working with Ken on the mind game appealed to me because so much of baseball is played out between the ears. The timing was good too. I was examining my own inner life.

I have a photograph of our 1979 Cal State Fullerton team just after we'd won the College World Series championship. This was the first time I'd come away as a winner after I'd had such a poor showing in the championship series while playing at Fresno State. So, after winning the College World Series as a coach, I should have been jubilant, right? You'd never know it by looking at this photograph. In it, I'm surrounded by my celebrating players, but I look like the grim reaper. My cap is pulled down tightly over my eyes and I have a death grip on the trophy.

I studied that photograph recently and compared it to a similar one taken after my second College World Series championship victory with Cal State Fullerton five years later. In the 1984 photo, I'm smiling from ear to ear as I'm being carried by the players. My body is relaxed and open to the crowd. I'm waving to the fans. Joy beams from every Garrido pore.

What is the difference between those two winning moments? Why was I so uptight and dour in 1979 and so open and joyful in 1984? Well, in that first College World Series championship victory, I was still in the same place where Dante Powell had spent most of his time in college. I was living in fear and coaching from it too.

In the 1979 photograph, I'm clutching the trophy because I'm afraid someone will rip it out of my hands and tell me I'm a loser and that I'd better start walking because it was a long way back to Fullerton.

In the 1984 photograph, there is no past, there is no future; I am living in the moment and relishing it.

Fearful, angry Augie won in 1979.

Joyful Augie won in 1984.

In between, I undertook a journey of self-assessment and reinvention. It's a journey that continues. My story is still being written, but now I hold the pen firmly in hand. Prior to 1984, I wasn't in control of my emotions; they were running my show. It's a shame because that 1979 victory should have been sweet. It was my first College World Series championship. We'd come such a tremendous distance in building the baseball program at Cal State Fullerton. Many still feel that team changed the course of college baseball because Fullerton was a small commuter school back then with a minuscule budget for the baseball program.

We beat up on the teams from much bigger schools with deep pockets. We won with players who'd mostly been overlooked by UCLA, USC, Arizona, and Arizona State. Our guys supposedly couldn't throw as hard or hit as well, but they were hard workers and they were competitors. They'd spent all of high school watching the higher-ranked guys walk away with the professional contracts or the scholarships to prestigious schools, so they had something to prove, and they did.

I should have been enjoying their success along with them during and after that great season. I was in turmoil instead. Every time we took the field in the 1980 season, I was afraid we would lose. By the end of games I was a mess. Every run scored by the other team frightened me to death. Even when we won, I was a nervous wreck. We played a team we should easily have beaten, and when we won by just a single run, 2–1, I was trembling in fear that we might have lost it. I was deathly afraid of disapproval, and most of the disapproval was coming from within. I didn't respect myself and that made me overly sensitive about others disrespecting me. The rewards were never enough.

I'd also been struggling in personal relationships. No surprise there. I was one of those guys you see in self-help seminars who stand up and say, "I'm successful. I'm at the top of my game. I've got more money than I ever dreamed I'd have. So, why am I such a miserable wretch?"

Usually people in that frame of mind blame their spouse first, figuring it must be her fault or his fault. Then, when they ditch the spouse and still aren't happy, they blame their job or their surroundings or their friends or anything but themselves. I went through some of that, but I'd finally reached a point where I looked around and came to the only logical conclusion. Since it wasn't likely that everyone else on the planet was wrong, maybe I was screwed up.

CLEARING THE FIELD

After my first College World Series victory left me feeling hollow and scared, I realized even more that I was miles and miles from the person I'd hoped to become. To self-correct, you have to self-assess. I'd been avoiding that. To upgrade a bad attitude into a good one, you must first make an honest self-evaluation, which can be painful but ultimately rewarding. Often men in particular shy away from introspection. They "don't want to go there," but to keep moving forward, it's necessary to understand the source of attitudes and behaviors that are self-destructive. This also requires admitting that you don't have all the answers, which may also be difficult for some people. A willingness to change and a dedication to continuous self-improvement are also part of this process.

My self-defeating attitudes were a form of self-defense. I was all about the rewards because I thought they'd win me acceptance, yet when we won it all, I went back into my default mode, fearing someone would rip back the curtain, expose me as a fraud, and snatch it all away. The old themes of abandonment and rejection were still playing as my background music.

With my life unraveling, I finally grabbed the string and followed it inward. I hoped to reinvent myself as someone not quite so miserable in his success, and maybe a guy who could trust in love. I undertook a spiritual journey and sought some help from those around me. Now that was scary territory for me. As a kid, I'd always been creeped out in church so I grew up wary of walking through that door. My dad was a Catholic, and when we went to his church, the robed priests spoke Latin and waved incense burners. I didn't understand a thing they were saying. The rituals and mysticism gave me the willies. My mom's church was even scarier. Her father was a self-taught Pentecostal minister. His services had a lot of screaming and yelling and speaking in tongues.

Since I was still intimidated by organized religion, I worked my way back by reading the Bible and trying to understand how to apply it to my daily life. I found it comforting and enlightening, but I still didn't get how its lessons could be put into practice day in and day out.

So, I looked around for someone who had a handle on that, which led me right back to church. I found guidance from two nationally known ministers, both of them noted authors and inspirational speakers with churches in the Los Angeles area.

Dr. Lloyd John Ogilvie was then leading the First Presbyterian Church in Hollywood. He also hosted his own television and radio shows, which I tuned in. His teachings helped me get a handle on how to apply the Bible's lessons to my daily life, as did those of Chuck Swindol, who then had a radio ministry based out of the First Evangelical Free Church in Fullerton. I listened to their broadcasts and I bought boatloads of their audiotaped sermons and inspirational speeches. Both offered practical lessons on how Christianity worked in daily life.

Their guidance gave me a sense of peace as do the sermons of Pastor Joel Osteen today. They helped me recognize how my childhood response to fear worked up to a point for me, but then became self-defeating.

Chuck Swindol, whom I met with on a couple of occasions, offered four steps for dealing with fears that I found useful. His method is based on his strong faith and that of his many followers and admirers. But I believe it has value for anyone, whether religious or not. The steps below are based on those developed by Chuck, but the interpretations are my own, geared more to secular life.

Step One: Admit the fears, recognizing them and their source.

The ability to step back, recognize your feelings, trace them to their source, and examine how they are affecting your actions is critical. If something is bothering you, rather than fleeing from it, you need to understand it. This doesn't mean you should dwell on fears or get caught up in them, but you should try to understand their origins and how they affect your performance. In my case, the twin boogeymen were fears of rejection and abandonment. Because of them, I didn't feel worthy of either success or love so I tended to sweat it when either entered my life.

Step Two: Commit to dealing with the fears.

Whatever your spiritual beliefs, and even if you have none, you should never feel that you are alone. Nor should anyone ever be too proud to ask for help. I need it. You need it. We all need it from time to time. For Christians and other spiritual believers, God or other deities are a natural source of assistance and comfort, but help also is available in the next room, next door, and down the street. Don't be afraid to reach out to your family, friends, teachers, coaches, and professional therapists and counselors.

Step Three: Release fears.

Again, religious faith is the go-to source for millions of people, but you can release your fears in whatever way works best for you. Letting go is a choice you can make. Sometimes it helps to visualize the process. During my coaching days at Cal State Fullerton, I once had a team that was all but overwhelmed with fear. Pitchers couldn't pitch. Hitters couldn't hit. Fielders couldn't field. They were committing errors upon errors. They seemed to think one bad turn deserved another. They were being buried by their fear of failure, so I decided to turn the tables.

I rented a hearse and casket and had it driven out to the pitcher's mound one day at practice. A funeral dirge played over the sound system. Black armbands were passed around to the players.

Then, with the team gathered round, I told the dearly be-gloveds that we were gathered together to say a last farewell to all of the dropped balls, missed pitches, wild tosses, lousy swings, and runners left on base. I quoted a couple of appropriate Bible passages. I told them that what was past had passed and that this marked a new beginning. Then I had each team member place a bat and a ball in the casket to give closure to their calamities. The designated pallbearers (DPs) loaded the casket back into the hearse and escorted it out of the ballpark and into the great beyond.

The slump ended there.

Step Four: Close the door, refusing to dwell on fears anymore.

You have the power to choose what you focus on. Old fears will arise. New fears will creep in, but they are feelings, not facts. You can refuse to give them power. When they try to steal back into your thoughts, take a walk, ride a bike, go to a movie, call a friend. Do whatever it takes to release them. Whatever you dread may seem real to you, but you are responding to a feeling, not a fact. If you refuse to give feelings power over your thoughts and actions, they will lose their hold on you over time.

THE FEARLESS FIELD

Some fears are more debilitating than others. Those rooted in abuse or tragedy may require years of professional counseling to manage. I don't pretend to have all the answers on restoring emotional health. I leave that to the experts. However, as a teacher and coach, and as someone who had his own demons to deal with, I understand the power of emotions and their impact on performance.

That is why I talk about a "Fearless Field" where boys and girls and athletes of all ages play out of joy and passion without the burden of expectations set too high or motivations rooted in fear. To play at the highest level in any sport, you have to sweat and grind it out while developing the skills and knowledge you need. Still, the most fulfilled and the happiest players I've known are those chasing their bliss around the base paths, across the field, and up and down the court.

I see two major factors responsible for creating a Fearless Field. The first traces back to my own experience. The coaches and parents of the youngest athletes are critical in creating a playing field where failure is not a finality but part of the continuous process of success, where opportunities are seen as unlimited, and where fulfillment resides not in securing victories but in striving to do one's best each moment of the day and every step of the journey.

A big part of my dream is that every parent, coach, teacher, and mentor lives not through their young charges but for them. As adult guides we need to realize that we can hurt our children even when we think we are acting out of love for them. Nearly all parents want to do what is best for their kids, but sometimes their own insecurities and desires blind them. Parents and coaches need to be aware of whether they are concerned with the child's success and happiness or their own.

The coach or parent who rages from the stands or yanks a boy or girl from the field after a loss or mistake is not doing it for the child's benefit. Adults need to recognize when they are confusing their goals with the child's. Parents whose egos are invested in their children's athletic success risk spoiling sports for the children and, worse, damaging long-term relationships. Too often, parents whose children are still developing as athletes treat them as if they are professionals in the major leagues.

Only one in twelve thousand high school athletes ever becomes a paid professional, and only 5 percent of young baseball players who sign a pro contract ever play a single major-league game. When parents take the playfulness out of sports, they rob their children of an important aspect of their development. Increasingly, researchers are finding that we are hardwired to play. A 2008 *New York Times Magazine* story titled "Taking Play Seriously" noted that scientists who study play in animals and humans alike generally agree that play is more than a way for kids to unleash energy. "Play, in their view, is a central part of neurological growth and development—one important way that children build complex, skilled, responsive, socially adept and cognitively flexible brains," the story said.

Through play, we learn to interact with others. We also learn about ourselves, how we fit in, how to control our actions and self-correct. Surveys have shown that most young people care more about playing than winning. The wise mentor encourages boys and girls competing in sports to have fun and to do their best. I encourage our baseball players and you the reader to do the opposite whenever possible. Approach your work as play. Not in a frivolous way, but in a manner that engages you completely so that it isn't a labor but an expression of your talents, creativity, and knowledge.

Often, though, parents and youth coaches corrupt the purpose of play by putting far too much emphasis on the results instead of the experience. The real danger comes when a parent's love and acceptance are withdrawn if the child doesn't meet athletic expectations. I wish my father had brushed away my tears and encouraged me to "get 'em the next time" instead of berating me and telling me I embarrassed him. I wish many of the players who've come to me did not carry the same scars.

Every coach has horror stories about players' parents, and I'm sure most players' parents have horror stories about coaches. All the parents I've dealt with had the best intentions. Most do a great job supporting their kids and the coaches trying to develop them. Still, others have good intentions but their actions are counterproductive, even destructive. I'm not concerned about things parents may do or say that make my staff's jobs more difficult, but I am concerned about what they do in the name of love that negatively affects their sons and daughters.

You've no doubt encountered "helicopter" parents who hover over their young athletes, doing all they can to remain in total control. Most of these parents are focused on the wrong things. Some are living through their kids and smothering their individuality. Others are all about the results and not the play. The mother and the father of a talented young athlete would naturally want the child to be successful, especially if that is the child's dream too. Yet, when there is unrelenting focus on winning a scholarship or a professional contract, there is a real danger that the individual will lose passion for playing. The intense focus on developing athletic skills can thwart the development of the person, the teammate, and the balanced individual capable of one day handling all that comes with success.

I've seen hyperinvolved parents of college athletes dominating every aspect of their lives, from whom they date and hang out with to what they eat and the hours they sleep. As much as they insist, "We're only doing it for our son," the result too often is that the young man never develops the self-confidence and self-respect necessary to guide his own life.

I once had a young pitcher who arrived on campus with a 95-mile-per-hour fastball, a truckload of raw talent, and a level of anger off the charts. The more his parents pushed to be involved with him on campus, the worse his behavior became. He constantly demanded to be the center of attention whether it was during practice or on the bus. He sucked the air out of every meeting and event.

On the field, it was worse. He threw his bat and helmet after a failed trip to the plate. If he was pitching and walked one batter, it was all over. By the time I'd replace him, he'd be bouncing balls across the plate or throwing them over the backstop. He went from a potentially great player to one barely able to function.

I had many conversations with this young man. I don't take sides with our players against their parents, nor do I try to manage family relationships. The point I made to him was simply that he had to do something to control his anger and his fears. We arranged for him to get professional counseling and it helped him some, but when he left school, he still had a long way to go in learning to manage negative emotions.

Monitoring thoughts and impulses that come from negative experiences is critical to taking responsibility for and control of your actions. Be aware of the filters through which you see the world. If you aren't satisfied with your life, those filters may need adjusting. Be aware of the negative experiences that influence your attitudes and actions, understand how they can detract from your performance and the quality of your life. Replace negative messages that incite fear with those that nurture passion and excitement.

GETTING IT RIGHT

Most parents find the right balance. Instead of dominating and pushing, they encourage and advise. They provide the support that allows their sons and daughters to make mistakes, to fail, and to find their way. One of the joys of my job is seeing the powerful bonds that form when this occurs. One of the best father-son relationships I've seen on our teams arose out of circumstances that could just as easily have been disastrous.

We've all heard of fathers who were themselves great athletes and the sons who struggle to follow in their footsteps. Rebellion, resentment, and disappointment often result. But it doesn't have to be that way. It certainly wasn't the story with one of the best, brightest, and most well-balanced players I've had the pleasure to coach.

All-American pitcher Huston Street grew up in Austin, home of the University of Texas, where athletes who excel are heroes for pretty much eternity. James Street, Huston's father, is one of the most beloved members of that elite Longhorns fraternity. He quarterbacked the Longhorns for twenty straight victories, leading them to a national championship and a Cotton Bowl win over Notre Dame in 1969. If that were not enough to guarantee his UT fame, James Street also was a star pitcher whose Longhorns teams made it to the College World Series in 1968, 1969, and 1970.

Huston grew up attending football and baseball games with his father, who often signed as many autographs as the active players. After one Longhorns football game, they had to stay for three hours so his father could talk to all of the fans and friends gathered around him. Yet, it was James Street who stood waiting for his son to sign autographs back in Omaha a few years ago.

In the 2002 College World Series, Huston came in as our closing pitcher and saved all four of the Longhorns' victories, including in the championship game. Huston is considered one of the best closers in NCAA history. He was named the 2002 series Most Outstanding Player, and a writer from *Sports Illustrated* crowned him "a Longhorns legend, right there with his pop."

Now with the Colorado Rockies, Huston was named 2005 American League Rookie of the Year. He has had injuries and some ups and downs, but I never worry about his mental health or his attitude. This young man is wired for success and his parents have every right to be proud.

After helping lead his Longhorns teammates to the 2002 CWS championship, Huston told *Sports Illustrated,* "I've never thought of it as pressure, having a dad who did so well. He's my best friend. My role model. My adviser. My hero. It'd be an honor just to be mentioned in the same breath."

I'm sure Huston Street's parents feel the same about him and his four brothers. While the athletic accomplishments of that family are amazing, their relationships are what we should really honor and emulate.

PLAYER COACH

The second group whose role is critical in the creation of a Fearless Field is the players themselves. As coaches, we can give young people encouragement and we can provide them methods for disabling fears and redirecting emotions in a positive direction. It's up to each player to put those tools to use.

Just to be clear, my Fearless Field is not really a field without any fear at all. But it is a place where fear is no longer a debilitating force. I wouldn't want to banish fear entirely because the emotion can be quite helpful and sometimes just plain necessary for survival. The fear of falling and the fear of fire, for example, are clearly healthy fears that are worth hanging on to.

When I tout the Fearless Field, I'm advocating that we teach our athletes how to effectively manage unhealthy and debilitating fears of losing or making a mistake, of disapproval or rejection. Those fears all came into play in my first year of coaching baseball at California Polytechnic State University in San Luis Obispo. No surprise then that this was my worst year as a baseball coach. We went 15-33.

That was 1970, also known as the year I lost control of both our players and their coach. They didn't seem to care what I said. They wore what they wanted, came to practice late, or missed it altogether. When they did show up, they practiced as if they had hangovers. Then they played as if they were late for a party. They didn't seem to believe in my approach to the game. Mostly, each was pursuing his own agenda, and as a result the team was playing far below its abilities. I seriously wondered whether I should go back to work in the shipyards with my dad. I even thought about becoming a dentist, since coaching that year was so much like pulling teeth.

Fortunately, our crisis led to a breakthrough. As often happens when things look at their worst, I was forced to make a change. I couldn't keep doing what I was doing if I wanted to change the results I was getting. So, I went searching for answers and found some in a gem of a book that is often cited as a major influence by coaches and athletes of my generation. Many consider *Psycho-Cybernetics,* first published in 1960, by Maxwell Maltz, M.D., to be one of the books that pioneered the field of sports psychology.

Oddly enough, Maltz wasn't into sports and wasn't a psychologist. He was a plastic surgeon who wrote the book to help clients who weren't satisfied with their lives even after he'd corrected whatever physical flaws they'd sought to repair. Sensing that his clients and maybe others needed guidance on self-motivation and building self-esteem, Maltz wrote what is considered a classic self-help book. In it, he offers ways to break self-destructive patterns of behavior. He also encourages readers to build their self-image by always doing their best and striving for their goals.

I was so enthused by Maltz's methods that I ordered my entire baseball team to read his book. Then I held discussion classes three nights a week, going over the contents chapter by chapter. I even tested our players to make sure they were absorbing it. They learned about focusing on doing their best in the moment instead of playing to win or trying not to lose. We applied Maltz's methods to build their confidence when they were stressed, and to manage their fears on the field.

After reading Maltz's book, I began teaching our players that what they fear, they create. If they fear being hit by a pitched ball, they will be hit. If they fear striking out, they will strike out. If they fear being picked off, sure as hell, they'll get picked off. I told them that the demon is fear. The warrior is confidence. Those two emotions battle it out inside you. If you have confidence, you will perform at the level you aspire to. If you have fear, you will never achieve that level. The problem is that confidence is often fleeting while fear hangs on. Confidence has to fight like mad to win the battle against fear. It is faster but not as strong.

Our players took the message to heart. The next year, we went 39-11.

Baseball isn't just about baseball. The physical aspects are critical, of course. But it is usually on the spiritual side that the magic happens. The confidence of the players and the chemistry between them, the constant struggle to maintain confidence and manage fear, determines the level of performance.

In the second game of our 3-game sweep of Oklahoma early in the 2010 season, our center fielder, Connor Rowe, broke free of a hitting slump with a nice two-run double and a single. It was a game most notable for great pitching, but I saw those two hits as an important step for him. I walked up to him after the game, grabbed the top of his head, and chanted a little mantra to him.

"Confidence. Confidence. Confidence."

He smiled, knowing exactly what I meant, appreciating the moment.

Coaching is like conducting an orchestra. Each player has to have knowledge of the position he is playing and a vision for his role within the team's framework. Rhythm and timing are equally important. The key is to simplify each individual's duties so he can perform consistently. The ultimate reward is the respect you develop for yourself and those around you.

Emotions and feelings come and go. Most serve us well, and even if you wanted to keep them at bay, there is no wall you can build to shut them out. My goal as a teacher and coach is to give our players tools so that they are in control of their emotions and feelings rather than being guided by them. We teach them that they gain self-control first through awareness, which is being conscious of the emotions affecting behavior. Control is also exercised through thoughts by consciously playing supporting and positive messages and shutting down those that are not constructive. If fears creep into your thoughts, manage them by using the energy they generate to do something positive. When you are frightened, your heart rate increases, pumping blood to your extremities preparing you for flight or to fight. If we can tap solar power, wind power, and even the methane gas pumped out of mountains of garbage, we can harness the energy of fear.

Ken Ravizza and I have worked to make players aware of their emotions and the thoughts that prompt their actions. We redirect their emotion-generated energy into a positive force that our players can use to remain alert and motivated on the field. We've developed customized routines, or mechanisms for channeling that energy, including visualization and imagery techniques that many top athletes use instinctively.

You've no doubt heard professional quarterbacks talk about running plays in their minds before a game so that when they call those plays in a game, they've already visualized how the defense will respond. As I noted earlier, we train players to use those mind-generated images and scenarios to mentally walk through situations that occur during competition. The goal is to build confidence and also to hardwire them to respond with proven methods in each situation. We encourage them to "see" themselves completing a play in the field, throwing strikes, or hitting the ball cleanly. We also ask them to imagine the sounds, emotions, and physical feelings of completing those tasks successfully.

Ken uses the circle of focus and other techniques with professional baseball players too. He has consulted for years with Tampa Bay Rays major-league coach Joe Maddon and his players. One of his most recent success stories was with the outstanding young third baseman Evan Longoria, the American League Rookie of the Year in 2008. Ken actually began working with Longoria when Evan was still a college player at Long Beach State University. Although he is now a bona fide star, Evan was not drafted out of high school and received no scholarship offers from Division I schools. He first went to a community college instead and worked on building strength and improving his baseball skills.

When Longoria moved on to Long Beach State, Ken helped prepare him for success by teaching him mastery of the mental game. Learning to forgive himself for mistakes and failures was a major step. Ken also taught him about finding focus points on the field to help him relax his mind, which tended to race with distracting thoughts during idle moments in games.

Evan has the ability to self-analyze and self-correct, along with a fierce determination. He has been open to Ken's methods and applied them to great effect. He established himself as a star in college, and soon the professional scouts were on his trail. He was the third pick in the first round of the June 2006 major-league draft. After a brief stint in the minor leagues, he moved up to Tampa Bay, where he hit .272 with 27 home runs and 85 RBIs in 122 games.

Like every player, Evan had a sharp learning curve in the minor leagues, but he also had the benefit of a structured approach to dealing with the mental challenges of the game. Late in the 2009 season, Evan broke his wrist and had to sit out thirty games. Ken noticed while watching a game on television that Longoria was still so focused on honing his skills that he sat in the dugout and mentally went through every at bat that his replacement had while he was on the injured reserve list.

"Every time his replacement came up to bat, I'd see Evan would put on his batting glove," Ken said. "I knew he was visualizing himself at bat, mentally playing each pitch. Then, when his at bat was over, he'd take off the glove."

Once Longoria returned to the lineup, he hit a home run on his first trip to the plate. And his second. In the 2008 season, Evan went into a slump during the World Series. But the great thing about the skills he'd learned is that they will help you through those inevitable downturns. Ken calls this "learning to be comfortable being uncomfortable." The idea is that sooner or later, we all hit a rough patch. We can't control that. But we can prepare ourselves so that we can control how we respond to it.

When Longoria makes a fielding error or just feels that he's not in control of his emotions, he says he takes just a couple seconds and focuses his vision and his mind on the top of the left-field pole. That's his designated "focal point" on the field for the simple reason that every field has a left-field pole. During his at bats, if he feels the need to focus his mind after a bad swing or a called strike, he'll step out of the box and unstrap his batting glove as a method for mentally letting go of that mistake.

The way players respond to adversity impacts them, but it can also impact their opponents. If a pitcher sees a batter walk away with his head down after striking out, that gives more power to the pitcher and his teammates. Ken and I coach our players to control their body language after at bats, and we even make them practice walking away from the batter's box with body language that signals confidence, not defeat.

The mental game can also save physical wear and tear on players. Ken used visualization techniques to help California Angels pitcher Doug Corbett in the early 1980s. He'd been on the disabled list for three straight seasons because of injuries to his throwing arm. Ken taught Doug how to practice pitching mentally rather than physically, saving his arm for games and reducing the risk of injury. After Ken worked with him, Corbett earned 4 saves and went 12⅔ innings without giving up a run.

Coaches in many sports and at all levels use visualization. My longtime friendly rival Skip Bertman, the former baseball coach and athletic director at Louisiana State University, once told his players to lie on the floor of their locker room prior to the first game of the year. He then had them close their eyes and imagine themselves on the field for the College World Series championship at season's end. Skip, a huge advocate of visualization techniques, told them not only to "see" that in their minds but to also imagine the smells, sounds, taste, and touch of the experience. This is an exercise you'd do only at the beginning of the season because during the season you want your players to concentrate in the moment, winning each inning and each game as you go.

MONKEY MIND

My quest for tools to master emotions began out of self-interest. I realized I needed those tools personally. As I noted, I read the Bible and listened to inspirational and motivational tapes, but I also looked beyond Christian teachings to other sources, including Buddhism. There, I learned about living in the moment, and about quieting the mind.

Most of us lug the past around while chasing the future, and as a result we often fail to appreciate or enjoy the present, which is where we live minute by minute. Nowadays, everyone is a multitasker. We are overwhelmed with work and more work while also being bombarded by information and instant communication from Twitter, text messages, and e-mail that can find us no matter where we are.

I'm a movie buff and I've read that movies often reflect the lifestyles of the era in which they are produced. No surprise then that so many of today's films are like the *Bourne* series starring Matt Damon, in which viewers feel as if they were on a thrill ride. The action flies by in rapid-fire scenes that our eyes can barely follow across the screen. The movies do reflect real life. Life seems to fly by faster and faster and our brains struggle to keep up. Buddhists compare our run-amok thought patterns to swarms of monkeys skittering through the trees. They call it the monkey mind.

The average college baseball player is certainly not immune to scattered thoughts and distractions. So, we try to help them control their monkey minds and calm themselves by practicing mindfulness, which is a form of meditation borrowed from Asian cultural traditions. In the simplest terms, mindfulness calls for shutting out distractions, observing your own thoughts and actions in the moment, and understanding the process.

Applying this can be tricky in practice because the goal is to improve performance by doing a task unself-consciously without analyzing it or looking for rewards. It's about understanding where you are instead of thinking about where you've been or where you are going. I've seen a cartoon that captures the spirit of mindfulness. It shows a pair of monks sitting together and meditating. One of them is younger and he looks to the older monk, who says, "Nothing happens next. This is it."

The practical use of mindfulness in coaching is to teach our players to be aware of their thoughts; particularly the fears, insecurities, and other negatives that can distract them and make it difficult for them to perform at their peak levels. To teach this, we created a subtle drill that helps our players practice mindfulness. It's a bit like in the original *Karate Kid* movie where the martial arts master has the boy sand floors, paint his house, and wax his car. The kid doesn't see the value in this at first, but the master reveals that he has been teaching him mindfulness by having him repeat movements that are essential to karate without being aware that his muscle memory is being trained.

Our mindfulness drill is disguised as a simple game of catch. I can watch two players doing this drill and quickly tell you who is capable of being in the moment and who is not. The drill calls for each of the players to throw the ball first to the other player's left side, then to the center of his body, and then to his right side, keeping that pattern going for the duration. Players who can focus in the moment will follow that pattern, but those who are unfocused will quickly slide out of it, letting their minds and the ball wander.

When I see a player break the pattern, I'll often talk to him to see what's going on, because usually something big is on his mind. Often it is a concern, a fear, or a doubt. Sometimes, he's fretting about a big test coming up or a personal problem he's dealing with. When I do this, players wonder if I'm a mind reader. They'll tell my staff, "Coach Garrido is inside my head, how does he do that?" It's a matter of taking a basic skill and attaching mindfulness to it.

I was a bat-throwing, plate-kicking, helmet-smashing player at points in my career. I didn't want to be that kind of coach, and I certainly didn't want players like that on our team. You can win that way, of course. Hothead coaches Bobby Knight and Billy Martin certainly did. Yet, they never experienced the sort of long-term success or widespread respect of John Wooden or Phil Jackson, two much cooler heads.

At times in my playing career fear had me so tightly in its grip that if I made an error or struck out, I couldn't shake it. I carried it like a bad virus into the next inning and even the next game. Fear-ridden people who respond like that are often characterized as their own worst enemy. Those who master their fears, the cool heads, are their own best friend. I try to teach our players to focus on the things they can control and to let go of whatever is beyond their reach. Being prepared, fit, and focused in the moment are things we can control.

CLEAR THE MECHANISM

I was actually able to see our mindfulness techniques put to work on the set during the filming of Kevin Costner's 1999 baseball movie *For Love of the Game.* Kevin and director Sam Raimi recruited me first to serve as a technical adviser for the movie, and later, to my surprise, they gave me a minor role as the Yankees manager in the film, which was a thrill for this longtime Yankees fan.

In the film Kevin plays Billy Chapel, a forty-year-old star pitcher for the Detroit Tigers who is nearing the end of his career. Nagged by a hand injury and relationship problems, and aware that he might be traded, Chapel has to pitch against the New York Yankees in Yankee Stadium in his team's last game of the year.

Despite all of the distractions and doubts, Chapel, a master of the mental game, dominates the Yankee batters. He is so focused in the moment for each pitch that he doesn't realize until the bottom of the eighth inning that he's working on a perfect game.

One of the techniques Chapel uses to stay focused is to tell himself, "Clear the mechanism." This is a phrase from *Psycho-Cybernetics.* Clearing the mechanism is a method for emptying the mind of fear and other distractions. It's managing the moment by mentally slowing it down. In *For Love of the Game,* Sam Raimi demonstrated the effects of the pitcher's calming and focus techniques by slowing the action to a crawl, reflecting what was going on in the character's mind. He also muted the crowd noises, showing how Chapel focused only on pitching to the catcher's glove.

Maxwell Maltz likens this process to clearing an adding machine or calculator before you do a new computation so that the old numbers don't affect the new ones and give you the wrong answer. The *mechanism* referred to is the brain, which Maltz calls the human *success mechanism.* He suggested methods for quieting the mind by mentally clearing out old fears and negative distractions.

In the movie, Kevin does this by tapping the ball in his glove. This may look like just a nervous habit to most fans, but it is a trigger we've often used with our players to signify releasing emotions and focusing in the moment. Both J. P. Howell, now a pitcher with the Tampa Rays, and Huston Street of the Colorado Rockies, used similar triggers while playing for the Longhorns. Our players are also taught to find a focal point, whether it's the ball, a flagpole, an ad on an outfield wall, or the rubber of the pitcher's mound. They'll look at it, get their breathing under control, get their focus off inner thoughts, fear, and self-doubt, clear their minds, and release everything but the task at hand. We tell them to "get outside of your head because that is where the competition is."

When Huston Street was feeling nervous about playing in the College World Series as a freshman, his father offered this sage advice: "You're gonna see all those people in the stands, and you're gonna think, 'This is the big show—I gotta do more!' But all you've gotta do is throw strikes and get people out just like in all the other games you've played. Here's what I want you to do. Pick out a stitch on the catcher's mitt and focus on hitting it. Forget about all those people and what's at stake. Hit that seam."

HOLLYWOOD CHALLENGE

One of the greatest obstacles to our growth as athletes and as individuals is our fear of moving from what is comfortable—even if we aren't fulfilled—to what is uncomfortable—even if it could fulfill us. The key to overcoming fears and insecurities so that you can make a leap to a higher level of accomplishment and fulfillment is to break the task down into steps that you can comfortably manage. Our coaching staff often teaches that method to players whom we've asked to try a new position that may be unfamiliar to them.

Young men who've spent their lives playing one position and bet their futures on staying put will often rebel or at least express fear in those situations. I then pull out my speech about stretching and growing and testing yourself to know yourself. If that doesn't work, I have to explain that although I've spent my life playing and coaching just this one sport, I've experienced this sort of challenge in a big way, a crazy way.

If ever a guy was in over his head, it was me on a movie set for the first time in my life, telling a famous director and famous actors and a vast crew of veteran filmmakers what they needed to do and how they should do it.

When Kevin Costner signed on as the lead actor in *For Love of the Game,* he recommended that I serve as the technical director for all of the baseball scenes and story lines. I had no experience in this sort of thing, and in my naïveté I figured my job would mostly be to make sure the Hollywood players ran the bases in the right direction and touched every one along the way.

Director Sam Raimi, the brilliant mind behind all three *Spider-Man* movies, among many others, quickly set me straight and sent my head spinning. Our first meeting was on the Warner Bros. lot where Sam had an office for his production company. After getting to know each other a bit, Sam told me that he knew little about baseball so he would be counting on me to ensure the authenticity and accuracy of all the baseball scenes—and there are a lot of baseball scenes in this movie.

I was prepared for that responsibility, or so I thought. I was not prepared for the first assignment that Sam handed me: "We need a couple baseball teams for this movie, Augie. I'd like for you to find the players for each team, bring me eight-by-ten colored photos of each player in uniform, and their full résumés with playing experience. I'd appreciate if you'd get that done before we meet again next week."

I'm sure Sam must have seen the expression of sheer and utter panic that washed over my face after hearing that assignment and the time line that came with it. I thought he was testing me to see if he could rely on me so I sucked down a glass of water, drowned my fears, and accepted the mission. Then I drove out of the Warner Bros. lot feeling like Hollywood's biggest imposter.

I have no idea even where to start! What the hell have I agreed to do here? I had seven days to identify and recruit two full teams of baseball-savvy athletes willing to spend several weeks on a movie set. The first two days I beat my head against walls trying to develop a plan. Then, in a panic, I dialed a friend, a great friend, the best friend in the world as it turned out—Jeff Moorad. At the time, Jeff was a sports agent who represented some of the biggest names in baseball. I explained to him the assignment given me by Sam Raimi.

"How do I find these guys in a week?" I said.

"That shouldn't be a problem, we can handle it here in my office," Jeff said. "We'll get you all the players you need."

I know people often think sports agents cause problems, but in this case Jeff solved a big one, or so it seemed. His office staff delivered. They recruited two teams of prospects for our movie versions of the Detroit Tigers and the New York Yankees. They even collected all their résumés and photographs. Jeff never billed us for any of this help. He now owns the San Diego Padres, so he made out okay.

Thanks to his staff, all I did was pick up all the materials they'd put together and take them back to Sam Raimi. I was eager to please. I suspected that this tall order on short notice was a test. Sam wanted to see if he could trust me to deliver throughout the production of the movie. It was kind of like when my dad threw me in the pool for the first time and said, "Okay, swim."

If Sam was impressed, he didn't let on. Later I learned that he had bigger problems than fielding two movie teams, namely, the field itself. The director was negotiating for exclusive rights to use Yankee Stadium for eight weeks, and the guy at the other end of the table was George Steinbrenner. I thought their negotiations were unrelated to my duties but I was wrong. At the last minute, Steinbrenner threw in a requirement that no player in the movie could wear a Yankee uniform unless he was a former Yankee, a current Yankee, or an actor who had never played for another major-league organization.

The Steinbrenner Movie Rule effectively shot to hell the team of players for the Yankee team that Jeff Moorad's office had put together for me. Luckily, we had not signed any contracts with those players. We had to start all over. I went back to Jeff, and once again his expert staff got the job done, following the Steinbrenner Movie Rule for both teams, meaning the actors on the Detroit team had to have a Detroit affiliation or no major-league affiliation. As it turned out, what appeared to be an unreasonable demand actually proved to be helpful because it set the bar high for authenticity. Sometimes things that appear to be overwhelming challenges actually do force us to perform at a higher level. Our two movie teams took pride in representing their organizations and in doing things realistically, which gave the production of the baseball scenes not only an authentic feeling but more heart and soul.

I leaned on Jeff Moorad's staff heavily to build our teams, but I did put together the hiring of the Yankee groundskeeping crew for the movie—the real crew—and I recruited a friend of mine, professional umpire Rick Reed, to be the head umpire for the movie's baseball scenes. Yes, coaches and umpires can be friends—as long as they are in different baseball universes. Rick, who is now a supervisor for major-league umpires, also helped me recruit the rest of the movie's umpires from the pro ranks, Jerry Crawford and Rich Garcia, along with one actor ump, who was teased unmercifully by the pros throughout the production.

Once we'd recruited candidates for our movie Yankees and Tigers, we had tryouts in Los Angeles and New York. We put them through the same skill tests we used in baseball tryout camps in college and for the Olympic teams I helped put together. Some of the players were actors who had never played in the major leagues, so we had to be sure they looked like real Yankees and not like thespians who'd wandered over from a dinner-theater production of *Damn Yankees*. I did what smart coaches always do. I hired someone else to do most of the work; well, not exactly, but I did hire two former ballplayers to be the designated team captains. José Mota, who played for me before a stint in the major leagues, was the Tigers team leader. I asked the players to help the actors look like athletes and I asked the actors to help the athletes with their acting.

After we put the teams together, we held rehearsals at Pace University outside Manhattan. They have a beautiful ball field where we spent a week with the players performing every baseball scene in the movie—twenty-six of them featuring fifty-one pitches.

I had no idea how to proceed so I started at the beginning of the game, which allowed me to get the sequencing worked out, but drove any number of producers and at least one of my best friends a little crazy. Kevin had places to go and people to meet so he wasn't thrilled with my ponderous pace, and he let me know that the star was bored. Fortunately, once we were rolling, things went like clockwork. We rattled off all twenty-six plays in fifty-eight minutes. The rehearsal went well, but later I saw how it gave me false confidence. We ran the plays with the experienced baseball players. None of the actor players were on the field. They would prove to be somewhat less adept when we began filming in earnest.

In Los Angeles, I worked like every other Hollywood mogul wannabe, with a full-time assistant out of a trailer office on the Warner Bros. lot. I was learning as I went, and there was a lot to learn. I'd worked with game plans and playbooks, but storyboards were a whole new deal. I had no idea how complex moviemaking is, but I quickly grew thankful for storyboard artists and their ability to take the intricacies of plot and production down to a series of small steps more easily absorbed by a guy whose movie experience had been restricted to viewing the polished films, not the messy production.

Camera angles had never been much of a concern for me. Nor had quality of the lightning or the requirements of labor unions, safety regulations, and wardrobe mistresses. It also never occurred to me that movie scenes are shot out of sequence, which entails a much greater degree of organization than the average moviegoer might fathom.

The script called for Kevin's character to pitch a perfect game, but in reading the script, I was unable to answer highly detailed questions, such as who was batting in what order in such and such an inning. The wardrobe people would come to me and ask whom they needed to have ready for such and such a scene, and at first I didn't have answers for them. I had to get a much better grasp of every pitch, swing of the bat, and fielding play in this fictional game. To do that, my assistant and I put together the entire game scenario in a baseball scorebook, pitch by pitch, inning by inning, breaking it down for the movie so I always knew where everyone was supposed to be and what they were doing at every point in the game.

I had no experience in making movies. That was my weakness. But I overcame that by going with my strengths, by breaking the script out into at bats and innings. If there were holes in the script, such as no explanation of who made an out and how it was made, I filled them in so that the entire game scenario made sense. I mapped it out in a scorebook so it made sense to everyone and everyone could track the game in their scorebook. The lesson in this is that when you take on an unfamiliar and daunting task, the way to handle it isn't to suddenly try to become an expert in a whole new field. Instead, break it down so that you can go with your strengths.

After we laid out the scripted baseball scenes in detail, I discovered that the screenwriters had players batting out of order throughout the movie. No wonder I'd been confused. They had the same batters coming to the plate inning after inning. That had thrown off my baseball brain, and I knew baseball fans watching the movie would be baffled too. I worked with the screenwriters and other production people to rearrange the sequences so it all made sense. Then we did storyboards so we always had a clear picture of each scene. Once we'd done that, I figured we had it under control.

That was wishful thinking and pure bullshit. Once you get on location, everything is subject to change. Once I'd earned the director's trust, he had no problem dispatching me to deal with any problems even remotely within the realm of the film crew's designated baseball expert. I can still hear Sam Raimi's voice screeching out across Yankee Stadium, "Aug-eeeeie! Aug-eeeeie! Has anybody seen Aug-eeeeie!"

My job as technical director for the baseball scenes was a daily exercise in problem solving. Fresh challenges came each and every day, but I enjoyed them. We had plenty of resources so it was simply a matter of finding a way to make things work.

Still, I often tripped over my own feet, especially in the early going. I pissed off half the unions in New York City out of sheer ignorance over their rules and procedures, but thankfully they forgave my rookie mistakes. As things progressed, I grew more confident and did manage to make some contributions to the movie's authenticity. For example, a "blooper play" in the movie might have made the real movie-bloopers list if I hadn't figured out that it was not feasible.

As scripted, the left fielder went back and leaped in the air while trying to reach a ball hit high and deep. The screenplay had the ball bouncing off the left fielder's glove and barely going over the fence and the fielder crashes into the fence, dislodging the protective pad, which falls on top of him. This was supposed to be a play that caused the left fielder no end of embarrassment because it was replayed over and over on ESPN.

Sam Raimi loved that scene, but early in our discussions I had to tell him it would not work as written.

"Oh my, why not, Augie?"

"This play is supposed to take place at Fenway Park," I said. "The left-field fence there is ninety feet high. That would be a hell of a jump for Michael Jordan, let alone for a major-league baseball player." In addition, there are no fence pads in left field at Fenway.

Sam looked at me over the rims of his eyeglasses, made a face as if he'd just swallowed a poison beetle, then moved on to other matters. So, a few weeks later, on the set with the full cast and crew, I had to raise my concerns once more. We were in about the third day of production in Yankee Stadium when the crew rolled out this huge slab of wood.

"What is that?" I asked the director at my side.

"It's supposed to be the fence at Fenway," said Sam Raimi. "We're filming the blooper scene today."

The set designers had done their homework. The fake fence was ninety feet tall, just like the real thing.

"Sam, is the left fielder Spider-Man? Because if he isn't, I don't know how he is going to leap to the top of that fence."

"Oh my!" said Sam. "We're not going to be able to do this, are we?"

What followed was a scene that didn't make the movie, but it should have. As word spread of our problem, we were suddenly surrounded by Sam's loyal production team—all of whom were trying to come up with a solution. Everyone from the sound crew to the caterer's dishwasher seemed to be throwing suggestions at us.

Sam, who is normally not a command-and-control sort of director, finally raised his hands in the air and demanded silence.

"Okay, I see what we have here," he said sternly. "It's Let's All Play Director Day! So, let's all take turns deciding what we should do. Everybody gets a chance! You go first! Then you and then you!"

The officially designated director of the movie made his point. The eager mob fell silent. Unfortunately, Sam then turned to me. "Augeeeeie, what should we do?"

I noted that the fence pad falling on the player had been done previously in movies, but no movie had ever reenacted the infamous "Canseco bounce" play in which a deep fly ball smacked off the head of outfielder Jose Canseco and ricocheted over the fence for a home run.

"The fact that it really happened in a game will make it more believable for the movie fans who know their baseball," I said.

We hauled off the fake Fenway fence and improvised our own version of the Canseco bounce for the scene. Directors are used to having their artistic vision fulfilled, even if it may not be physically possible. While filming another baseball scene, Sam demanded that one of our ballplayers hit a home run to an exact spot in Yankee Stadium.

Placing the ball was only part of the challenge. Sam wanted him to bat left-handed, even though he was a natural right-handed hitter. The targeted area was in a difficult spot to hit for someone batting left-handed. I tried to explain that to Sam, but he would have none of it. Fortunately, Vic, the batter, put one close on the fourth attempt, and Sam decided it was good enough. They later went back and had a pitching machine throw a ball exactly where they wanted it to land.

Vic thought he was off the hook, but Sam had decided to give him another challenge.

"What's your name again? Oh, Vic. Okay, now I want you to stand in the batter's box and stare at the pitcher like you are in a game and he's thrown a pitch at your head and you are so mad you want to kill him," the director ordered.

Vic was a gentle soul from South Carolina and was a ballplayer, not an actor. Hard as he tried, he couldn't emote anger well enough to suit the director. When he offered that he never got that mad at pitchers in games, Sam was amused.

"What's your name again? Vic! Well, Vic, maybe we can just do what they do on MTV. We'll just film you standing there with the bat in your hand and then we'll have the film editors put in a little bubble and it will say, "Vic doesn't get mad at pitchers!" And then, Vic, because you don't get mad at pitchers, I won't have a (blank) movie!"

Sam wasn't trying to be funny. He was really ticked off. But the entire cast and crew were rolling on the ground laughing at his artistic fury over the batter who just couldn't "do" mad.

My technical advice was rarely challenged during production, mostly because my primary supervisor, Sam, didn't know much about baseball. But one of the biggest scenes in the movie was revised against my advice after I was overruled by a higher authority, or at least one with a higher seat in the ballpark.

The final play of the game was written so that Kevin was pitching with two outs in the bottom of the ninth. The batter hits a ground ball up the middle, and the second baseman backhands it with his glove and flips it to the shortstop, who grabs it bare-handed and throws it to first, but he short-hops it. The first baseman still manages to scoop it up, ending the game and keeping the no-hitter intact.

So went the plan in the screenplay until a higher authority on the set offered that the script wasn't realistic. The expert with the higher point of view was Hall of Fame television sports broadcaster Vin Scully, who'd been hired to play himself as the play-by-play broadcaster for the game. Kevin and Sam were watching a clip of the play as it was scripted, and when they showed it to Vin, he offered, "I've only seen that done three times in my life, and for that to be the last out in a perfect game doesn't seem very likely."

I wasn't there to offer my counterpoint, so Kevin and Sam went with Vin Scully's ruling. They rescripted a less dramatic final play. I didn't much like it, but who was I to argue? Then, just two weeks before the movie came out, the Cleveland Indians made the original play exactly as scripted. They pulled it off in a televised game so the highlight clip was played over and over on ESPN and other media. It would have been perfect timing for the movie, except Vin Scully, a great sportscaster, talked us out of using it.

My movie job had perks, but a definite downside too. First the perks: Jeannie and I were asked to accompany Kevin and Sam to the major-league All-Star Game, where Kevin introduced the lineup. We gave a sneak preview of the film to the all-stars, then we went to the movie's premiere in Los Angeles. We walked the red carpet. Those were the big perks and created great memories.

The downside was that my involvement in this movie during our team's off-season was drawing serious heat from critics back in

Austin. I'd taken over a struggling team at the University of Texas, and some complained that I shouldn't be distracted by the glitter of Hollywood. They felt I didn't have my day job fully under control. Most of this criticism came from talk-radio callers and hosts and some of the local newspaper columnists.

I wasn't satisfied with the Longhorns' performance either, but I felt I could hardly turn down the opportunity to work on the film with Kevin and Sam. Still, it had turned out to be a bigger job than I'd expected. The athletic department was supportive of my role on the film, and with the help of DeLoss Dodds, our athletic director, we developed a plan so the university could benefit from my fling with Hollywood. I proposed the plan to Kevin and Sam, and they both agreed to it, which was generous of them considering all the demands on their time.

That is how we came to stage a second premiere party for the movie in Austin, as a benefit to the general athletic fund, which sends money to every men's and women's sports program at UT. We sold out the Bass Concert Hall and turned it into a huge movie theater for the event, which raised $480,000 for the university. Jack Valenti, a Houston native who was a longtime president of the Motion Picture Association of America, said it was the second-largest fund-raiser in the history of the film industry.

My moviemaking experience was a brief interlude in my baseball coaching career, but stepping out of my comfort zone to help with the film gave me a tremendous boost of confidence. I was way out of my element in Hollywood and on the set of the movie. I had never been around so many highly creative people who place no limits either on their imaginations or their ability to put their ideas into action and bring their dreams to reality. I'd like to think that at least a little of their magic dust rubbed off on me. At the least, I intend to pretend it did. I learned from them that there is no reason to fear something just because you haven't done it before.

I was glad to return my full focus on the Longhorns when the baseball season rolled back around. Still, I highly recommend stretching yourself if given the opportunity to try something above and beyond what you do every day. You might surprise yourself, and you might reap huge benefits. I surely did.

One of the things I've observed with many coaches and top athletes is that for all of their physical talents and knowledge of the game, they often sell themselves short in other areas. They tend to accept the *dumb jock* label even when their intelligence is obvious. Some of this reflects that life is usually good for top athletes during their school years, so when they run into challenges later on, they haven't developed the skills necessary to overcome adversity.

I ran into a fellow college baseball coach recently, a well-respected coach who is twenty years younger than me. He made a point of stopping to talk because he wanted to thank me. He was so sincere his words choked me up. He said he'd once heard me talk about the necessity of "expanding our boundaries," just as I did when I took on the advisory role for Kevin's baseball movie. "Coach, that changed my life," he said. "After I heard you say that, I realized that I could change the way I did things. I could be more than I had been. It's really made a difference in my life and I wanted to thank you for that."

I encourage you to never accept limitations and to always welcome the opportunity to push yourself and to grow. It's never too late to be better. I work on it every day, and some days I even take more steps forward than I do in the other direction.

LAUGHING AT FEAR

Sometimes the most effective solution to overcoming fears is to defuse them with humor. During the 1995 College World Series, our Cal State Fullerton players were looking a little uptight on the team bus as we rode from our hotel to Omaha's Johnny Rosenblatt Stadium to play USC in the championship final. So, to get their minds off any fears, I dropped my pants and flashed them in the locker room with my elephant boxers bearing images of our team mascot.

They cracked up. Then before we took the field, I told them to enjoy themselves and not to do anything differently from what we'd done all year. After all, we'd only lost nine games all season so I liked the odds.

"It's just another game, boys, go out and have fun," I said.

Our scrappy guys took down the golden boys of USC 11–5 to cap off a wonderful season with the NCAA title. The players thought that my dropped trousers was one of the best performance-enhancing stunts ever pulled until Ken Ravizza went and pulled his own stunt. Knowing him so well, I'm sure it was based on solid psychological research and scholarly study, but I can't say that I found it all that amusing, especially since he pulled it on me. In 2004, Ken and my successor at Cal State Fullerton, Coach Horton, decided that the baseball team members needed help clearing their minds of mistakes and errors.

So, they installed a portable toilet in the team dugout. It wasn't a full-size Porta Potti. It was a small toy toilet, like one you might put in a large dollhouse. It was realistic and even came with its own sound effects. This was not a high-minded, intellectual concept. It was about as down and dirty as clearing mechanisms get.

Each time a player struck out or made an error in the field, he went to the little toilet and "flushed" his flub, releasing all ownership so he could have fun and focus on the rest of the game. The Fullerton players liked it so much they used the clearing commode for the entire season. They even began carrying "mini-me" toilets on their key chains. Unfortunately for me and my Longhorns team, Fullerton's potty training was all too effective. They won the 2004 College World Series by beating us in the championship series.

CHAPTER FOUR

The Game of Failure

When a pitcher releases the ball and sends it on a four one-hundredths of a second journey toward the batter's box, he simultaneously destroys the past and creates the future. In that moment when the batter sees the ball coming and reacts, that's life. That's everything. That's the moment of performance that teaches us how to live all the other moments of our lives.

The sad thing is that most players, and most observers of the game, don't understand how to evaluate that performance. They don't know how to comprehend what it means. Consider a hitter who goes 0 for 5 in a game. Did he have a bad game? If you're judging purely by immediate results, then, yes, but it's wrong to judge that way; wrong and shortsighted.

What did the hitter learn in those five trips to the plate? Was he working on something specific each time? Was he getting his timing down? The placement of his feet? The rhythm of his swing? Was he preparing himself to succeed on the next pitch, the next at bat, in the next game, for the rest of his career?

Baseball is a game of failure. If you play it, you will likely fail more than you succeed. The hitter is unsuccessful seven out of ten times and still considered successful—that is a truism of the game—but the hitter only has to win one out of three pitches. The pitcher can throw strike one and strike two, but the hitter can beat him on the third pitch. The challenge is you have to be present on the third pitch to beat him.

To succeed in this game, you must simply devote yourself to playing your best. You cannot control whether you win or lose. You have to give up control because in trying not to fail, you will never consistently win. That's true in the batter's box, it's true on the free-throw line, and it's equally true in daily life.

It was certainly true of Phil Nevin. A native of Placentia, which adjoins Fullerton, Phil was a great athlete in high school who was heavily recruited to play both baseball and football. He came to Cal State Fullerton widely considered to be the best freshman baseball player in America.

I returned to Fullerton from the University of Illinois as baseball coach just before Phil's sophomore year. We clashed. He wasn't content to be just a ballplayer. He was trying to be coach, athletic director, and umpire. He wanted to take charge of every aspect of the team and the game. His attitude was not working for him. He was trying to do too much.

Phil, by far our most gifted athlete, wanted to lead the team, so we clashed. Fortunately, he didn't shut down and walk away. He learned that trying to control all outcomes is a formula for failure. He let go of that misconception.

Once he focused on being a ballplayer and controlling what was controllable, Phil won the Golden Spikes Award and the Most Outstanding Player of the College World Series. Then, he became the first player picked in the 1992 major-league draft. He is now managing the Detroit Tigers AA team and he is a dynamic leader in that role.

Phil had a good twelve-year career in the big leagues. But he only accomplished all of that after he learned that failure is not something you can control or avoid, it is simply something you have to learn from and build upon. To realize that is to free yourself for success. We have little or no control over what happens to us; all we can do is learn from our failures and move on.

SUCCESSFUL LOSERS

[Augie] hates to lose, like we all do. You know he hates it with a passion. But he understands that losing is part of it. He teaches you that losing is part of it, but he also teaches you that losing is part of learning.

PHIL NEVIN
Cal State Fullerton
Detroit Tigers

When I look back at Phil Nevin's college career and the Fullerton team he led in 1992, I see another lesson about losing. In most ways, 1992 was a golden year for us. We had a great team with five future major leaguers. Coincidentally, that was the year Kevin Costner dedicated our new Titan Field baseball park. Maybe it was Kevin's blessing that sent us off on a 46-17 season. We also made it to the championship of the College World Series. But we lost to Pepperdine University, finishing second.

If winning the championship was our ultimate goal, and it is always is, the 1992 team members were losers. Except they weren't and they aren't. In the years since, the guys on that team have become one of the most successful bunch I've coached. Whether it was in sports, real estate, banking, medicine, or community leadership, the 1992 "losers" seemed to achieve more after college than any group of "winners" I've ever coached. They were a strong-willed bunch and I believe their losing the College World Series made them determined never to finish second in any other aspect of their lives. They also seem to have bonds as strong as on any team I've coached. Every now and then I'll hear about one or another of them doing something special, enjoying success, and I'll wonder again whether the fires were stoked back in Omaha in 1992. Finishing second is tough in my business. It can be gut-wrenching to come so close and fail. For some, it's like a near-death experience, so when you survive it, you never want to feel like that again.

I can't say for certain if that's exactly what drives each of those 1992 Fullerton team members as individuals, but as a group, it seems clear to me that they have benefited over the long term from what they experienced. I believe some benefits are derived from failure. You can choose them. You can choose to work harder. You can choose to learn and move forward. You can choose to nurture the unique bonds of teammates who've won and lost together. Sometimes, as in the case of this 1992 team, great things happen to those who lose. If you handle failure with the right attitude, it can lead to success.

IT'S THE PROCESS

Competitors want to keep score. I understand that, but outcomes aren't that important. It's the process and the moment that count. If you need an example, I'm available. I've coached for more than forty years and I've won five national championships. I'm considered a pretty good coach. But the hard truth is that I've failed to win the college championship thirty-five times. Sure, I've won more than 1,725 games, but I've also lost more than 795 games.

So, if you're using outcomes as the measure, the math says I stink as a coach.

Do you need more evidence?

I once had a Longhorns team that made 29 errors in its first thirteen games.

I had another Texas bunch that hit only 19 home runs in twenty-six conference games.

Bunch of losers, right?

That first team made it to the finals of the 2004 College World Series.

The second group won the 2005 national title.

Baseball is both an empowering and a humbling game. It's a little like a wild animal; just when you think you've tamed this game, it eats you. That's why I love it, but I also maintain a healthy fear and respect for it. In the same way, I have both a fear and a respect for failure. Mickey Mantle put it in perspective when he noted that during his eighteen-year career he had almost 10,000 trips to the plate. He struck out about 1,700 times and walked nearly 1,800 times. "If a player averaged five hundred at bats a season," Mantle said, "that means I played seven years without ever hitting a ball."

Our players are often shocked when I tell them I don't care whether they get a hit or make an out. I don't want them seeking my approval when they step up to the plate. I want them to focus on mastering the skills of the game pitch by pitch.

If a player strikes out with the bases loaded, which every player does at some point in his career, how does he move on from that moment to the next at bat, or the next play in the field? How do any of us rise above a setback, defeat, or failure? We learn from it and move on with the understanding that there is always another day, another pitch, and another play when we will do our best and hope to succeed.

My coaching staff tries to take the failure that occurs in every game and turn it into a positive. We want each player to see that striking out, being thrown out, committing an error in the field, walking a batter, throwing a home-run pitch or a wild pitch—all of that reveals information that can make you better. You can grow from it. The alternative is to give up and walk away, and there is no joy in that.

WINNERS AND LOSERS

That said, I want to be clear that winning is always my goal as a competitor and as a coach. It isn't how I measure my worth as a person, but it is certainly a major part of my job-evaluation forms. If our Longhorns teams don't win consistently and if we aren't in serious contention to win the College World Series this year or next year or the year after, I won't be coaching at the University of Texas much longer. I don't harbor any illusions that the alumni love me win or lose. They love me not if, but *win*. And win we must!

I don't have a problem with that. We are expected to win games and championships. The University of Texas has one of the best-funded, best-equipped, best-staffed baseball teams and athletic departments in the NCAA. It's a tremendous university in one of the most dynamic cities in the world, and great athletes are eager to play for us. By every measure, we should win.

Yet, much to our dismay, games sometimes end before we've managed to score more runs than the other guys. Then we must pay the price of losing, whatever it is. There is always a piper to pay for losing, whatever your job may be. For the record, I believe in the undeniable importance of winning, just as I believe also in the undeniable importance of losing. Let's look at each of them.

THE UNDENIABLE IMPORTANCE OF WINNING

For me as a coach the most valuable thing about winning is not job security (though it may be a close second). Seriously, the best thing about having a consistently winning team is that it creates an exciting environment for teaching and learning. Sure, having a winning team is fun for me and my staff, the players, the fans, the media, and our entire community. You feel better when you win, no doubt about it.

Still, the magical part of winning is the way it affects our practices, because when we are winning, I can be more critical of flaws without crippling our players. When the Longhorns are winning, we can practice more aggressively the things we are doing poorly because no one is embarrassed or depressed or feeling vulnerable. What the hell, we're winners. Sure, we may have a hard time hitting a ball to the outfield, but we are winning, so let's figure out what we're doing wrong and win some more.

The winner's mind-set allows you to focus on the weaknesses. You can't do that if you are losing because then you have to focus on strengths or risk arousing fears. For a team that is winning, the most positive effect is the confidence and the nurturing environment it creates for further development. Winning helps coaching. When you are winning, you can look to get better. When you are losing, you have to be careful going into the negative stuff, you have to stay as positive as you can. If you are having a rough time, focus on what you are doing well. When you are in the flow and doing well, work on your weaknesses.

My livelihood as a coach depends on winning, but I would rather not think about winning. One of my challenges as a coach is to remove winning from the team's consciousness and focus on the process instead. Otherwise, you allow fears of not winning to arise, stirring up all the pressures and stress that accompany those fears.

I'm not alone in this philosophy, by the way. The late basketball coaching legend John Wooden went four decades without a losing season, yet he banned the word *win* from his vocabulary. A fierce competitor, Wooden fought to win every game, but he believed that the focus for his players should always have been on doing their best and fulfilling their potential. If they played their best and lost, Wooden considered the game a success. If they won but played miserably, he felt they'd failed.

That approach makes sense to me. Going 0 for 4 at the plate in a baseball game doesn't mean a player failed. Maybe that player smashed four pitches so hard that they sailed right into the waiting glove of the center fielder playing deep. Maybe the other team made spectacular plays to get him out each time. That's part of the game.

In a capitalistic society, we learn to measure everything by results. I grew up seeing that the world was a different place for the winner than the loser. I didn't have the presence or the knowledge to understand then that if I'd done my best, there was no reason to feel guilty if the game shrugged at my efforts and sent me home in defeat.

[Augie] says all the time that once the pitcher lets go of the ball, he can't do anything about it so what are you going to do about it? No matter who is on the mound or no matter what team you are playing, you are always playing the game of baseball, you are never playing an opponent. I had to buy into that philosophy, and when I finally did, it made all the difference in the world.

SETH JOHNSTON
University of Texas
San Diego Padres

YOU CAN'T ALWAYS GET WHAT YOU NEED

Baseball, like life, doesn't give you what you need. Baseball functions like the banking industry. When you don't need money, you can borrow all the money you don't need from a bank, but when you need money, the bank won't give it to you. My game is just as cruel and uncaring as the meanest banker in town.

If you enter the batter's box focused on your need for a hit, odds are the baseball gods will not deliver. When your mind is on the results, you will likely neglect the process. If, however, you concentrate on seeing and squaring up to the ball, winning just that pitch and letting the results take care of themselves, it won't matter what happens because you'll know you've done your best. When you stay with the process, your ego and self-esteem are not connected to the outcome.

When our team of coaches send our players out to the plate, we don't tell them they'd better get a hit (most of the time anyway). We tell them to have a quality at bat. That might mean letting four bad pitches go without swinging. It doesn't mean they have to get a hit. A quality at bat involves evaluating pitches and reacting to them. It means squaring up and hitting the pitches that are hitable. Whether you get a hit or not, you can have a good at bat. You can have a good at bat just fouling off difficult pitches. The objective is not to get a hit; you can't control that because of all those fast, agile guys out there with huge gloves. A quality at bat is evaluating pitches thoughtfully and reacting to the ball. It is controlling what you can control. Still, if your team members consistently have quality at bats, you will increase the likelihood of winning.

Each baseball victory is an accumulation of details done right. Sometimes it is difficult to recognize the nuances. The umpire, for example, has a big effect on each hitter and his mentality. The umpire crew is effectively another team on the field. They are the guardians and the shepherds of the rules of the game. They are there to maintain the integrity and essence of the game within the framework of the rules so that both teams have an equal chance to win. They play a key role. Yet players can be weakened by a wrong call by the umpires if they feel their ability to win has been compromised. I tell them that the umpire's call is part of the game. If you think it's a bad call, it's just another adversity that you have to overcome to win. Is it fair? Maybe not. Is it right? Maybe, maybe not. But it is part of the process. Winning is the ability to grind it out and overcome adversity throughout the entire course of the game.

Every inning and every pitch produces opportunities to win. To win, you must stay in the moment because that moment can change everything. So winning has to be part of your reality, yet winning can also be the single biggest reason why you lose. Ken Ravizza talks constantly about "winning the next pitch." You have to be present to win the next pitch, in the process of pitch to pitch. That is the game within the game of baseball.

One of the dangers of winning is that you tend to sweep poor play under the carpet after a victory. Often, you don't pay attention to breakdowns in the fundamentals until you lose. You may be declared the winner because you scored more runs, but if you aren't doing the fundamental things right and staying with the processes that you've developed, you won't keep winning for long. Winners need to be just as focused on constant improvement and striving for excellence as losers. As Lou Gehrig said, "If you're not getting better, you are getting worse."

Everyone knows of the high school homecoming king or queen who had it all during the teen years, who ruled the roost, dated the best, captained the teams, and led the pack, but then, in the years that followed, suddenly went into decline and struggled to reclaim social prominence, or to find fulfillment. What happened? Often, this person had little experience with failure or rejection and, as a result, never developed the skills necessary to succeed as a grown-up.

As a coach, I've seen this in players who come to me out of high school where they played as stars on dominant teams that rarely, if ever, lost a game. They came to me wearing the "winner" crown but found themselves competing for positions or against opponents of much stronger character forged in failure, which brings us to . . .

THE UNDENIABLE IMPORTANCE OF LOSING

Some claim winning is everything, but if that were true, why do winners keep coming back for more? They must know they risk becoming losers, right? So winning must not be everything. Testing ourselves and defining ourselves is the "everything" of competition.

Developing our talents to their fullest and then losing ourselves in the deployment of them may be what sports and life are all about.

Winning is what happens when you are willing to risk losing. Without a doubt, nearly every level of our society has a low tolerance for losing, especially at the University of Texas, whether it's the fans, the player's parents, the players themselves, or the school administrators. I've had more experience with losing than I like to think about, yet my successes have come from losing, in the same way that my knowledge is born of ignorance. You must lose to learn what it takes to win, just as you must realize what you don't know before you can seek the knowledge you need.

It's no secret that my first three years as baseball coach at the University of Texas was more the stuff of Dumpsters than legend. I'd followed a genuine legend, Coach Cliff Gustafson, who retired with more wins than any other coach in NCAA history. I was second behind him in wins when I moved to Austin. I'd become bulletproof as coach at Cal State Fullerton after winning three College World Series championships. Unfortunately, I neglected to pack my Kevlar vest when I moved to Texas from California. My car radio rarely played in those days because every sports talk show seemed to be all-Augie, all the time. They weren't singing my praises. Mostly they were calling for my head, minus the UT cap.

The University of Texas baseball team is a major-league team in many respects, including media coverage and fan loyalty. The Longhorns had been to the College World Series more times than any other team.

I'd taken on a beast that often appeared to be a cross between an octopus and a centipede with hundreds of legs wrapped around me, squeezing the air from my lungs, choking me, and pulling me apart at the same time. Pressure? What pressure? The eyes of Texas were upon me, and I wasn't holding up well to the scrutiny. I tried to make light of it even as dark clouds dogged my every effort to take control of this program and bring order to it.

As I've noted previously, rejection and abandonment have been issues for me in the past. They reared their ugly heads once again. I'd won love and respect in California, but apparently my grades didn't transfer. I was discouraged by criticism from fans, alumni, and the media. I developed this sort of alien dementia, seeing myself as the eternal outsider who might never be allowed inside greener Longhorn pastures. I'd hoped that my experience and base-ball knowledge would buy me some time and patience, but there apparently wasn't enough money in that bank. I should have seen it coming since those who'd followed similar coaching legends such as John Wooden at UCLA, Bear Bryant at Alabama, and even Dar-rell Royal at Texas had had substantial challenges. Fear and lack of trust created chaos, and once rock-solid programs struggled.

The talent pool at Texas had diminished by the time I arrived, and many lacked patience for player development that involved losing game after game. I didn't handle it well. I was pressing the players to win games to take the heat off.

Some were calling for my head on talk radio. I claimed that I was the Longhorns' coach for the long haul, as long as it didn't involve a U-Haul. I even joked that instead of building a house I might buy a bus painted "stealth gray" so I could move it every night without being seen.

I wanted to be liked. I'm human that way. To make it through this tough transition I had to stay focused on the mission and maintain good relationships and open communications with the players and coaches instead of being distracted by my detractors. They didn't line up with hatchets and knives to form a gauntlet every time I walked on campus, but the disapproval was hard for me to take. I turned it around when I followed my own advice and focused on the things I could control.

FAILING TO SUCCEED

The formula for dealing with failure is straightforward and time-proven.

1. Acknowledge the failure
2. Analyze what went wrong
3. Consider your successful recoveries from past failures and setbacks
4. Make the adjustments you need to make based on what you learned
5. Keep adjusting until it works
6. Focus on doing your best in each and every moment

You overcome failure by mastering the skills necessary to succeed. You focus on the process, not the outcome. If your efforts to recover don't work, break it down step by step until your mastery of each small step eliminates failure from the equation. Build upon each small success until you have momentum. That momentum brings confidence. Once you have that confidence, the next failure is just a pit stop, a learning experience, on the road to success. When you take that position, every failure motivates you to find solutions and to up your level of performance.

Focusing on solutions rather than problems is critical. When all you do is obsess over what went wrong, you're like a guy trying to drive a car forward by looking in the rearview mirror. A solution orientation forces you to look ahead, and when you look ahead, you can move ahead. Don't obsess over what went wrong; instead, ask yourself, *What do I need to learn from this?* and move on. Ask yourself, *How can I turn this setback into an opportunity?* Then visualize yourself achieving your goals.

The ability to come out of failure fired up with courage, determined to manage your fears productively, and committed to success is a life-changing gift. It won't keep you from failing. You will lose but you won't suffer. Your failures will only motivate and inspire you. You focus on solutions, not problems. You won't be a loser because your energy is positive and your confidence is solid. You are willing to know what you don't know and to do what needs to be done.

My first season at Texas was 1996. We went 29-22. The next year was worse; we dropped to 23-32-1. In 1999, we began fighting back, going 36-26 for the season. We made the turn at the turn of the century, and it came none too soon. We were 46-21 in 2000, and the Longhorns made it to the College World Series for the first time in seven years. We didn't make it to the championship game, but we made a statement.

Two years later, we went 57-15, won the Big 12 regular-season and tournament championships, and took the College World Series championship, bringing that trophy to Austin for the first time since 1983. Three years later we did it again.

When the Longhorns won the national championship, the governor of Texas proclaimed me a citizen of the state and they inducted me into the Texas Sports Hall of Fame, and their acceptance meant everything to me. Although my mother was a Texan to the bone, I arrived in Austin as a Californian. My first three years as coach of the 'Horns were difficult, so I'm all the more grateful for the successes and for the support I've received through thick and thin. The athletic administrators supported our staff while we were taking heat from the fans and the media.

Still, uneasy lies the head that wears the coach's crown. Losing is not a good career strategy, yet it is undeniably important because it is through adversity that we grow. I had to change. The team had to change. Losing forced us to make those changes. We were under fire so we fought back. We looked for solutions and kept looking until we found those that worked. I'll never forget those first three years in Austin. They motivate me every day, and they remind me that both wins and loses have value, but one is much more fun than the other.

At the beginning of the 2010 college baseball season, the Longhorns were ranked number one in nearly every poll. I hate it when that happens. It is a mixed blessing because high expectations tend to tighten up legs and arms. Playing not to lose will most often assure a loss by creating pressure.

By early March, we'd dropped to third in the polls even though we were 7-2 going into the Houston College Classic tournament. In our first game, we beat ninth-ranked Rice University 2–1 with some late-inning heroics that made me overlook the negative things that I saw us do during that game. If we'd lost, I might have paid more attention.

Then, in the second game of the tournament against our host Houston, we lost in the first two pitches. Their leadoff batter sent the first pitch to right center field. The outfielder bobbled it just enough to allow the hitter to make it to scoring position at third base.

On the very next pitch, the 'Horns' Brandon Workman threw a slider that bounced off the catcher's glove and rolled down a little slope behind home plate. The catcher had to chase it and the runner scored from third. Two pitches and we were down one run, and we never recovered. That put the score at 1–0 and that's where it stayed.

Brandon only allowed two more hits in the entire game, retiring the next 14 batters. But we couldn't buy a run. We left 7 runners on base. The heartbreaker was that we could easily have won the game on the last play, but an outstanding defensive effort shut us down. Our hitter, Paul Montalbano, had runners on first and second and a 2-1 count when he hit a high, hard shot at Houston's shortstop. Unfortunately for us, their kid made a great leaping catch and ended the game.

Two games, two dramatic endings. One win. One loss.

After the win in that first game with Rice, we celebrated without giving much thought to how we'd played. Following the loss, my mind was swarming with negatives and *shudda*s as in "We shudda done this" and "We shudda done that." Every strikeout and bad at bat was magnified. I felt terrible. Yet, if Houston's shortstop hadn't made such a great play and grabbed the line drive for the final out, we would have won it and I would have felt just fine.

Comparing those two similar games with different outcomes and very different impacts on my psyche made me realize once again that winning and losing each have value. Win or lose, you can choose to respond like a winner or a loser. I've seen players handle it both ways. Few things are as rewarding to a coach as seeing a young man come back from a failure stronger, wiser, and more determined to succeed.

COMEBACK KID

Chris Carmichael, an honor student from a small town in Georgia, was a good baseball player in high school, but the scouts overlooked him. The only scholarship offer he received was from Howard University in Washington, D.C., where the team practiced on their football field and took hitting practice indoors most of the time because of the cold climate and bad weather. Still, Chris became a standout player in his first two years at Howard. He was their most valuable player, hitting .373 during his freshman season and making All-Conference.

When his Howard baseball coach left for another job, we accepted Chris as a junior transfer to Texas based on a scout's recommendation. He struggled in his first year with an injury that put him behind the competition, which was tough for his position. This sharp young outfielder with an almost perfect grade point average considered himself a failure because he lost his starting job. He wanted to do well, and he was upset with himself. Because he wasn't playing or performing up to his own standards, Chris fell into a funk.

As a game of failure, baseball is a fickle mistress. I tell our players that often, maybe too often. Yet, it's true; someone fails on every play. Sometimes several people fail. The pitcher fails to get a strike. The batter swings and misses. The base runner is thrown out. The fielder makes an error. The coach gives the wrong sign . . .

It sometimes pains me to admit that my favorite sport is so cruel. Baseball has contributed many of our culture's favorite idioms and synonyms for failure: *striking out, dropping the ball, a swing and miss, whiffed,* and *out at home* to name just a few. Yet, as I also tell our players, if you are willing to learn from your failures, they can lead to success. After all, baseball has also inspired phrases such as *hit a home run, knock it out of the park, a great catch,* and *batting a thousand.*

The coach's role is to provide, organize, and impart the information a player needs to succeed, but on the playing field only the player can succeed. He will also fail because baseball will make sure he fails, many times. That is the value of baseball, because success is something we reach through failure. On our teams, we encourage failures in practice and *even in games.* By that I mean we want players to understand that taking risks is how they find out more about themselves. You can only take risks if you know that failure isn't final, that it should be considered part of learning, a step toward success. When you are doing your best and you fail, you need to find the message of the failure. What else do I need to learn? What adjustments can I make?

When you think like that, you create a no-fail environment because failure isn't like death, it's not the end of anything. Instead, it's an experience in education, an opportunity to learn if you stay with it.

We encourage players to carry their best performances with them so they can recall them and build upon them when they need to figure out why their best isn't enough and what they need to learn to keep improving and growing.

To have fun playing baseball and going through life, you can't be afraid to risk failure. Instead, you need to focus on your growth, your development, and performing at your best with the attitude that the results will take care of themselves. If you win, great; figure out what you did right and keep doing it better and better! If you lose, learn from it and put it to work in the next practice.

A baseball player who goes to the plate determined not to strike out is probably doomed to do just that. He is focused on failing rather than succeeding. I encourage our players to go into a game to have fun, to unleash their talents, to play at their peaks. If they do their best and still lose the game, they should tip their hats to their opponents and then go home and figure out what happened.

If you have a problem overcoming failure, mistakes, or setbacks, you probably have unrealistic expectations of yourself and of life. Everyone fails, especially when one is learning and seeking to grow. No one is perfect, especially in baseball, where the best batting average in major-league baseball in 2009 was .365. That's not perfection. I don't demand perfection of our players, but perfection is what we strive for. It's a goal, not an expectation. The batter only has to beat the pitcher on one pitch to succeed, while the pitcher has to beat the batter three times. The batter can lose two out of three to the pitcher and still win. So, a batter who fails as often as seven out of ten times can still be an all-star. When you look at it that way, failure isn't such a big deal, and it certainly isn't a permanent state.

GAME ON

Baseball offers many ways for players to discover things about themselves. It is especially helpful in showing them whether they've learned to effectively deal with failure. In a baseball program as competitive as that at the University of Texas, it's survival of the fittest, and if you aren't strong enough to overcome setbacks and missed opportunities, the Longhorn herd will leave you behind.

Chris Carmichael was left in the dust. His junior year was a disaster. Then he missed all of his senior season after he broke his wrist. Because he'd been injured all season, Chris was eligible to play one more season for us as a fifth-year senior, but I met with him for a heart-to-heart talk.

"We gave you an opportunity but it didn't work out," I said. "I won't lock you out of the lineup next season, but there are no guarantees that you'll play much. There's some stiff competition for your position."

We had a frank discussion. Chris agreed that he had not handled failure well. He acknowledged his mistakes and asked for another chance to prove himself. I granted his request because he seemed committed to the team and doing whatever we asked him to do to help us win. I could tell that he'd taken this to heart, done some serious thinking, and taken a big step toward adjusting his attitude.

He didn't disappoint me, or himself. Chris worked as hard, if not harder, than anyone else on the team in the off-season and in the preseason too. He was back in the lineup for our 2002 opener, and he played well for the first month or so, hitting .316. Then, I had to replace him with another player who'd earned a shot.

Chris returned to the bench, but I noticed a difference in his attitude this time. He did not hang his head or complain. His attitude wasn't just good, it was inspiring and contagious. Obviously, this savvy young man had committed himself to being the best player and the best teammate he could be.

I know Chris didn't think he'd been treated fairly but he never showed any resentment. He had a strong religious upbringing and I think his faith helped him. It was interesting because Chris quickly slipped into a leadership position on the team even though he was no longer a starter. In practice, he dove for balls, encouraged his teammates when they were down, and cheered for them when they did well.

His enthusiasm and dedication became a vital part of our team. Chris figured out how to make as big a contribution, or even bigger, to the team on the bench as he'd made when starting for us. As the season progressed, everyone on the team, including me, looked to Chris to lift us up and keep us in games through the sheer force of his positive spirit.

He was a blessing to have around, but he still didn't get to play much. During the 2002 College World Series, the starter ahead of Chris went into a major slump. It was tough because the harder he tried, the worse it went for him. He was a great kid too, so it was painful to watch.

I didn't want to take out the starter, but when we reached the championship game against a tough South Carolina team, I didn't have a choice. He was struggling so badly you could feel the tension when he went to the plate. The player was in a downward spiral and his failures were affecting his teammates, who empathized and felt badly for him.

It happens in sports and in life. Sink or swim. When the big drain opens, you have to fight your way out or go down the pipe. Everyone was sympathetic to the player's plight, but I had to step up and make a change to protect the team. I had to get him out of there. It was a hard decision, one of the hardest.

I knew there would be second-guessing from our fans and the media. That's an occupational hazard in coaching, and I've developed an immunity to it.

Chris had earned the chance with his performance off the field. (We need his spirit.) I didn't care whether he hit or struck out, I just knew that whatever happened, Chris would trot back to the dugout with a smile on his face and help take the stress off his teammates with his good attitude. I put him in left field not knowing what might happen, only that he would keep doing his best.

In the fifth inning, our first batter reached first base on an error. The next batter walked. Chris was up. As he stepped to the plate, he did a little nervous dance. I could see he was trying to keep his emotions in check and not succeeding.

Three pitches later, with the count 1-2, Chris absolutely drilled a three-run homer over the right-field fence to help win the championship game for us. I still get chills when I think about that scene. Chris leaped in the air in pure joy when the ball cleared the fence. He chased our two other runners around the bases, pointing at his cheering teammates in the dugout as he came around third.

Then, just as he reached home, Chris spun around with arms extended, doing a windmill as he touched the plate before the Longhorns herd piled on him. He didn't know it at the time, but our comeback kid had just danced into the history books. He'd only had one other home run that season, but his homer on college baseball's biggest stage was the sixty-eighth of the season for our team, breaking a school record.

It was my fourth College World Series championship win, and one made all the sweeter because of moments such as that and players such as Chris Carmichael. He learned a great deal about the game that season, but even more about himself. At our team banquet that year, Chris's father pulled me aside. In an earlier discussion, he'd made it clear that he felt Chris deserved more playing time so I wasn't sure what to expect.

"I have not liked you very much," he said.

"I can understand that," I replied.

"But you have had more of a positive influence on my son becoming a man than anyone else he has met, and I appreciate that."

They can carve that on my tombstone if they'd like. You can have all the trophies and plaques. Chris taught himself what he needed to know. I simply did what I thought was best for the team at the time. It was difficult. Still, it warms my heart to know that what he learned will benefit him well beyond his playing days.

Because Chris practiced and played like a champion, he prepared himself to be a hero. He was ready for that opportunity because of his attitude and his preparation.

One of the main reasons I've never wanted to coach on the professional level is that I can still reach and teach most young men in college. I can use the game to help them better themselves. Major-league baseball is a business. They use people for the betterment of the game. I don't think the game is that important, but our players' lives are. Different industries, different goals. One is America's pastime. The other is America's future.

Coaching in a university setting allows me to teach life skills along with baseball. My staff and I work to help our players be whom they are meant to be, so every day is exciting for us. We've found that most of the learning that takes place in both life and baseball occurs when there has been a failure. That's when we go into problem-solving mode on the field and in our daily lives. When we suffer setbacks or hit a wall, it forces us to self-analyze and look for solutions. If you don't do that, you don't go anywhere. You're stuck.

Sometimes when we experience failure in our work or our relationships, we go into crisis mode. You may discover, as I have, that those times that seem to be the hardest—the failures that hurt the most or have the harshest consequences—often result in the most positive changes over the long term. That's when we are given the opportunity to make better choices and find a better path.

WALKING THE TALK

For better or worse, parents, coaches, teachers, and other mentors also serve as examples. We can hardly expect our young charges to respect us or to take us seriously if we don't walk the talk, not just on the field or in the classroom but in our private lives too. That's a scary thought for those of us who are all too human and less than perfect. It's also a tremendous responsibility. As a coach, I talk to our players often about doing the right thing in every situation, being honest, learning from mistakes and failures, and striving always to be the best they can be.

I had the opportunity to walk that talk after making a serious mistake in judgment on January 17, 2009. That day, I left a downtown Austin restaurant and bar just before 11 p.m. on a Saturday, after several hours of talking with friends. I'd had wine with my meal and should have taken a cab home, but I didn't.

I'd only driven my SUV a block or so before a city patrol car with the DWI Enforcement Unit pulled me over. I hadn't turned on the headlights, which would normally come on automatically, but the parking valet had turned them off. The patrol officer smelled alcohol on my breath. He gave me a field sobriety test and ruled that I failed it. The officer arrested me on the charge of driving while intoxicated.

My first thought was that I'd really screwed up. I was in the wrong place at the wrong time doing the wrong thing. As it all sank in, what weighed on me the most was that I'd endangered other people by driving after drinking. I felt bad about that. I drank wine that night and I should not have been driving.

I was determined to acknowledge that serious mistake and to be up-front about it. I knew that was my responsibility as a coach, a mentor, a public figure, and as an adult. I wasn't happy with my poor judgment. I disappointed many people. I worried about what the university president and the athletic director, my staff, and our team members would think. I knew this would be a major distraction for our team just as we were about to begin a new season.

I spent the next several hours in the city jail, where I was well treated. I talked baseball and even signed a few balls and caps. The next morning my lawyer bailed me out. My SUV had been impounded, so I walked the few blocks to my house from the jail, thinking that freedom is a great thing and wondering why I'd risked mine. I had some trepidation about what the next few days would bring, but the more I thought about what had occurred and how I'd handled it so far, the more encouraged I became. It wasn't just a learning experience for me, it was also a teaching experience, a chance to demonstrate the actions and qualities we'd talked about so often.

I knew there would be criticism in some corners and maybe outrage in others. I could not do much about that, but I felt confident that I could make the changes necessary to recover from this and to be a better person and a better coach. I felt strangely uplifted because it was an opportunity to prove that personal responsibility and honesty are the right paths for dealing with mistakes, failures, and adversity. I was eager to see whether what I'd advocated actually worked for me.

Several hours after leaving jail, I met with the president of the University of Texas and with the athletic director—my bosses—and with the members of the baseball team. I apologized for my mistake, and I reminded the team members about the cornerstones of our team and athletic program. I gave them my word that I would put into practice what I had long preached.

"I know you are confused and in a lot of different places right now, but hear me and challenge me on this. I stand before you in a difficult time because I have made a bad choice, a very bad choice, and it is a difficult mistake to make. However, I am not a hypocrite. I have told you to do what is right. I made a bad choice. I knew what was right and did what was wrong, and when you do that, you lose respect, trust, and freedom and the other kinds of things that you work hard to develop, like your integrity. I'm telling you right now that I will fight to get all of that back. I *will* do what I told you to do when you make a mistake. You have had a lot of coaches and you have to be honest when you think about it. You have heard them talk the talk, but you may never have had the opportunity to see them live what they've preached. I will do that and together we will see if I can walk the talk. We will see whether doing that produces the respect and trust and all of the other things we want."

I felt it was important for me to take full responsibility for my actions and to show that I'd learned from the experience. The university suspended me from coaching for the first four games of the 2009 season. I pleaded guilty. Since this was my first offense, and a misdemeanor, I was fined $500. My driver's license was suspended for ninety days and I was sentenced to four days in the county jail with credit for time served. I also agreed to meet with Mothers Against Drunk Driving and to participate in a statewide educational program on the dangers of drinking and driving.

Looking back, I was glad that the patrol officers stopped me so quickly. Far too many lives have been ripped apart by drunk drivers. I won't ever again put my hands on a steering wheel after having a drink, so that is a step forward and I'm glad to have the opportunity to be a responsible citizen in that regard.

The University of Texas president, the athletic director, and our team members stood by me, and I appreciated their support and kindness. Probably the most striking thing about this whole humbling experience was the huge outpouring of affection and support from the community and those closest to me. My most emotional moments came when I reflected on that and thought about how important it was for me to repay that love. I felt like a man who'd been to his own funeral and discovered that he meant more to others than he'd realized. I was shocked by how many people expressed their concern and care for me. It's motivated me to do all I can to be worthy of such compassion and affection. Every failure or setback holds a lesson to be learned and applied. I encourage you to find those opportunities and take advantage of them too.

CHAPTER FIVE

———————————— ■ ————————————

Be a Player, Not a Prospect

When the 'Horns were tanking and I was struggling during my first year as their coach, Darrell Royal, the Longhorns' retired football coach and athletic director, stopped by during practice. A legend on campus and across the country, Coach Royal never had a losing season in twenty years of coaching at UT, where the football stadium rightfully bears his name.

"What sort of team will you have this year, Coach?" he asked.

I had no idea, so I hemmed and hawed and finally mumbled something about having some great athletes with a lot of potential.

Royal's face reddened. He looked down at his boots, then turned his laser gaze on me. "You know, boy, that poh-tential you're talkin' 'bout right there will get your ass fired around here."

I should have chosen my words more carefully. This was, after all, the same coach famous for saying, "*Potential* means you ain't done nothin' yet."

No wonder college coaches tend to flinch when they hear a scout, a parent, or a high school coach tout someone as having "great potential." Too often, it means that they're pushing someone who is gifted but not engaged, a prospect but not a player.

Whether you are running a business, an organization, or a sports program, having the best team isn't about having the best prospects. CEOs and coaches alike need players, not prospects. If you want to be considered a star in your field, whatever that might be, you need to be fundamentally prepared and fully engaged.

In the sporting world, the professionally packaged prospect may have the perfect combination of height, speed, and strength, but too often the batteries—heart and soul—are not included. On the other hand, I've seen many college players who were never considered top prospects go on to sterling careers as major leaguers because of their commitment to stay in the game and help their teams win.

Personal branding and the packaging of people as products is a trend long fostered by marketing gurus and self-help seminars rooted in a Madison Avenue mentality. We're told that image is everything by pitchmen who put goods in packages, stamp a brand on them, and sell not the product so much as a lifestyle and an illusion. Somehow, somewhere, someone decided people should be packaged in the same way. Books and magazines touted the selling of the president and Brand U personal-branding strategies. The next thing we knew, high school athletes were being bred, born, and boxed up as "prospects." Too often, though, when you open the package, you find more air than Jordan.

The Prospect Mentality tends to put appearance over substance and the individual above the team. At one point during my tenure at Cal State Fullerton, our coaching staff and team became infected with that mentality, and it was like a bad virus attacking every aspect of our performance.

The entire coaching staff was caught up in this corrupted vision of our purpose. We acted as if we were a running a finishing school for the major leagues. Our coaching family was dysfunctional. We confused the players because we were confused about our roles. The staff had recruited a bunch of topflight athletes and we were carried away with their potential. We were coaches whose goals were to develop MLB prospects rather than teamwork and life skills, which is always a mistake.

Our staff did not provide those young men all they needed to support long-term careers in the major leagues. We didn't work hard enough to forge them into team players instead of individuals with potential. As a result, they didn't become as confident as they needed to be to handle the pressures when they moved up.

We allowed them to play for the future instead of in the moment, and our record showed it. As I recall, we were just a little over .500 that season and we had much more talent than such a record would indicate. Our prospects looked better on paper than they played on the field.

FINDING BALANCE

I learned a lesson that year and it has stayed with me. I'm glad for the opportunity to help young men prepare themselves for professional careers, but I'm more focused on the man than the career. I am no longer in the prospecting business. I'm all about creating players who are well-rounded and deeply rooted human beings.

A friend contacted me a while back for advice about his triplet sons. They are still in grade school but already immersed in baseball. The dad is a Hollywood writer and producer with ample resources. Naturally, he wanted the best for his three athletes.

"What can I do to help develop their baseball skills?" he asked me. "Should I get them personal trainers and coaches?"

I could tell my response caught this dad by surprise.

"Enroll them in karate classes or some other demanding martial art and yoga," I said. "They'll learn to control their breathing and to focus on the moment. It will also help their flexibility, agility, balance, and emotional control."

I explained to this father that you can hire the best hitting and pitching coaches that money can buy, but if young athletes are not mentally engaged and equipped with the proper attitudes, the game will get the best of them instead of the best from them. The balance of mental and physical skills taught in martial art (and the breathing and flexibility taught in yoga) serve as an excellent foundation for an athletic career and life in general. The attitudes and self-perceptions of young athletes are much bigger factors than any combination of knowledge, talent, or skill in determining the quality of the people they become. Three-hundred-dollar spikes, four power shakes a day, and a closet full of Under Armour makes for nice packaging, but all that window dressing won't turn a prospect into a player if his head isn't in the game. Success in sports and in life still relies more on attitude than accessories.

GAMING THE SYSTEM

I don't blame young athletes for buying into the branding and prospect-packaging mind-set. They and their support teams are products of a system that has strayed far from the spirit of amateur sports. The playful joy of pickup games in vacant lots have been all but lost to a factory farm system designed to crank out grade A prospects. It's not all bad, of course. Many benefit from the high level of competition and expert advice they receive, but sometimes I worry that they aren't having enough fun while competing.

Major-league baseball considers college baseball and high school baseball and everything before, after, and in between to be a part of its developmental system. The major-league owners and teams and the league itself spend millions and millions to find, assess, and rank the top young athletes in the world for their annual draft. They run a finely tuned, well-controlled machine with scouts who prowl the summer leagues as well as the high school and junior college games in the United States, the Dominican Republic, Puerto Rico, Cuba, and anywhere else you can hear the crack of a bat and the smack of a ball in a glove.

The major-league scouts are determined and skillful. They try to take the cream off the top by signing kids right out of high school and then teaching them what they need to know in the minor-league system. Even the top baseball colleges such as the University of Texas seldom land those players ranked by scouting services in the top fifty of their age group, those considered to have the highest potential for success as professionals.

College baseball normally recruits in a slightly lower range, those ranked average to slightly above on professional scouting reports. We take pride in helping many of those young men refine their skills and knowledge of the game so that they do eventually get drafted and signed by major-league teams. We're glad to see this because it is their goal to play on the big stage, and because the financial rewards are life-changing, not to mention mind-boggling.

In recent years, we've seen top high school players signed to professional contracts for $7 million or more. Each of the first twenty-six players chosen in the first round of the draft can expect multimillion-dollar deals. No wonder many parents chase the MLB lottery. Considering the staggering sums involved, you can hardly blame them.

Fortunately for my profession, some players still turn down substantial major-league contract offers to play college baseball. In 2009, a Houston high school pitcher, Matt Purke, known for his fiery competitive spirit as much as for his 94-mile-per-hour fastball, turned down a reported $4 million contract offer from the Texas Rangers. Instead, he decided to pitch for Texas Christian University. (I do admit to having mixed feelings considering that Matt whipped up on us and helped his team end our 2010 season.)

Rather than spend ages eighteen through twenty-one in the minor leagues refining their skills, some players choose to do it in a college setting while, hopefully, also earning a degree that will come in handy later in life. Most believe that they will be in position for an even bigger pro contract once they've played college baseball for a couple of years, and that they will move up faster in the big leagues because of their college experience.

That theory holds true if the athletes come with the right attitudes. In a recent year, three prospects joined our team after turning down professional contracts worth hundreds of thousands of recruitment dollars. Two of those prospects never got over their potential. They devalued themselves in college. They didn't want to break the seals on their packaging. They considered themselves brands ready for market so they weren't willing to stretch and grow. As a result, each of them signed for less money than he would have received straight out of high school.

The third young man came to us as a prospect but he became a ballplayer. He was willing to run any drill and play any position to help his team win. He had a great attitude and an inspiring love of the game. This athlete turned down a major-league contract of $750,000 to play for us. Three years later, he left campus with great memories and lifelong friends, and a major-league contract worth more than $1 million!

When a top baseball prospect comes out of high school in Texas and most other states, it is likely that he's already had a long playing career. Most who show early promise are moved quickly from public Little Leagues into pay-to-play "select" baseball leagues. In showcases around the country, these select league teams play. The players, or their parents, pay a fee to participate. Every major-league team and every major college has representatives there. This is where the top players get exposure. Often these league teams are run by former college and professional players. Many of them are in the full-time business of training young athletes. Teams have indoor and outdoor practice facilities with batting cages, private lessons, and strength and conditioning coaches.

These private coaches and trainers usually work with the athlete in the off-season, independent of the local high school athletic departments. They can play an important role in an athlete's development. Each state has its own system, but nearly all of these private leagues, personal coaches, and trainers and scouting services are focused on grooming and delivering prospects to major-league teams.

Their measures of an athlete's potential focus on:

- Running speed
- Physical size
- Throwing-arm strength
- Hitting power
- Batting technique
- Pitching technique

The major-league scouts do their best to keep tabs on every player coming up through the elaborate system. They even subsidize leagues that require players to use wooden bats because that gives them a more accurate feel for a prospect's true hitting power. The top prospects often have a personal coach or adviser who stays with them even if the player goes to college instead of signing a professional contract. These advisers try to guide the prospect's career so he'll eventually attract an offer from a major-league team. Since the focus is on the individual player's development rather than the team's development, the adviser's goals may not match those of the college coach.

When they clash with me, my point is usually this: If your kid makes it to the major leagues, his success will depend on his ability to perform on a team, not by himself. So, he'd better be a player as well as a prospect because a true ballplayer does whatever his team needs him to do to help it win.

This is why I think playing college baseball is a better route for some players than the minor leagues. The minor-league managers and coaches are great teachers, but they are charged with developing individual talent more than with building winning teams. If a team comes together, that's fine, but the emphasis is on getting individuals prepared for the big stage. College baseball is more about winning as a team and promoting cooperative effort.

I also have no doubt that playing college ball is more fun and creates a more well-rounded individual than the minor leagues do, but I may have a certain bias there. Without a doubt it's more challenging to be enrolled in classes while also playing baseball for your school team. But the payoff is generally that a player comes out of college prepared to be more consistent and predictable over the long term; and major-league contracts are based on predictability.

Being a baseball player requires mastery of fundamental skills for both offense and defense. Physical and mental preparation and a good attitude are essential. The prospect often receives well-intentioned and specific advice about the position he needs to play and how to play it. A private coach or other adviser—maybe the mailman who played a couple years in the minors—may tell the prospect he needs to be a shortstop, so when his family pays for him to go to a select team, they will insist that he play that position. Often, young athletes and their families will become set on a position, feeling it is that prospect's best shot.

As a college coach, I reserve the right to position our players where I think they can best help our team. Certain parents and their prospects have a hard time with that because their primary goal isn't to help the team, it's to groom their kid for a big contract and signing bonus. I can quickly tell whether a young man is a player or prospect by his response to one question: "If I tell you that I want you to play a different position on our team than the one you customarily play, what will you tell your teammates when they ask you why you switched positions?"

The bona fide ballplayer will instinctively answer, "Because Coach felt it would help the team win."

The prospect won't usually have an answer for me because he doesn't want to be moved to another position. He will see it as a threat to his future earnings. He is involved in the team but not committed to it. When you consider what's at stake, it's hard to blame young athletes with that mentality, but some bona fide prospects do rise above self-interest, do what's best for the team, and thus raise their own value.

The 2010 Longhorns team had one of the best and deepest pitching corps we've ever been blessed to coach. Finding a closing pitcher we can rely on is always tough, but this embarrassment of riches made it even tougher. The Longhorns pitching coach, Skip Johnson, had to ask one of our real stars and most vaunted prospects to step out of the starting rotation and take on this vital role for us.

Fortunately, Chance Ruffin has a terrific foundation as both a prospect and as a ballplayer with a great attitude. He also has good genes. His father, Bruce, pitched for twelve years in the major leagues after playing on the Longhorns' 1983 national championship team.

As a sophomore, Chance went 10-2 as a starter, leading all of our pitchers and setting the bar high for the next season. Naturally, he viewed himself as a starter this year too, but my assistants Tommy Harmon and Skip saw that this natural leader and fiery competitor had the personality to lead us to victory in the crucial final innings. Tommy, who is the associate head coach and recruiting coordinator, knows these guys better than anyone. He talked it over with Chance and his father, and they agreed to designate Chance as our closer because it would have a greater impact on our team and be best for his future career in the MLB.

I agreed with the coaches' choices because Chance is mentally tough but playful in spirit. You can tell that he enjoys every aspect of the game. Yet, when he takes the mound, he has a killer instinct. Tommy nicknamed him Ruffin Ready, and Chance chose the Trace Adkins song "Rough and Ready" to be played whenever he comes to bat at home games.

The coaching staff was convinced that Chance was our closer, but Tommy and Skip had to sell him on the new assignment. He'd had a great run as a starter and Chance was wary about wearing out his arm. Once we assured him that we would use him carefully, Chance stepped in and stepped it up like a true ballplayer and team leader.

This young man went all in. He dedicated himself to doing whatever we needed him to do. The difference in the commitment levels of the pure prospect and the true player is that the prospect is all about his major-league potential and the true player wants to help his team win.

PLAY IS IMPORTANT

Potential may land you on a team, but commitment keeps you in the game. To be fully engaged, you must enjoy the process. You can be loaded with ambition, talent, and potential, but still be a load on your employer if what you do for a living doesn't live inside you. If it doesn't inspire and excite you, I'd suggest you consider a career switch before the boss shows you the door—even if the boss is you.

The joy of doing what you love keeps you authentic. You feel the same rapture you felt as a child discovering what it is you were meant to do. That little rascal is the part of you that wants work to be play. When you tap into that youthful spirit, it energizes you. I always know when I've found other people who understand this when they radiate playfulness and enthusiasm. It is especially evident to me in the personalities of our players. The prospect is like a scared kid looking over his shoulder for assurance that whatever he is doing is right. The ballplayer is the little boy having fun, lost in the moment, unaware of time or place, focused and fully engaged.

Psychologists call this state of mind *flow,* and some say it is the closest thing to pure happiness that many of us experience. There is also growing evidence that playfulness and play itself are critical aspects of emotional intelligence. Studies have shown that children who are not allowed to play spontaneously and independently from adult control have difficulty socializing as adults. A study of death row inmates found that none of them played normally as children. They were emotionally stunted in part because they had never played freely, according to psychiatrist Stuart Brown, who conducted the study and founded the National Institute for Play as a result of his research.

When was the last time you saw a group of kids playing a pickup game of baseball in a schoolyard, a vacant lot, or an open field? I look for them all the time, but it's a rare sight these days. The *New York Times* reported that psychologists and social scientists are increasingly concerned that kids are less and less involved in that sort of "spontaneous play," which is an important part of socialization. A recent Nielsen report said that children six to eleven years old now spend an average of twenty-eight hours a week using electronic devices. Another study found that over twenty years our kids lost twelve hours of free time a week, which included eight hours of outdoor play and unstructured activity.

Think back to your own experiences as a child. Wasn't it more fun to play without adults telling you what to do and when to do it? When young people play without adult interference, they are free to make up their own rules and to break them too. They learn that the world doesn't revolve around them, and that other people respond to them based on their own attitudes and experiences. Playing games with other kids is where we learn that we don't always get our way, we don't always win, and that life doesn't always give us what we want.

Through play, we learn social skills and we learn who we are, where our talents lie, and how we can express them to create our identities and our place in the world. If we as adults suppress those gifts or the expression of them, we cannot flourish. If what you do feels like drudgery, like hard labor or a life sentence, then you are still a prospect and not a player. If your focus is purely on the outcome and you take no joy in the process, you are cheating yourself of your destiny.

The young men recruited to play for the University of Texas baseball team are prospects, outstanding athletes with a legitimate shot at earning a lucrative contract from a major-league team. Not all of those athletes are also players dedicated to doing their best and being the best in all aspects of the sport because it gives them joy. Players who love to play the game are generally the athletes who enjoy long and fruitful careers in the big leagues.

FAKING IT

One more key characteristic distinguishes prospects from players in sports and in life. Prospects can fake it for a while, but sooner or later they stop showing up. They may say all the right things and may even excel up to a point or in flashes, but if their hearts aren't in it, the rest of them will eventually withdraw. They are not committed because they are in the game to please someone else, or they've simply burned through the oil that keeps great athletes going, the love of competition.

All prospects must be team players if they are to succeed beyond signing day. This point is often lost on those grooming their children or themselves for careers as professional athletes. The same situation occurs in many other realms. You load up on expectations and goals, piling up points for the résumé to build your brand, but then when it comes time to be a producer instead of a prospect, you hit a wall. As we say in Texas, you are all hat, no cattle. You've got the résumé and the grooming, but you are not ready for prime time. You are not fully engaged or committed.

Even worse, the pure prospect generally comes equipped with a certificate of entitlement stamped DESERVE RESPECT. Yet, the game, like life itself, respects no one. It is equally cruel whether you were ranked number one among Little League catchers or you held no rank at all. The same is true of the cold, cruel world, where the only respect you get is that which you earn. Prospects get no automatic props. Players earn respect through commitment.

Attitude is critical. No one owes you a shot. So, my advice is to forget the packaging and go with your passion. You can't be so focused on outcomes and attaining position or prestige that you have no emotion invested, no juice in the game, no enthusiasm or joy for doing what you do.

My father was a child of the Depression years and was convinced that work and play were the north and south poles. They never met. Work was work. Fun was what you did after work. He hated his job. He had no idea that you could make a living doing something that you actually enjoyed. I figured that out early on and went with it, much to his dismay.

As much as Dad hated working at the shipyards, he wanted me to work there too. I don't think he was misery and I was company; I think he just didn't believe there was any other way. He couldn't understand why I didn't jump at the opportunity to join him in the shipyards. He'd shown me a path I didn't want to take, especially after I thought I'd found a better one.

DOGGING IT

My father grew up at a time when paychecks were scarce and children went to bed hungry, so his view wasn't unreasonable and made sense for him. Women and men often stick with jobs they don't love because, for whatever reason, they aren't able to pursue their passions. Bills have to be paid. I understand that and I respect those who accept their responsibilities. I find it more difficult to respect those who have every opportunity to pursue their passion but refuse to commit to excellence.

I coached at the University of Illinois for three years, but it seemed longer. I struggled in my first year there. I couldn't seem to teach my Fighting Illini players the fighting spirit, a good work ethic, or winning habits. They weren't as mentally tough as I wanted them to be. Worse, they didn't appear to be interested in learning anything I had to teach them. We had a problem there.

Finally, I decided to let Jimmy, my dog, offer a lesson. Jimmy was a yellow Labrador retriever. One day, I brought him out to the practice field where the players were going through their usual lethargic workout.

"I have a team of prospects but no players," I said. "No one on this team understands what it is to be a true ballplayer. But Jimmy does."

I then let the dog out. I picked up a bat and whacked a tennis ball into the outfield. My four-legged symbol of unleashed joy nearly ran over his own ass going after it. Jimmy was so excited. He snatched the ball off the grass at a dead run, spun around, and brought it back, tossing it in the air to me.

I hit another tennis ball into the outfield and Jimmy tore after that one too.

Again and again and again; I hit tennis ball after tennis ball, and no matter how far it traveled or where it went, Jimmy flew after it, fielded it, and fetched it home.

(I should note that no dogs were injured in this experiment.) Jimmy's tongue may have been a-draggin' but his tail was a-waggin' at the end of the exercise. He was dead tired but still game. He certainly wore me out.

"Now this is a ballplayer," I told my clueless team. "He has a ballplayer's attitude. The rest of you can go home and stay there until you come back with Jimmy's attitude. Otherwise, you will never be true ballplayers."

That little lesson motivated them for a couple weeks, but soon my Fighting Illini team was back to playing more like the Sleeping Sioux. This time, I called out the band. The Marching Illini Band was a heck of a band with 350 members. Their practice field was near ours. They were out doing drills and playing their instruments that day, so I plugged into their energy.

"How many of you have been to football games?" I asked my drowsy team.

A few of them defied gravity and managed to raise their hands.

"Have you ever watched how people cheer and yell when the Marching Illini take the field? Do you have any idea how hard it is to play an instrument correctly while marching in unison and maintaining a precise formation in a full band uniform?"

I then made the case that the University of Illinois baseball team could not shine the brass buttons of the Marching Illini.

"If we were band members, our performances would get us booed off the field because we don't give a rat's ass about doing our jobs with excellence and enthusiasm," I said.

I didn't have to pull any other rabbits out of my hat. The Lab and the band did the trick. My Fighting Illini baseball teams won Big Ten championships in two of the next three years.

THE PLAYER

Some young men need strong guidance to become true players rather than mere prospects. Others surprise you with their own drive and dedication. Mark Kotsay was a good athlete who played football and baseball in high school, but he was not a superstar. At the age of fifteen, he participated in a baseball camp at Stanford. Their coaching staff told him he would never be a Division I player. Neither Stanford nor USC recruited him. Kotsay wasn't big enough or fast enough, according to most coaches and scouts. He didn't have the basic "tool sets" used by the pros as predictors of success in the major leagues.

My former assistant coach George Horton, who is now the head baseball coach at the University of Oregon, did the recruiting for our baseball team at Cal State Fullerton. He has a keen eye for talent. George thought Mark Kotsay was our kind of under-the-radar, blue-collar kid.

I wasn't so sure. I wasn't at all impressed the first time I saw Kotsay on the field. Midway through his freshman season, Kotsay was starting in right field for our team. He proved me wrong in about every way possible.

Kotsay may not have been a prospect, but he certainly was a ballplayer. He overcame whatever limitations he had by playing every practice and every game with total commitment, intensity, joy, and enthusiasm. He played any position we asked him to play, anywhere on the field. We even used him as our closing pitcher, not because of his arm but because of his heart. Mark was the leader and most vital player on a Fullerton team that won a national championship in 1995. That team is widely ranked among the best college baseball teams of all time.

In his sophomore year, Kotsay won the Golden Spikes Award, baseball's equivalent of the Heisman Trophy. He was named both the College Player of the Year and the 1995 College World Series Most Outstanding Player. His performance in that series is considered one of the greatest in College World Series history. He had 9 hits, including 3 home runs, in 16 at bats. He batted .563 and made a string of spectacular defensive plays in center field. Did I mention that Mark also pitched 3⅓ scoreless innings of relief, picking up a save?

During the fiftieth-anniversary celebration of the College World Series, he was voted the most valuable player in its entire history! That's a player, not a prospect. Kotsay is motivated by challenges. He made himself into a major-league star through sheer force of will and strength of character. He was not the fastest guy, but he caught the most balls in the outfield. He didn't have the strongest throwing arm, but he threw out more opponents than any other player.

When the experts talk about the greatest college baseball players of all time, Mark Kotsay is usually near the top of that list. He was a warrior on the field, a leader who elevated the performances of everyone on his team. Mark was the ninth player chosen in the major-league draft in 1996, selected by the Florida Marlins. The kid who wasn't considered a prospect in high school received a $1.125 million signing bonus, the largest ever given to a Fullerton player at the time. Fourteen years later, Kotsay was still playing in the major leagues, most recently with the Chicago White Sox, where he is respected as a veteran leader.

Mark has had a great career as an outfielder and first baseman. What you may not know is that he is widely considered to be not just the epitome of a true ballplayer, but also a great husband, a great father, and a great person.

Kotsay had a tough disciplinarian for a father too, and they had their clashes, but Mark talks often about the love they share. He told me that every night his father, after returning from his late shift as an East L.A. motorcycle cop, would come to Mark's room and put his hand on Mark's forehead or shoulder as he slept, to let him know that his father was safe and there for him.

We are all products of one system or another, whether its one designed to create professional athletes, nurses, software programmers, or corporate managers. You may have to go along with the system because that's reality, but you should never let it distract you from what really matters. Don't lose sight of what is important to you as a person. Keep your value system intact. Don't sell out to please others. Nurture your self-esteem by developing your talents and following your principles.

Be a player, not just a prospect. Mark Kotsay is my prototype for the true player and, beyond that, a great human being. If you are building a brand, I'd suggest you follow the Kotsay model.

CHAPTER SIX

━━━━━━━━━━━━━━━━ ▮ ━━━━━━━━━━━━━━━━

Small Ball/Big Game

The text message to my cell phone arrived just after Game 5 of the 2008 World Series, which I had been watching on television.

"Hey dude, did you see that bunt?" it said.

The text was sent by Tampa Bay relief pitcher J. P. Howell, who played for us at the University of Texas. A free-spirited Californian nicknamed Ice Cube in his Longhorn days, Howell had just laid down a successful sacrifice bunt in the series. It was his first bunt as a major leaguer. He wanted to share the moment with me, and I'm glad he did.

Pitchers rarely even bat in college baseball, but Howell, an All-American at UT, had to learn to bunt just like everyone else. Our teams generally bunt more than any others. We've been known to bunt 80 times in a 56-game schedule. Our offensive strategy is based not on hitting but on scoring runs. We strive to get our leadoff batter on base as often as possible so we can put him into position to score by bunting and stealing bases. It's a simple philosophy but it takes focus and consistency and a selfless team effort.

With this approach, everyone contributes. The whole lineup is involved in producing runs. That's a good thing because baseball is a game of cycles and momentum. When we get nine players fully

engaged in the game offensively and defensively, we've got something cooking and it isn't hot dogs.

This is part of my "small ball" strategy, which is often characterized by sportswriters and fans as an old-school or a throwback style
of fundamental, grind-it-out baseball. Some players love it. Some
hate it. But all of our players know that by the time they leave our
fold, they will be able to do it consistently and accurately, or they'll
be spectators.

I emphasize bunting for many reasons. First of all, it is an un-
derappreciated but potentially lethal offensive weapon, especially
in college ball. It advances base runners, scores runs, and steals the
momentum from the opponent. Second, I insist that our players
learn to bunt because it requires commitment and mental tough-
ness that makes them better all-around athletes and better people
too. I see it with every team. Once the players master bunting,
it gives them confidence that carries over into all aspects of their
game and even into their lives.

AUGIE-BALL

My fondness for bunting traces back to my days playing fast-pitch
softball as a kid and also to my first coaching job at a California
high school. It's tough to score in softball because the bigger,
heavier ball doesn't travel as fast or as far as a baseball when you hit
it. As a softball player, you take anything you can to get on base. It
is no shame to walk in softball. In fact, it takes amazing self-control
not to swing at that big white pumpkin as it floats within range.
Bunting is an even finer art in softball because the infield is tighter
and the pitcher is closer. Usually, though, softball pitchers aren't
the speediest guys.

When I took my first coaching job after my minor-league career ended, I found that my Sierra High School team lacked not
only power but hitters too. The school was in Tollhouse, a small,

unincorporated community in Fresno County, in the foothills of the Sierra Nevada. Their Chieftains baseball team was largely made up of young men whose families lived in remote areas scattered in the mountains. The rugged, beautiful area included a 150-acre Native American reservation, the Cold Springs Rancheria of Mono Indians of California. I taught English and also served as a freshman football coach for three years.

I found my pitchers by asking all of the physical education teachers to have their boys throw a softball. Two of them threw it more than three hundred feet. They were signed on as pitchers. Then, I thought I'd found a potential shortstop in a young man named Johnnie Burroughs, but when I asked him to stay after school to field ground balls, he told me that he had to catch the bus home.

"No problem," I said. "I'll give you a ride home after practice."

After an hour of hitting grounders, I put Johnnie in the car and started driving, and driving, and driving. Turned out that Johnnie lived sixty miles from school. I never again volunteered to drive one of our players home, especially after I learned that Johnnie lived closer than a lot of his teammates.

Sierra High School turned out to be a good place to start my coaching career because these kids needed to learn the basics of catching and throwing, hitting and bunting. I taught them how to play baseball, but only after they taught me how to teach as a coach.

With these inexperienced kids, bunting was often our only option. I taught them to bunt because it seemed like our only hope, but then a remarkable thing happened—they became good hitters. One of the most challenging aspects of hitting is making the critical "eye shift" just as the ball enters the strike zone so that the player sees the bat and the ball connecting.

Bunting proved to be a great way to train the eyes of our players, allowing them to make the shift without losing track of the ball. Learning to bunt gave my high school kids more confidence at the plate. Standing at bat is like sitting behind the wheel in a race car with the engine revving. It is exciting, but you have to be in control physically and emotionally or you'll crash and burn. Bunting teaches that self-control.

Once the kids saw that they could make a contribution on offense, it helped them play with more intensity on defense. That's the way most people operate. Mastery in one area tends to help you focus on others, which is another reason to focus on developing strengths. I was simply trying to give my high school players the opportunity to be successful in one area, putting the ball in play, and it carried over into all other aspects of their play. They learned to see, time, and hit pitches better. Their bunting skills helped make them better base runners, better hitters, and just better all around. They gained confidence and had more fun with the game.

GRINDING IT OUT

Bunting appeals to me because it is democratic. You don't have to be a great athlete or bat with great power to do it successfully. I'll give the bunt sign to any player at any time, whether he's a cleanup power hitter or a strikeout artist. I once told a reporter that if I'd coached Babe Ruth, he too would have seen the bunt sign from me. I am an equal-opportunity advocate of the bunt. I think everyone should have the same opportunity to contribute to the offense. Of course, fans often hate it when players bunt. They cheer home runs and boo bunts. That's another reason I like to bunt. It takes the ego out of the game.

Home runs are great. They are easy to teach. The player hits the ball and then all he is required to do is touch each and every base—simple! Homers get all the glory, but bunting is the essence of baseball and of life. It is both a fundamental skill and a test of character. You can't always go for the glory. Before the forty-story skyscraper goes up, someone has to prepare the site, dig deep into the dirt and mud, and prepare the foundation. The bunt sets up the score. It's the groundwork, the small move that sets up the big score. It's the salesman building a relationship with a client one day at a time. It's the entrepreneur nurturing a mere idea into a profitable business.

More than any other offensive play in baseball, bunting requires selflessness, not to mention guts. The batter must stand and face the ball coming as fast at 90 miles per hour or more. Then he has to put the bat—along with his fingers, hands, and face—in the ball's path at just the right angle so the ball comes off the bat without much force and stays in the infield.

We recruit terrific athletes. Most of them have been playing baseball nonstop since they were old enough to pick up a bat. Yet, we still teach the fundamentals every day in practice, both the mental and physical aspects of the game. I want our players to be aware of what is most valuable to them. Is it a bat, a ball, a glove, or the ability to use those things? None of the above, I would say. It's their minds and their ability to use them. That's what makes the use of a bat, a ball, and a glove brilliant.

BUDDHA AT BAT

Too often, we make our lives difficult or overly complicated. Baseball is like life in that the secret isn't to try to hit a home run every time, it's to grab every opportunity to succeed in the moment, moving from base to base until you reach home.

Once you master whatever it is that you love to do, it doesn't matter whether you win or lose, succeed or fail; what matters is the joy you get from being present, pursuing your passion, and performing your best. Small ball offers ample lessons in this, particularly with one of baseball's most Zen-like plays, the sacrifice bunt. Done correctly, it freezes time and creates a space all of its own, a place dreaded by pitchers and infielders because it leaves them stymied. The sacrifice bunt is a selfless act that creates possibility by putting runners in position to score.

A great example of this occurred when we were playing Rice University, always a tough opponent, in the 1996 NCAA Midwest Regional. We'd been ranked as the top team in the nation for most of the season but then we lost 10 of 14 games. Mark Kotsay had driven in 9 runs in the previous game against Delaware, but Rice held him to 1 hit. In the seventh inning we were leading by just one run, 4–3. Kotsay walked with one out. Another future major leaguer, Jeremy Giambi, then stepped into the batter's box. He laid down a perfect bunt that put him on first and Kotsay on second. We followed that bit of small ball with another: a double steal. With both runners in scoring position, there was no danger of a double play. That eased the pressure on the next batter, Brian Lloyd, who'd hit a three-run homer in the first inning. All he had to do was hit a sacrifice fly to score another run or two. Instead, he hit another three-run homer to seal the game and keep the Titans in contention for the postseason.

That's the power of bunting. Small ball can make for a big game. Giambi's little chip set off a series of plays that led to three runs scoring, a key victory. Small successes add up to big victories on and off the playing field. To me few coaching moments are more enjoyable than watching one of my batters lay down a sacrifice bunt that moves a runner into scoring position while totally confounding and frustrating the opposing pitcher and his infielders. Priceless!

Basic skills must be mastered in whatever you do, work or play, physical and mental. Often, these tasks are a challenge to learn and to perform consistently, and they may not elicit the sort of rapturous praise that greater accomplishments bring. A great bunt rarely sends a crowd jumping to its feet the way even a single-run homer does; just as a basic pick-and-roll play in basketball doesn't have the emotional impact of a slam dunk. Yet both are highly effective when done right.

Teams have won championships time and again by consistently wielding basic but effective tools such as baseball's bunts and basketball's pick-and-roll. The same applies to life off the playing surface. Mastering the physical, mental, and emotional fundamentals builds confidence as well as competence. Every surgeon must learn to sew stitches before he can operate on a patient. Every race-car mechanic first learns how to change the oil and the air filter. "Chopsticks" is still the first tune many pianists play. The simplest tools may prove to be your best down the road whether you are working in a trade or building a career.

GO WITH YOUR STRENGTH

If you believe Ted Williams, *Sports Illustrated,* assorted physics professors, and kinesiologists—not to mention hundreds of guys making bets in bars—hitting a baseball is the most difficult skill in all of sports. Retired Yale physics professor Robert Adair, author of *The Physics of Baseball,* noted that the ball and the bat make contact for just one one-thousandth of a second, but the ability to make that successful contact takes years and years of training.

A fastball thrown 95 to 100 miles per hour reaches the batter's realm in 0.4 seconds. Considering that it takes 0.15 seconds for you to voluntarily blink an eye, that 0.4 seconds doesn't leave a player much time to assess the location and speed of the pitch and swing into action so that the bat and the ball meet at exactly the right place at exactly the right time. Then there are the variables. Is it a breaking pitch? A knuckleball? A changeup?

Professor Adair holds that when a fastball thrown in the upper 90s leaves a pitcher's hand, the batter has just two-tenths of a second to process essential information before initiating the swing. When you look at it from that perspective, the value of small ball becomes pretty obvious. After all, the goal isn't to get hits; it's to score runs, right?

If the most difficult skill in all of sports is hitting a baseball, why should we beat our heads against the wall every at bat, every inning, every game, by trying to win with the most difficult weapon? If that strategy were effective, most wars would still be fought with bows, arrows, and spears.

Why not go with the most effective weapons in your arsenal? Why not focus on strengths instead of weaknesses? This philosophy applies to life as well. Nobody hits a home run every time he steps to the plate, so why swing for the fences when it is so much easier to lay down a bunt, take a walk, or hit a ground-ball single and get on base? My contention is that we should use the best weapons available to us. Whether it's your gift for math or science, a talent for teaching, or the ability to quickly bond with strangers, seize upon that strength. Build momentum by building on whatever comes naturally to you.

BUNT MASTERY

Practice isn't what we do just because there's no game to play. Teams practice because that is the only way to keep improving and to get an edge on their opponents. We know that if we don't practice, we lose ground because the other teams out there are working to get better even if we aren't.

In his book *The Genius in All of Us: Why Everything You've Been Told About Genetics, Talent and IQ Is Wrong*, author David Shenk writes about the importance of "deliberate practice." He says that whatever we want to do well, we have to do over and over because this produces changes in the brain and makes new levels of achievement possible for us.

Shenk is a science writer and offers the latest research showing that our inherited genes are influenced by environmental stimuli, nutrition, hormones, and nerve impulses. He claims this gives us more control over our destinies than we might think. Genius and talent are the product of "highly concentrated effort," also known as practice. Repeated attempts to learn and master new skills and new levels of skill result in frequent failures, but that is where learning takes place; eventually practicing a new task produces changes in the brain, making new heights of achievement possible, Shenk writes.

His book notes that Beethoven wrote sixty to seventy drafts of a single phrase of his music. He also cites the practice and work-out regimens of athletic greats such as Ted Williams and Michael Jordan, who were known for their relentless pursuit of excellence. Williams practiced hitting until his hands bled.

It's often said that games and championships are won in practice first. The same holds true in life. If you aren't getting better every day, you are losing ground. The person who wants your job is building a résumé to take it. The guy who wants your girl is working on a way to win her over. What are you doing?

This is about never taking anything for granted; it's about always trying to be the best you can be at whatever you do. The better person you become, the better the jobs and the people you will attract. If you believe in yourself, others will believe in you too. There is no resting on your laurels in sports or in life; you have to keep pushing to be the best that you can be. Every day, find a way to better yourself in some way.

DIFFERENT STROKES

Unlike certain other authors, I sweat the small stuff. I believe that mastering the small things, rather than focusing on the flashy big strokes, sets us up for consistent and long-term success in baseball and life. We teach our players that this is a small game played on a big field. Games are won or lost by inches and steps. The player who runs full speed even on "routine outs" sets himself up for opportunities that a slacker who doesn't make the effort will never be able to capitalize on.

It's the same in life. Big achievements come when you master incremental steps one at a time. This helps build confidence, which is vital in sports and in every other aspect of life. Catching, throwing, and hitting the ball are basic skills that most people can master at some level, but to play at the highest level in college and the major leagues requires a much deeper mental and physical awareness. I've always had to break things down until they no longer intimidated me, then work my way through the smaller tasks, building upon them over time.

NORTHERN EXPOSURE

Some of us may have to learn the hard way, but that doesn't mean we always have to take the hard way. My cold and calculating small-ball coaching philosophy was forged in Anchorage, Alaska, appropriately enough. I served as manager of the Anchorage Glacier Pilots summer-league amateur baseball team for the 1975 and 1976 seasons. In my final season with them, we made it to the National Baseball Congress championship game. We were playing our archrivals, the Fairbanks Goldpanners (I kid you not). We'd won something like 17 out of our last 20 games against them, so we were fairly confident going into the championship game. But the Goldpanners grabbed us by the nuggets and wouldn't let go.

We had 15 hits. They had 5. And they won.

Look at those numbers again, because therein lies the truth of baseball. We had three times the number of hits they had, and they went home with the trophy. It was a hard lesson, but I studied that failure inside and out and then I mined a little gold from it. The stats in that game made it clear to me that to win baseball games, a team must concentrate not on getting hits, but on "productive outs" that put base runners in position to score. If hitting the ball is the hardest skill in all of sports, but it doesn't bring victory, why should that be the focus of our offensive efforts? Why not home in on something easier that is just as likely, or even more likely, to produce runs, such as bunting, getting walks, and base-running?

Getting rocked by the Goldpanners awakened me to how baseball games are won or lost based on runs, and there is more to generating runs than cranking out the most hits. So, I decided to refocus my coaching strategy. I began keeping stats on how many hits we had versus how many runs we scored. If we make seven outs for every ten at bats, what are we accomplishing with those seven failures? What are we producing and how are we handling them mentally? The statistics of hits versus runs show the relative importance of hitting, bunting, baserunning, productive outs, and runs batted in.

Early in our 2010 season, I checked those stats for our Long-horn team. We were 14-3 and ranked No. 3 in the nation. We had racked up only 6 hits more than our opponents so far in the season, but we had scored 26 more runs. Eye-opening, isn't it?

Consider that baseball is a series of battles over ninety-foot stretches of terrain, the distance between the bases. Every ninety feet gained is critical. So any opportunity to claim one of the four bases is one worth seizing. The base runner's job is to keep advancing while also doing everything he can to distract the pitcher and throw off the timing of the defense.

We encourage our players to always be thinking and striving to reach the next base, then the next, until they score. The focus isn't on simply getting a hit, it's about scoring runs. We want them to be speedy but also smart. Our players on base need to have a plan and to visualize what they intend to do before stepping off the bag. Once they are off the bag, they need to be focused on the pitcher and to trust their ability to carry out the plan.

Small ball is about taking small bites. Small steps lead to big things. First base first. Second base second. One bite at a time in ninety-foot chomps. If your strategy relies on doing the big flashy things such as belting home runs, great pitching will beat you every time. But with small ball, you can kill them with a thousand cuts.

SWIFT LESSON

The seeds of small ball were planted in Anchorage, but they didn't begin to take root until I reached Omaha. In 1982 I coached a big-hitting, fast-running Cal State Fullerton team in the College World Series, which was being televised for the first time on the new ESPN network. Unfortunately, we discovered that our Titan team was not ready for prime time.

All season we'd relied on home runs, big hits, and speed around the bases to rack up victories. In our first game in the CWS we ran into a fully loaded Wichita State University team that clobbered us 7–0. Then we faced Billy Swift, a right-handed pitching machine for the Black Bears of the University of Maine, Orono. The fourteenth of fifteen siblings in the Swift family lineup, Billy was a three-time All-American with a full arsenal of pitches including a sinking fastball and a high-velocity slider. He would become the second player chosen in the 1984 major-league draft and enjoy a long and successful career. Billy mauled us in the second game. I remember that game well. It was the day I learned you can't steal first base, much as we tried. The Titans went down 6–0 and our tournament was over before you could say, "Orono!"

In both of the games we lost big in that College World Series, we faced precise pitchers who threw consistent strikes. They shut down our hitting machine and kept the runners off the bases. In that painful trip to the CWS, Fullerton went eighteen consecutive innings without scoring a run.

While we were packing our bags to head home, the sportswriters naturally asked me what the hell happened to our home-run kings.

"Well, I've always told you that our goal was to be the best at whatever we do, and right now, we are the best at being the worst," I said.

THE GAME IS THE GURU

I am in awe of the game of baseball. You just can't control the game. The more you know, the more there is to know. The simpler you try to make it, the easier it gets. No one plays it well consistently. It plays everyone instead. It's too damned hard a game, which is what makes it so much fun. Win or lose, there is always a challenge, always something to learn.

We were out of that 1982 CWS so fast that we used the same airsickness bags coming and going. On the way home, I chucked the home-run strategy and pulled out my small-ball playbook. Alaska and Omaha had inspired me.

After our Fullerton home-run hitters went hitless for most of the 1982 College World Series, I began emphasizing small-ball strategies in practices during the 1983 season. My players weren't enthused at first, but slowly they came around. Then, in our third game in the 1984 College World Series, we unleashed small ball in a big way. We were 1-1 in the series at that point, having beaten Michigan before losing to Texas. Next up was the University of Miami. We had to tame the Hurricanes to stay in the tournament.

Miami's pitcher was averaging 15 strikeouts a game so we weren't about to intimidate him by swinging away. We gave our hitters the green light, but only if they bunted. Five straight Fullerton batters bunted. The Hurricane players screamed every synonym they could think of for *wimpy,* but we just kept laying the ball down at their feet. We scored 5 runs, and none of the bunted balls traveled more than sixty feet. We rattled the Hurricane's pitcher so badly he never recovered. We beat them 13–5 on our way to successive victories over Arizona State, Oklahoma State, and the Texas Longhorns to win the championship.

Today, the Longhorns practice bunting for twenty minutes during every practice in the preseason and at least twice each week during the season itself. Every player is required to master bunting. Our coaches want each member of the team to understand the importance of this fundamental skill, the play that sets up the score.

The 2009 Longhorns were masters of small ball. They bunted with absolute relish. We went into the College World Series that year ranked next to last in season batting average among the eight CWS teams. We were only eighth in that category among our Big 12 opponents. But we led the nation in sacrifice bunts.

We'd set an NCAA single-game record with 7 sacrifice bunts to beat Texas Christian University and win the opening game of the superregionals that year. After that game, our season bunt total was 95. Twice in that game we pulled off safety-squeeze bunts to score runs. The frustrated TCU coach called the safety-squeeze "indefensible."

Most of our offensive rallies then and now involve at least one bunt to get a man on base or to advance the runner. Brandon Loy was our leading sacrifice bunter on that 2009 team of overachievers. He had 24 of them in the regular season, but every member of the team had at least 6. Brandon Belt, our best hitter, had 9 sacrifices in the regular season.

GROUNDED IN SUCCESS

Someone asked me that year if our players resented being asked to bunt. My response was "Not if they want to play." Still, many baseball experts and pseudo-experts say that bunting is passé as a baseball tool, but most of them are talking about bunting in the major leagues, where players are bigger, stronger, and more experienced. The college game is slower. It's a matter of using what works where it works, and small ball is effective in college baseball. In the 2009 regular season, we had 22 fewer at bats than our opponents, but we had 125 more hits and 154 more runs. That happens when you keep people in position to score. The game is controlled by runs, so you need the total package in your offense. Productive outs are a big part of that package. Opposing fans sometimes mock us when we go to the small-ball strategy, but that's only because it hurts them to be bunted into submission. It's no secret that other teams in our conference and across the country have similar strategies now.

Bunting is not just an offensive weapon. It is a tool for making our batters and our teams successful. That's always a primary concern for me and any coach—teaching methods for finding success on and off the field. One of my favorite things about bunting is that it requires players to be unselfish. The natural desire of my baseball players is to go for the glory and swing for the fences. Bunting is an entirely different act. It's a finesse tool that requires an unselfish act; especially if it is a sacrifice bunt. That's taking one for the team. It builds unity.

As with any good offensive weapon, it's not just about what bunting does for your team, it's also about what it does to the opposing team. The threat of a skillful bunter at the plate draws in the first and third baseman, which opens up other areas of the field. It gives your opponent something else to think about, to worry about, and that is always a good thing.

Bunting is especially effective in distracting the pitcher and, hopefully, frustrating him, disturbing his rhythm and shaking his confidence. Bunting neutralizes good pitchers. Pitchers take it personally when you bunt on them and make them scramble to make a play. If it's a good bunt, the pitcher sometimes looks a little silly because even if he gets to the ball, it's too late to do anything with it.

The toughest bunt to defend against is the one laid down in bunting's Bermuda Triangle, the zone between the pitcher, second baseman, and first baseman. We love to see all three of those defenders rushing for the bunted ball at once because that means no one is covering first base and it is ours to claim. That's a beautiful bunt placement because it forces those three key defenders to jump on the ball, and they each have to decide who grabs it, who covers the base, and who just gets the hell out of the way. It's one of baseball's toughest defensive plays, and if the opponents don't make it, their confidence can be badly shaken for the rest of the game.

OFFENSIVE GOAL

Bunting is helpful in each of the three offensive phases:

1. Getting on base
2. Advancing to a scoring position
3. Crossing home plate to score

You can bunt to get on base. You can bunt to advance runners. And you can squeeze-bunt to score a runner from third base. A bunt will not work each and every time; the game of baseball isn't that kind. We try to play the percentages so our players have a chance to trigger a rally and keep it going. The baseball gods always have the final say.

Teaching players to bunt calls for some tact and applied psychology. You can't just round up your worst hitters, take them off to a corner of the field, and say, "Okay, you losers, since you couldn't hit if they rolled it to you, we will learn to bunt." That's probably not a good strategy. If you coach just your poorest hitters to bunt, you'll destroy their confidence. Besides, every player should know how to bunt, and each should understand that it's an extremely useful offensive weapon that allows everyone on the team to contribute to that golden goal—putting runs on the scoreboard.

Every player on our team practices bunting in game environments, and we practice it until each player is comfortable with it. Fundamentally, bunting is a pretty simple task as long as you don't mind squaring up to a small, hard object hurtling at you at a speed likely to leave a nasty bruise if not broken bones and ruptured parts. Along with remaining calm and unafraid, the player must stay balanced, positioned for a clear view of the pitch, with the bat out front so he can watch the ball strike the bat. We teach players to set the angle of the bat versus the ball early. The most common mistake is to not be in position before the ball arrives. When that happens, the bunter often loses sight of the ball, then rushes to make contact. We encourage them to have a routine with definite checkpoints that keep it simple but establish timing and rhythm.

We want players to be cagey to keep the defense guessing as long as possible. If the infield stays back, we try not to tip them off as long as possible if we are bunting for a base hit. But if the infielders are pulled in tight, we don't worry about being sneaky because it is better to have the timing right. Either way the batter can only wait so long before taking a bunt position. It's important that the bunter position himself in the front of the batter's box before the pitch reaches him. This allows for better bunting angles within the foul lines in fair territory.

TARGET PRACTICE

In Austin, we have a batting cage specially set up just for bunting practice. We give each player specific targets to aim for when bunting. We make up bunting target games to keep it interesting and enjoyable because most players don't find bunting glamorous. The "Baron of the Bunt" just doesn't have the same ring for them as the "Sultan of Swat." Our instructions are simple enough. We tell the bunter to "be firm" with the bat. The goal is to send the ball to the ground quickly. This encourages the bunter to stay on top of the ball, allowing the ground to do the work of draining its energy so it doesn't roll far. We plant the thought that the quicker he makes the bunted ball bounce, the more time it buys him to make it to first base and the base runner to advance.

It's fun to win, and it's especially fun to bunt and win because it drives your opponents nuts. Bunting also sets up the defense for failure by drawing them in and putting them on edge. It plays with their minds while building confidence and, hopefully, momentum for the members of your team. The small-ball weapons also tend to bring a team closer together because everyone can contribute by bunting, walking, and stealing bases.

RISK AND REWARDS

Small ball opens up new and unexpected opportunities for athletes. One of my goals is for our players to be confident that they can make choices that will bring them joy and happiness. Yet, I also want them to know that if they make a poor choice, they can still learn from it and take steps forward. This gives them the courage to take risks, to do what they know is right even if it means finding out they are wrong.

Texas was playing Oklahoma in a 2007 regular-season Big 12 conference game. With two outs and the bases loaded in the second inning, Chance Wheeless, our big-hitting first baseman, caught the Okies by surprise. He laid down a perfect bunt single that scored a run and helped us win the game. Chance decided on his own to bunt. If I'd ordered him to do it, I might have scared the hell out of him, but he took the gamble because he had the confidence, along with the proper first name.

———————————————■———————————————

CHAPTER SEVEN

Step Up, Superman

Chance Wheeless was tough as well as versatile throughout his Longhorns career, but on one particular day he was Superman. In the sixth inning of our game against Baylor University in the 2005 College World Series, Chance hit a weak ground ball into the infield, then went down on his knees in agony. Our first baseman had injured his right shoulder in a game two days earlier. After that first time, Chance dislocated his shoulder nearly every time he took a good swing, popping it in and out of the socket, causing intense pain.

We were in the semifinals. Baylor had beaten us three times in the regular season. Chance wanted to keep playing, but the injury was obviously bothering him. In the next inning, he lost a throw in the sun, setting up two runs for Baylor.

We went into the bottom of the ninth tied 3–3. This was a crucial moment. If we scored and won, we were in the championship series. If we failed to get a run and lost, we were facing a long ride home and an even longer wait for next season. The year before we'd been in the finals of the College World Series, only to return empty-handed.

Going into that last inning, Chance was supposed to be our leadoff batter. He was normally one of our best hitters, but because of his injury, I'd decided to put in a pinch hitter. It wasn't a tough decision. Chance was hurting so badly, I thought I'd be doing him a favor.

"I'm going to have someone pinch hit for you," I said, expecting him to express relief.

Normally Chance is not an outspoken guy. An old soul, brilliant of mind and just a terrific athlete, he was also laid-back. His teammates called him Sleepy.

On this day, though, Chance was not about to give it a rest. "Coach, I've played against this pitcher my whole life. We grew up together. I've always hit him hard."

"What about your shoulder?"

"It won't matter."

Nobody would have blamed me for simply thanking Chance for his offer, then sitting him down and sending out the pinch hitter. After hearing his determined response and talking it over with the team trainer, I had to honor his courage and my own principles. One of the greatest honors and responsibilities we have as coaches, teachers, parents, and mentors is providing our young charges with opportunities to discover who they are. Chance Wheeless was asking for just such an opportunity. He was confident that he could get on base despite his injury.

His desire to help the team regardless of his pain confirmed for me the remarkable power of the human spirit. He shocked me, actually. For six seasons at Texas, I'd lamented a lack of leadership and guts on our teams. I'd often said how hard it was to find young guys who were willing to stand up and take responsibility when things got tough. Now, this rangy kid who'd twice dropped to his knees in agony during the game was telling me he could help us win it. Who was I to deny him that opportunity?

Besides, he had my curiosity up. I wanted to see if he could really do it.

"Okay, Chance. Give it your best shot," I said.

The announcers expressed disbelief when the big guy ambled

to the plate with bat in hand. My assistant coaches didn't bother stifling their shock. Neither did the fans.

"Are you crazy, Augie?" one of our coaches said. "He doesn't have a chance with that shoulder."

"Hey, he wants to be a hero and I'm sure not willing to stop him," I said.

After the first two pitches, I was questioning my sanity. One was a ball. The other was a strike. Chance was gritting his teeth. I was grinding mine.

Then, the next pitch came blazing across the strike zone and Chance swung as if he were the Man of Steel. He just creamed it, sending the ball over the fence for a walk-off home run that won the game and put us in the championship series.

As I watched Chance trot around the bases to the cheers of his teammates and our fans, I thanked him. Then I thanked his mother and father and their mothers and fathers, his hometown of Bryan, Texas, the entire population of surrounding Brazos County, and everyone who had anything to do with this kid's being on the planet.

MEN OF STEEL

A writer for *USA Today* covering the 2005 College World Series game compared Chance Wheeless to the character of Roy Hobbs in the movie *The Natural.* I think it was an apt description, but I'll go with another fictional hero. Chance's performance that day confirmed my long-held contention that a Superman is inside every one of our players, and in every one of us. To celebrate that, we stage a Superhero Halloween each October in which our players scrimmage dressed as their favorite character. This has turned into a great event, but our little play party has a purpose too.

Our hope is that the laughter and enjoyment the players experience in the scrimmage will help them stay loose and playful in games. When they are nervous in real games, I often tell them to go out and play as if they were still the same boys who thought they were the baddest dudes in baseball. The dress-up day reinforces that too.

We've had the Halloween scrimmage about five years now. The players stuck to the superhero theme fairly well in the first few years. They showed up as the usual comic-book types: Superman, Spider-Man, Batman, and assorted X-Men. Being eighteen- to twenty-three-year-olds, however, they have tended to take the concept and run amok with it in recent years.

For a few years, our left-handed submarine pitcher and team comedian Keith Shinaberry dominated the costume competition. He showed up one year as a beefy, blow-up umpire who kept expanding like a balloon throughout the scrimmage until he finally popped all the buttons off his uniform. Then another year Shinaberry arrived in drag doing a strong impersonation of one of our most avid female fans. He stayed in character throughout the scrimmage, even running the bases with his purse flopping at his side. We've also had a couple Peter Pan impersonators and at least one Fidel Castro, which may not be the sort of superhero I had in mind originally, but then I did come dressed as the rapper Flavor Flav one year. Even more shocking was a recent costume worn by Coach Tommy Harmon, who strictly enforces the team dress code. Tommy, who bleeds Texas orange, may have given several players nightmares for life when he showed up sporting dangling dreadlocks in a dead-on impersonation of the Dodgers' Manny Ramirez, complete with wave cap, wristbands up and down both arms, and baggy pants covering his shoes! It was the best costume ever.

I encourage our players to believe that their inner superhero is just waiting for the perfect moment when preparation meets opportunity, potential is fulfilled, and destiny is realized. The game, like life, doesn't give us what we want. It doesn't give us what we pray for. It doesn't give us what we wish for. It doesn't give us anything other than opportunity, nothing more, nothing less, and that's enough. In fact, it's a great gift.

When I was a young man, opportunity was all I wanted. While I still relish it, I enjoy even more providing it to others. That's one of the joys of coaching. Young players are often vulnerable and even fragile, but if you help them find their confidence, they can become Superman in an instant. Chance's performance was supernatural—and not just because it gave us the confidence to win the 2005 College World Series. With his display of courage, Chance confirmed that each of us is capable of doing extraordinary things. More important, Chance reached down deep and found inner strength that he might never have known existed. I have no doubt that he will be successful wherever life takes him, in part because of what he learned about himself that day. Whatever he accomplishes, that moment will be part of it.

Our 2005 team not only had confidence, they found the fun in the game. They were the hardest-working bunch of guys, but they also had fun on and off the field. That group found a fabulous balance of competitive genius and boyish fun. And their coaches enjoyed the ride.

A SENSE OF BELONGING

Experiences like that showcase the higher value of sports. Participating in athletics isn't all about the trophies you take home, it's about the person you become. Your success in life is determined not by how others perceive you but by how you perceive yourself. I mentioned Phil Nevin earlier. He helped lead our Fullerton team to the 1992 NCAA championship game, though we came up short. When the Houston Astros were considering taking him high in the major-league draft, they asked him to attend a workout in San Francisco. Phil was an exceptional athlete, an All-American kicker on the Fullerton football team for three years. He was confident in his abilities. So I wasn't surprised when he returned from working out with other Astro players—guys who'd already been in the major leagues for several years—and said, "You know, Coach, they aren't really that good."

Phil wasn't bragging that he was better than the players already on the Astros. He was just stating that their skills weren't that much greater than his own, or those of his teammates. When he said that, I replied, "Well, you just told me that you are going to make it in the major leagues, Phil."

"What do you mean?" he asked.

"You just told me that you know you belong there, and that sense of belonging will get you through any hard times you might have."

Phil was the first player taken in that 1992 draft. He played twelve years in the major leagues and made the National League All-Star Team. He was right. He belonged. Phil's level of confidence is what it takes. Whatever you do, if you don't believe that you belong, you won't. If you are confident in your skills and your ability to keep improving, then odds are you will make it.

That sense of belonging is powerful. I've seen the true power of it in several young players whose fathers were major leaguers. Some of those kids may not have been as talented as their best teammates, but as sons of major leaguers who'd hung out with the best in the game, attended practices and sat in the clubhouse during games, they had a strong sense of belonging.

Other college players tended to be awestruck or intimidated by the major leaguers, thinking of major-league stars as superheroes or the legends on baseball cards. The sons of professional athletes simply weren't intimidated. They were confident, and that confidence carried them a long way. That confidence carries over into all aspects of life. A friend told me about six brothers who grew up working in a rural hospital founded by their physician father. Five of them became surgeons. The sixth is a lawyer who runs the hospital. They'd grown up working in the family business, treating people, so they weren't intimidated by sickness or surgery. Now several of their sons and daughters are either practicing medicine or are in medical school because, like their parents, they too feel they belong.

You don't need a Harvard study to tell you the power of that sense of belonging. In my small corner of the sports world, the players who succeed are those who feel that they truly belong at the top, whether it's in the major leagues, the business world, or their community. It's all about confidence. Once again, self-perception determines who you are and where you go.

NO LIMITS

Each of us is born without limits, but we tend to accrue them as we age, either because we put limitations on ourselves or we accept those placed upon us by others. Yet, time and again I see men and women blast through those limitations and rack up extraordinary achievements when they are provided encouragement and opportunity.

Given my own journey from child laborer in the California produce fields to coaching great student-athletes at major universities, I am a big believer in our ability to write our own stories. I'm not saying that everyone does it alone, by any means. We all receive assistance along the way, some of it merely human, some of it surely divine.

Some of the great joys of being a coach are those moments when I'm able to give a young man such as Chance Wheeless the opportunity to stretch and grow, to discover something about himself, to become a better man than maybe he'd imagined he could be. I encourage anyone who mentors young people to take every opportunity to set them up for success, to help them fight through limitations of any sort, and to provide them with whatever they need to be whomever they want to be. What a great honor that is, to have a positive impact on the life of a young man or woman; to be the person who lights the path, opens the door, or offers hope and encouragement.

Teachers, coaches, parents, and all other guardians and guides should do whatever is possible to instill young people with the confidence that if they make good choices, they will have joy and happiness. It is also our duty to help them understand that even if they make poor choices, they can learn from them and move forward. My staff and I try to encourage our players to believe in their destinies, to have faith in their abilities, and to understand that every step of the journey is a moment to be savored.

EN-COURAGERS

In my effort to be the coach I always wanted to play for, I do my best to convey to our team members that I am heavily invested in seeing them succeed for their own sakes, not just as athletes but as men, husbands, fathers, and members of their communities. I am not a professor of linguistics by any means, but I'll take a gamble and define *encouragement* as "the act of instilling courage in another." If I aspire to be anything, it is an encourager. I believe the relationship between the coach and the student athlete should be as intimate as their personalities will allow, which offers the greatest opportunity for growth. I would hope that every coach and teacher at every level, every parent and everyone with children in their charge, would seek to be the same.

Neither my father nor my college coach were the best at demonstrating interest in my personal welfare, but other teachers and coaches and one wonderful man in particular did that, not just for me but for hundreds of others. When I finally met my boyhood baseball hero, Joe DiMaggio, our entire conversation was focused on that particular encourager because he'd done the same for Joltin'

Joe when he was a young ballplayer in San Francisco. DiMaggio and I met in the late 1960s. Joe was then serving a brief tenure as a vice president and coach of the Oakland Athletics. I had just taken my first college job as head baseball coach at San Francisco State University. I was also enjoying a little part-time gig as a practice pitcher for the San Francisco Giants. They paid me $20 a day to pitch batting practice to the likes of Willie McCovey, Bobby Bonds, and Willie Mays. I would probably have paid the Giants five times that for the thrill of it.

I met DiMaggio at the Oakland A's practice facilities. He was wearing his coaching uniform and we spent a wonderful hour or so talking mostly about our mutual mentor and friend, Dante Benedetti. It's a strange and magical life when a boy grows up pretending to be his baseball hero, then meets him as a man and discovers that his hero and he share fond memories of a mutual friend and a legendary mentor and coach.

MR. BASEBALL

When the University of San Francisco held a dedication ceremony in 1985 to name their baseball field after Dante Benedetti, who'd been the coach there for many years, Joe DiMaggio showed up on his own for the ceremony. Though he rarely made public appearances and did not like to make speeches, DiMaggio stepped up to the podium and warmly hailed Dante as "Mr. Baseball."

Hundreds of guys, maybe thousands, felt the same way about Dante Benedetti. I was one of many who benefited from his benevolence. He was an encourager of the highest level, and a role model for the sort of coach and human being I wanted to become. Dante was a successful coach, but he was an even more successful person. He taught life lessons through baseball. Dante was a source of love, security, compassion, and understanding. Most of all, he was known for providing young people with opportunities to play baseball on the many teams he supported while also keeping them employed and fed. Dante stepped into my life and introduced me to a new species of adult male, one I'd rarely seen except for a few teachers.

I was seventeen years old and playing for the Benicia Mud Hens in an adult league, the San Francisco Winter League, because my dad wanted me to play against better competition. We had a game with a semipro team from San Francisco. Their pitcher was Marino "Chick" Pieretti, a native Italian who'd played six years in the major leagues before returning to San Francisco. He'd found a day job as a bartender at the New Pisa restaurant, a landmark and hangout for athletes in the North Beach neighborhood, but his main job was pitching for the restaurant's semipro baseball team.

I somehow hit two home runs off Chick that day, and after the game this big-shouldered bull of a guy came up to me smiling and said, "Congratulations! I'm impressed! Do you know you just hit two home runs off a major-league pitcher?"

The warm stranger then introduced himself as Dante Benedetti, owner of the New Pisa restaurant and sponsor of the team I'd just helped defeat.

"Would you like to play ball for us?" he asked. "I'll pay your bus fare and give you a job clearing tables at my place. You can sleep there too."

I learned that Dante was both a famous North Beach restaurateur and the patriarch of all things baseball in the San Francisco area. He was especially fond of Italian ballplayers, and he may have assumed that I shared that heritage. I certainly never tried to tell him otherwise. My father knew of Dante because he sponsored about a dozen baseball teams at every age level, and even better, he and his brothers had grown up playing ball with the DiMaggio brothers, who both frequented his restaurant.

With my dad's enthusiastic approval, I began taking the Greyhound bus into San Francisco every weekend. I'd leave Vallejo on

Friday night after school and start busing tables as soon as I arrived at the New Pisa. After closing, I'd curl up in a corner booth. They'd wake me Saturday morning so I could play two games before coming back to work the night shift. Then I'd play another game on Sunday before boarding the bus back home. Dante always had something encouraging to say before sending me off. "See ya next week, Augie!" he'd say.

I followed that routine for two winters, and I remember it as a golden time, just an exciting and heartwarming period. I felt as if I'd been adopted into this huge, loving family. Dante was born in an alley just outside the restaurant, originally owned by his uncle. He'd lived four doors down from it all of his life. After serving in the U.S. Marines, he came home and took a job at Saint Ignatius High School, where he taught Spanish, Italian, and "sports." He opened the restaurant each morning before school, and his sister managed it during the day until he returned to close at night. In between, he coached baseball in parks throughout the city.

He knew everyone, including many professional baseball players, who visited his restaurant whenever they were in town. Dante was like the mayor, the mother hen, and the dinner host for a huge community of family and friends. His entire extended family worked in the restaurant, where his mother was the head cook for many years.

He took over as head baseball coach at the University of San Francisco when they fired their coach as part of a plan to eliminate baseball from the athletic program. Dante said he'd coach for $1 a year to save them money. He funded most of the school's baseball team budget. He bought spikes and gloves for hundreds of kids who wanted to play ball. He and his wife, Florence, took in orphans and paid the college tuitions for many young people who'd never have been able to go on their own. Dante was the softest touch in the city, and people loved him for it.

This was an entirely new world for a kid from the federal housing projects in Vallejo. Every weekend I was playing ball against top competition, and at night I was meeting major-league players, celebrities, politicians, boxers, cops, firemen, and legions of other Dante Benedetti admirers. I observed Dante's interactions and his benevolent leadership. Finally, here was an adult whom I could trust to give me a ride home even if I played crappy and lost a game. Not only that, but he'd feed me even if I went 0 for 4 at the plate! With each meal and each game, there would be tidbits of advice.

"Baseball is like the game of life," he once said. "When that ball starts to roll, you have to anticipate, execute; and if you don't execute well, then you had better start practicing, because if you don't, you won't enjoy the game. It's the same in business. When you open up in the morning, it's like that ball starts to roll, and you've got to anticipate what you plan to do and then you execute effectively. If you can't anticipate and execute, you won't be open long."

Still, it was a poorly kept secret that Dante gave away more food than he sold. The neediest families in North Beach always knew they could dine on spaghetti until they were full at the New Pisa. Years later, when I finally took an assessment of my life and tried to figure out what sort of man I wanted to be, all I had to do was remember how Dante treated me and everyone else within his huge circle of influence.

As I rode that Greyhound into San Francisco on those winter weekends, I had the sense that I was entering a warm glow, a welcoming place. Dante's circle was full of laughter, love, and encouragement. I played just two years on Dante's team, but that made me a member for life of his inner circle. When I moved back to San Francisco to coach the baseball team at San Francisco State University, it was as if I'd never left town. Dante took me around and introduced me to all of the movers and shakers, and he became one of my best recruiters. It didn't hurt that his brothers were high school baseball coaches in the area and knew everyone who could swing a bat. And whenever I was in San Francisco, I never wanted for a good Italian meal.

Dante was a mentor and a role model for me. He showed me that an adult male could be kind, encouraging, and worthy of trust. He gave me not just opportunities but hope, and he did the same for many other people. Our relationship endured for many years because he loved baseball and coaching. Whenever I came anywhere near San Francisco, I stopped in to see him and to have a meal at the restaurant.

Dante lived a wonderful, fulfilling, and long life. After his death in 2005, at the age of eighty-six, his friends put up a plaque in his honor in Jasper Alley, where he'd been born. The inscription on the plaque is one of his favorite sayings: "If you are proud of where you came from, you'll always know where you are going, and you'll take pride in everything you do."

His legacy as an encourager lives on too, through the Dante Benedetti Foundation, which supports youth baseball teams, fields, camps, and clinics with funds donated and raised through baseball and golf tournaments held each year in this great man's memory. Dante was like a great character in a movie or a play, this gregarious, good-natured, but firm mentor who set many a wayward child on a straighter path, sometimes with tough love but more often with just love. Mostly, he was a stage manager. He saw to it that young people had a chance to stand up and test their mettle.

PITCHING THROUGH THE PAIN

I'm rarely disappointed when I provide a player with an opportunity to discover something about himself. If ever there was a kid who needed that sort of chance, it was Eddie Delzer. He came to Cal State Fullerton out of junior college, where he'd been a terrific pitcher and an All-American left-hander with a two-year record of 21-2 at Sacramento City College.

Like me, Eddie spent a good part of his childhood throwing a ball against a wall. His target was on a lumberyard shed in Lennox, the Los Angeles suburb where he grew up. The owners of the lumberyard had asked Eddie not to throw against the plaster part of the wall because he was chipping it with his hard tosses. So, he had to keep his pitches down, aimed at a lower section of the wall that was solid concrete. It was good training. Eddie developed a real mastery of the low fastball.

Still, he didn't get much attention from major-league scouts because he was only five feet seven inches tall and so skinny I joked that he weighed 133 pounds but only with his pockets full. I recruited him, stealing Eddie away from Arizona State, because he fit the profile of a Fullerton baseball player. He had a tenacious, bulldog attitude. Most pitchers were tall guys, but Eddie was determined to prove that heart meant more than height. He was teased a lot because he was such a small guy, but we knew he could take it. During practice one day, I was talking to a group of players in the infield when someone noticed a baseball cap on the ground near the warning track in the outfield.

"Hey, somebody lost a cap," a player said.

"Naw, that's just Delzer out there running wind sprints," someone said.

Eddie didn't take any ribbing for his pitching though. He had great control on the mound, but as we all learn, sometimes life throws us a curve and things happen beyond our control. On Christmas Day in 1982, Eddie's dad, who'd been his biggest supporter and booster, was shot and killed by some vicious thugs who crashed a holiday party. Eddie took it hard. He'd always played to make his dad proud, and with his father taken from him, Eddie found it difficult to take the field.

Our pitching coach, Dave Snow, and I tried to console Eddie. We convinced him to go to a grief counselor, but he struggled.

He nearly lost his eligibility for his senior year, but we lined up some tutors for him. Slowly, Eddie worked his way back, finding focus and rebuilding his confidence. You had to admire his determination. He fought his way back, and on the way he set a school pitching record of 18 strikeouts in a game that was still standing twenty-six years later.

We needed Eddie that year. Our top three pitching recruits had been signed to pro contracts just ten days before school started. Our bullpen wasn't deep, but we still had some talented pitchers including Eddie and Todd Simmons, another All-American. We managed to win the conference title and a trip to the 1984 College World Series in Omaha.

I clearly remember the fall of '83 and the season of '84, our first team meeting with Augie. He had this pamphlet made up, rules and regulations from grooming to curfew to dressing and time to prepare the field. The first sentence said that our goal in 1984 was to win the national championship. Our first team meeting; no ifs, ands, or buts—just this is what we are striving for and what are you going to do to be part of this team? Right away, I started thinking, *Is this guy nuts?* We haven't even touched the field for the fall practice and he is telling us we are expected to win the national championship?

JOSÉ MOTA
Cal State Fullerton
San Diego Padres
Radio play-by-play sportscaster for the Los Angeles Angels

RISING TO THE OCCASION

Our first CWS game was against the University of Michigan. We beat them, but we lost our next game to the University of Texas, the defending national champs. Since the CWS was a double-elimination tournament, we weren't out of it yet. Eddie was still having some trouble with nervousness, so we slowly brought him along as a relief pitcher to build up his confidence. Our sports psychology consultant, Ken Ravizza, worked with Eddie to help him remain calm and focused on throwing to the catcher's mitt while shutting out distracting thoughts.

We called upon him to pitch in the fourth inning in our next game against the Miami Hurricanes. He took the mound with a 3–2 lead, but the heart of their lineup was set to bat. In two innings, he gave up 1 hit and 2 unearned runs but struck out 5 batters. Our offense suddenly ignited for 13 runs. Eddie picked up the victory and we could see his confidence growing.

Next we played top-ranked Arizona State with Barry Bonds, beating them 6–1 with Eddie again pitching in relief late in the game. In our semifinal game with Oklahoma State, another top-tier team, Todd Simmons pitched great and we won 10–2 to reach the championship game.

We had planned on starting another right-hander in the final game, but he'd struggled earlier in the tournament and his confidence was obviously shot. In the meantime, Eddie was coming back strong. We were facing Texas again in the championship game. They'd already beaten us in this series. Dave Snow and I decided to give Eddie the starting assignment. We thought he'd rise to the occasion, but we didn't want him to have too much time to think about it. So, I didn't tell him he was scheduled to pitch until just thirty minutes before the game.

"Eddie, go warm up, you're the man today," I told him.

His knees were knocking in the dugout between innings, but

Eddie came through. He gave up one run in the first inning on a couple of slow-rolling grounders. Then, in the second inning, he struck out the side. As the game unfolded, he pitched better and better. We knew Eddie had it in him, but he unleashed more pitches with more control than we'd ever seen from him.

At one point I turned to Coach Snow and said, "Where the hell did this come from?"

Later, Eddie had an answer to that question. He had become a devoted practitioner of visualization. He said that when he took the mound that day, it felt as though he'd been there before, in the same game, facing the same team, because he always pretended every game was a championship game. "It was like I'd already played this entire game in a dream. I knew I could win it. I knew what pitches to throw each batter," he said.

Eddie shut down the Longhorns batters for seven full innings. He might have gone the entire game. He was still in command of his pitches, but as he went out for the eighth, he got a leg cramp that he could not work out. It didn't matter. Eddie proved himself. He was Superman that day. He put us in position to win. We brought in our closer Scott Wright, who was the son of a childhood friend of mine. Scott stepped it up that day too. He took us home with a 3–1 victory and the College World Series championship trophy.

It was a great victory for the team. For Eddie, it was life-changing. He learned something important, and it wasn't that he had great stuff on the mound. He pitched with a photo of his late father in his uniform pocket, and he'd shut down the defending champion Texas Longhorns while overcoming his grief. Eddie rose above and soared beyond all the pain and sorrow.

When the game ended, all the players rushed onto the field to celebrate. I went up to Eddie and said, "Son, well done." He smiled, walked a few steps, then crouched with his hands on his knees, finally giving up control, letting the tears flow.

I worried about Eddie and his life after baseball up until that game. I never worried about him again. I see him from time to time at Fullerton events. He still loves baseball. He still pitches, in the Men's Senior Baseball League's thirty-five-and-up division. He plays for a top-tier team, and for two straight years he helped his forty-five-and-up all-star league team win their division's national championship. Eddie also umpires high school and junior college games and does some private coaching with young players. He is healthy and happy, and I believe that CWS game against Texas is where his life came back together. He recently told me that it is still the high point of his long athletic career.

SUPER MAROUL

Sometimes I motivate our team members, but more often they motivate me. Chance Wheeless wasn't the only inspirational player on that 2005 championship team. Probably my favorite slump-recovery tale is that of his teammate David Maroul, one of the greatest Longhorn superheroes I've known.

I think Superman became such an iconic fictional character because most of the time he was just a regular guy like the rest of us. Before he could fly, he had to find a phone booth to make the transformation from mild-mannered Clark Kent. I can't think of any player who fit both roles better than David.

This even-keeled, low-key member of our 2005 national championship team was one of the best defensive third basemen in the country. He had a great throwing arm and he was a gifted fielder. The fans loved him. They called him the Vacuum Cleaner because of his fielding skills, but the coaches nicknamed him Ricochet because any balls that came to him at third base seemed to just ricochet to first because he had such a powerful arm.

Yet, the Fort Worth native had a tough regular season prior to our championship series in 2005. In our opening game that season, he scored the winning run but had to sacrifice his body to do it. David hit home plate in a collision with the catcher, banging his head and jamming a thumb in the play. When he returned to the dugout after that crash, he didn't know where he was.

"Did we win?" David kept asking. "What did I do on my second at bat?"

We took him to the hospital after the game and the doctors said he'd had a concussion. David missed the next ten games and that set him back. He'd joined our team the year before as a junior college transfer. Coach Tommy Harmon, who hunts baseball talent even better than he tracks deer, discovered David while scouting an opposing player at a junior college game. Tommy came back and said he'd found a fielder with the fastest hands he'd seen in a long time.

He convinced David to come play for us even though he hailed from a family of Texas A&M Aggies. The only other drawback was that he was not nearly as strong a hitter as he was a fielder. His defensive play was always exceptional and often spectacular. This kid could fire a rocket from third to first base even if he threw from behind his back, which he did in practice now and then.

But David struggled in the batter's box much of the time. We adjusted his stance and that helped him, but in his first year with the Longhorns, he had only a .223 batting average.

As a senior, David worked even harder on his hitting. Once he recovered from his concussion and thumb injury, his powerful arm and great glove won him a starting position again. He'd quickly regained his excellent fielding skills and his hitting improved, but he was still frustrated at the plate for much of the season.

David was all in for the team and wanted to contribute both ways, but he couldn't shake the hitting slump. Every time I'd ask him about it, he'd stay positive. "It's okay, Coach. I've been in slumps before and I'll get out of it."

The son of an airline pilot and retired U.S. air force lieutenant colonel who flew in Vietnam, David was the sort of self-assured player whom coaches stand by even when he isn't playing his best. Even when he was struggling at the plate, I'd see him encouraging his teammates, energizing everyone around him. Sometimes coaches have to throw their players life preservers when they see them going down, but that was never the case with David. He managed to stay afloat on his own, using the confidence from his defensive play to bolster his efforts to be stronger with the bat.

He finished the regular season as a star on defense but remained one of our weakest links on offense, with a batting average around .250. Then David found a phone booth somewhere along the riverfront in Omaha.

Once play began in the 2005 College World Series, we never again saw David's mild-mannered alter ego in the batter's box. He became a hitting and scoring superhero, with a series batting average of .500 that included 8 runs batted in. In the final two games of the championship series, he went 6 for 8. He hit decisive home runs in both of the final games, including a three-run homer in the last game that gave us the NCAA championship.

David, who had no fielding errors in the entire series, was named its Most Outstanding Player. Even better, his College World Series performance led to David's being selected as the cover boy for the EA Sports *MVP '06 NCAA Baseball* video game. Perhaps best of all, David was drafted by the San Francisco Giants. He is now working his way up through the minor leagues, but true to form, he is still contributing to the Longhorns as a tutor and mentor in the off-season. We're lucky to have him around.

■

CHAPTER EIGHT

The Tao of Teamwork

Our Cal State Fullerton team made it to the final four of the College World Series in 1994. Then we were knocked out in a devastating loss to Georgia Tech, a team loaded with future major leaguers. I blamed myself for that loss because we had a great bunch of guys. We had all sorts of opportunities to score, but we didn't take advantage of them. It was tough because fourteen of our players graduated or moved on to the professional ranks at the end of that year.

It was a long, long winter.

We began the 1995 season, then, with a limited pitching staff and a bunch of inexperienced players at key positions. I fretted for months before the season opener, wondering how we were going to win any games at all. My former player turned assistant George Horton would remind me later that I gave him hell at the start of the season, saying we didn't have enough quality players.

I had to eat those words and it was a long meal. (Don't worry, Coach Horton got his revenge.) According to most experts, the 1995 Titan team was one of the greatest in the history of college baseball. It wasn't natural ability, nor was it skill. More than anything, it was teamwork.

This pack of scrappy underdogs set out to prove something. They had great chemistry, and probably best of all, they had the

uncanny ability to pull together and support each other, regroup-
ing after losses and rallying to regain momentum. Whenever they
lost or won ugly, they figured out what they were doing wrong, and
then they did it right.

They weren't perfect, but they sure were fun to coach, and they
were never boring. That 1995 team started like a house afire. They
won 39 of their first 45 games. Then we went over a cliff somewhere in Kansas. Actually, it was in Wichita, against Wichita State.
They beat us twice. Then we hit the road and lost the first game in
a three-game series with Nevada-Reno. The players lost their confidence. We blew big leads in all three defeats.

We'd been ranked the No. 1 team in college baseball most of
the season, but we were in a bad slump. The pressure just seemed
to keep building. During our second game with Nevada-Reno, we
followed the same sad script. We built up a lead, then it was as if
they saw the train coming and jumped on the track.

Players were so afraid of making mistakes, all they could do
was make more of them. A pop fly turned into a hit because two of
our college outfielders ran for it, stopped, and watched it drop like
a couple of peewee leaguers. I'd been cajoling them and berating
them for two days to no effect. I didn't know what else to say.

They came off the field with their heads down, their shoulders
slumped, and fear in their eyes. In the dugout, I turned to our senior first baseman, D. C. Olsen, and said, "I've tried everything to
get you all to relax and have fun, to trust that you are a good team
and to just play baseball, but whatever I've said hasn't worked. Why
don't you give it a shot?"

D.C. stepped up and took charge, which was a little unusual.
A hometown boy from Fullerton, D.C. was a quiet and thoughtful
guy, a man of few words. He rang the bell and sounded the trum-
pet that day. His brief, emotional, and inspired talk is now part of
the Fullerton baseball legend. It is known as "The Stupid Speech."
It went something like this, only with frequent cuss words: "This

is stupid. Oh, man, we just have to get back to playing ball. This is so stupid. I can't believe we're playing this stupid. What the heck, how stupid can we get? Now let's get out there and quit playing so stupid and win this stupid game. We need to be ourselves."

D. C. Olsen will never be mistaken for Knute Rockne. But his humble speech inspired his teammates. Mostly, though, what D.C. said wasn't nearly as important as who he was. His teammates respected him not because he demanded it, but because he'd earned it. Our Fullerton team returned to the field and won that game. Then they won the next 18 in a row, including the championship game of the 1995 College World Series. On the morning of one of those games, D. C. Olsen woke up at 3:00 a.m. and passed a kidney stone. He still played that day, and he hit an out-of-the-park home run! It was a cannon shot and one of the players said he hit that harder than he passed his stone! D.C. was drafted by the Montreal Expos, who knew a ballplayer when they saw one.

We won the national title that year with a record of 57-9, and it wasn't because the team was loaded with major-league prospects. These were ballplayers and, most important, they were dedicated to winning as a team. It's no accident that the 1995 Cal State Fullerton baseball team is still so highly regarded. As D. C. Olsen and his "Stupid Speech" attest, this team learned to do it for themselves. They took responsibility for their success. Individuals sublimated their personal needs and goals and devoted themselves to the needs and goals of the team. I was their coach and their leader in name, but by the time we hit the College World Series, they were in control of their own destinies. That's the Tao of teamwork, the way it should work.

Baseball is often referred to as an individual sport played within a team context because when a player is at bat, fielding the ball, or pitching, his performance is generally isolated. No one blocks for him. His teammates can't slow the runner down or interfere with the pitcher. I am tempted to roll out the cliché about there being no *I* in *team,* but one of our smart-aleck players recently pointed out that there is no *we* in *team* either. The fact remains that baseball teams do not consistently win unless the players work together and support each other.

In the 2010 season, we picked up a tough win, our ninth consecutive victory, by staging an eighth-inning comeback to beat Texas State. The Bobcats jumped out to an early 4-run lead but we battled back in the eighth to win it 6–5. Afterward, I told our players that I wanted our pitchers who had struggled in this game to remember that even when they may not pitch as perfectly as they hope to, their teammates will be there to support them and to do all they can to pick them up and win the game.

The game requires self-sacrifice and communal effort, which are critical to the survival of group undertaking. Teamwork skills learned in baseball, then, are applicable to your career and your personal life, including marriage and parenting, unless you think you *never* have to clear out the dishwasher or load the baby stroller into the family van.

The universal truths of effective teamwork apply to athletes and business teams. These include:

- It's amazing what can be accomplished when no one cares who gets the credit.
- Every role is important, but finding the right person for the right role is critical.
- On a fully functioning team bonded by mutual respect, anyone can take the lead at any given time.
- Constant and clear communication is essential to a team's welfare.
- The greatest achievements are the result of united efforts, not individual performance, because you have someone to share the success with.

NO COACH REQUIRED

The twenty-five-hundred-year-old classic *Tao te ching* says, "With the best of leaders, when the work is done, the project completed, the people all say, 'We did it ourselves.'" One of the cool things about the 1995 Fullerton baseball team was that after D. C. Olsen pulled them out of their slump, these Titans totally committed to each other and took responsibility for the team's success. They went on to play in four tournaments including the College World Series, and one of our players was named the MVP in each one. Yet it was never the same guy twice. In each series and nearly every game, someone new stepped up to lead and inspire the rest of the team. It was a beautiful thing to witness, and to be a part of.

I've never run a corporation or a community organization but I think the 1995 Titans serve as a model for any sort of team. They came together. Individual egos melded into a team identity. They took responsibility for their own success. They openly aired their feelings without acrimony. They self-corrected. They celebrated each other's successes and supported each other when support was needed. One by one they stepped up fearlessly to lead when the moment called for a strong voice.

It's always interesting to look back on a season to try to identify the key moment in which a team pulls together. As I write this in the early stages of our 2010 season, the Longhorns team seems to be pulling together, but I have no way of knowing for certain. I do know that on a recent Saturday, our batters struck out 9 times against the Nebraska Cornhuskers. We lost 5–3. The next day, before our Sunday game against the same team, the nine guys in the starting lineup called their own meeting. No coaches allowed. They took a vow to focus that day not on getting hits but on putting men on the bases and advancing them into scoring position. The same two teams played in that Sunday game. We had 13 hits and scored 13 runs. Nebraska tried seven pitchers but they only claimed 4 strikeouts in the entire game. The Longhorns won 13–3.

That is the power of teamwork. I had a similar experience at Cal State Fullerton with our 1992 Titans. I mentioned earlier that this team became one of the most unified groups I'd ever coached, but they didn't start out that way. Phil Nevin was the star of that team, but at the start of the season he tried to do too much. There was tons of talent on the team, but in the first few weeks these Titans tended to coast. They'd beat the heck out of an opponent on a Friday or Saturday, then take the Sunday game off.

Day after day I chewed them out for selfish play and lack of commitment. They responded with yawns and eye rolls. Despite their best efforts to play below their potential, we won the conference title, but only because our competition kept folding. We weren't champions, we were just survivors. They were black belts in lollygagging, and their success only frustrated me all the more. They were not good representatives of the school. They weren't about what was right. I resented that they won and that they weren't doing things right.

"You don't need to practice because you don't care anyway," I chided them. "I'm taking you to the regionals, but only because my contract says I've got to serve as the adult chaperone. I don't respect you and I don't like you and I hope we get beat so you aren't rewarded for your poor behavior."

My lockout started on a Monday. I kept the padlock on the gate Tuesday. On Wednesday, they finally put together four guys who cared enough to form a negotiating committee. Nevin was one of them. Leadership had been lacking, so this was a promising development.

I still didn't believe they could turn it around and start doing what was right.

They promised that if I let them use the field, they would run their own practice and would work hard to do things the right way by showing respect for the game and represent the university in the proper manner.

"I don't think you are capable of that," I said, "so I'm going to come and just watch to see if you really can hustle and grind it out and scrimmage like you care."

I told them they didn't have the character to be the type of team they needed to be. But somehow they had a pretty decent practice, and they built on that steadily. To my amazement, this team that had been one of the worst in its overall behavior rapidly transformed into one of the best. They went on to win the regionals and make it to the finals of the College World Series, where we lost to Pepperdine University in the championship final. We didn't win the NCAA, but we all learned that when the members of a team step up and take responsibility for their success, the dynamic changes dramatically. They went from the worst to the best. Even the bus driver for our team and the flight attendants on the plane remarked on what gentlemen they were. It gives me faith in young people to see them turn around like that.

When players truly come together as a team, the head coach becomes little more than a cheerleader and occasional traffic cop. That's the way I like it; not because it lightens my workload, but because these individuals will have experiences as a fully functioning team that they will savor and tap into for the rest of their lives.

The lessons absorbed by members of a unified, unselfish sports team make them successful in society. Playing selflessly within a team culture helps young people identify who they are, where they fit in, and what they can contribute to a purpose greater than their own. In ancient times, we took our young on hunting and gathering trips or sent them on quests or war parties. These traditional rites of passage tested them so they could learn who they were as they prepared for manhood or womanhood. Today, being part of a competitive sports team is one of the few remnants of that tradition, and one of the few places where young people can safely test themselves to discover what they are capable of and where they fit into the world.

GROUP SOUP

Often coaches make the mistake of having the same cookie-cutter approach with each team. We find out who the people are and respond to them and react to them and build the team around their personalities. That can be risky if they turn out to be not very good or if they don't care. But I want them to be successful and to fulfill their own destinies. They must have their own goals because if the coaches try to drive them toward our goals, we will probably lose. After all, once the game starts, it's the players who take the field.

That said, I don't have a secret recipe for pulling a team together. Sometimes it's a constant battle throughout a season. Then in other seasons, magic happens. The quality of the team depends on the strength of the player relationships. Egos must be checked at the door. Sacrifices must be made. Goals must be shared. Doing what is right for the team must be the priority.

With a baseball team, you have so many people and personalities that the coaches rely heavily on the player leaders. We guide them by constantly reminding them in simple terms of the principles and mission that we've set out for them. Our goal is to win the national championship, and our coaching staff constantly restates that. Then we work backward. We can't control the score game to game, but we can control our performance pitch to pitch. We break it down to take fear out of the equation while building confidence.

COACHING TEAM

In most discussions of teamwork in sports, one critical level often seems to be neglected. The first team a coach builds is his group of assistant coaches. My success is a reflection of the great assistants I've worked with and continue to learn from. I provide my assistant coaches clearly defined areas of responsibility, then try to stay out of their way. I offer them more freedom than most coaches allow their assistants because I've been an assistant and that's the way I always wished to be treated. I sought responsibility but I didn't want anyone second-guessing me. Either my boss trusted me or didn't. You have to trust your assistant coaches because so much failure is involved. If you don't trust each other, you'll never be able to get over failures.

I've mentioned my associate coach Tommy Harmon, who oversees the recruiting for our UT baseball team. He's a Texas native and a former Longhorns All-American catcher. Following college, he was drafted in the first round into the major leagues, where he played for five years with the Kansas City Royals and three years with the St. Louis Cardinals. His coaching résumé includes being the youngest coach in the National League during his stint as coach for the Chicago Cubs.

Tommy has been coaching at UT for twenty-one years. He was an assistant to my predecessor Cliff Gustafson, and he has served as my link to the traditions and great history of the program. He is a Lone Star legend not only as a player and coach but also as a recruiter plugged into the professional scouting network. Assistant coach Skip Johnson, who oversees our pitchers, is a Denton, Texas, native who has had barbecue with every high school and junior college coach in the state. He and Tommy can find their way blindfolded to any baseball diamond within a five-hundred-mile radius of Austin. Skip is the primary reason the Longhorn teams have been known for their dominant pitching in recent years.

Another key member of our team, who rarely receives any public acknowledgment, is Randa Ryan, a Ph.D. who oversees academic support for members of the baseball team. She has the training and practical experience too since she and her husband,

Steve Klepfer, have four sons of their own. Randa has put together a program that has kept our players performing at a high level academically despite their hectic schedules. For the last eight semesters, our thirty-two-man roster has had a cumulative grade point average of 3.0, and that's a major achievement. The school gives her the resources she needs, and Randa runs a tight ship. She has been a blessing to the team.

I don't always see eye to eye with Randa, or with my coaching team, and that's a good thing because as difficult as it may be to comprehend, I'm not always right. Besides, being right isn't all that important to me anymore. I'd rather do what's best. My coaching team has plenty of experience, and they know the players well, so they are often aware of what needs to be done before I am.

Sometimes they even earn the opportunity to prove they know more than me on a really big stage. In the 2004 College World Series my former team, Cal State Fullerton, was coached by my former player and assistant coach George Horton. His team beat mine, the Texas Longhorns, for that championship. It was bittersweet to lose to a former assistant. It hurts no matter who beats you, but I was happy for George because winning the championship changes your life. He is now one of the most respected and highest paid college baseball coaches in the country.

Every veteran coach has a family tree of former assistants, and mine is fairly extensive given my length of service. If you traced my coaching DNA, you would find major contributions from my college coach Pete Beiden, who sired an entire generation of successful head baseball coaches during his years at Fresno State. But you might be surprised to trace more than a few strands back to Cerritos Junior College and its longtime coach Wally Kincaid, who was one of the most successful coaches in the state of California.

A true innovator and master of the fundamentals too, Wally won six state championships in his twenty-two years of coaching to a 678-163 record. His community college teams once had a

60-game winning streak that spanned three seasons. I never played for Wally. I never coached with him. But like any other coach with a lick of sense I recruited every player I could from his juco teams because Wally's kids knew how to play the game. It was no coincidence that several of them became my assistants, including George Horton and Dave Snow, both of whom went on to distinguished careers as head coaches.

Dave Serrano, who became head coach at Cal State Fullerton, was another Cerritos juco player who played for us at Fullerton, as was Dan Boone, an All-American pitcher. Many players on the 1975 Fullerton team that won the College World Series had played for Wally before I snapped them up. One of the few baseball coaches to have an undefeated season, Wally had a knack for turning out mentally tough, unselfish, and team-oriented players who'd been overlooked by bigger schools because they weren't tall enough or as athletic as more-sought-after prospects. I'm grateful because those tough-minded overachievers out of Cerritos helped me build the Fullerton baseball program into a national power. They were my gift from God that 1975 team.

Our competition was a little slow to notice, though. In 1975, our Titan team won the Pacific Coast Athletic Association championship and advanced to our first NCAA Division I regional playoff. It was like moving from the freight car to a first-class berth. Our first game was against the University of Southern California, on their field. They were the elite dominant school, the golden Trojans. We were the scruffy guys with dirt under our fingernails and grass stains on our knees.

The coaches and school officials had a party the night before the Titan-Trojan game, and Madeleine the organist for USC was there. She asked me if I had a copy of the sheet music for our fight song. I told her we didn't have an official fight song. I don't think Fullerton even had an organist back then, let alone a school band. I told USC's organist that our players did seem to like the Doobie Brothers.

When we took the field to be introduced, she played "It's a Small World," and the USC fans mocked us as Cal State Disneyland. We promptly whipped up on the Trojans and took the regional championship from Pepperdine. We didn't last long in the College World Series that year, but we got a taste of what it took to win it all, and four years later we did just that.

MAKING THE MISSION CLEAR

No false modesty is in my claim that my assistants often taught me more than I taught them. That's obvious when you look at how many of them have become successful head coaches. One of them, Bill Kernen, who was on my staff at both Fullerton and the University of Illinois, even spent a few years out of baseball and living as a New York City playwright. I know he didn't learn anything about that from me.

Hiring people smarter than me isn't all that difficult. There seems to be an ample supply of them. For me, and for most head coaches, the challenge is to leave them wild and free and let them be. My Texas tag team, Tommy and Skip, spend long, hard hours in the blazing summer sun scouting players and recruiting them. The messages the three of us deliver in recruiting are critical. The foundation of every team is built upon clear communication. You have to tell new recruits clearly and repeatedly where you aim to go, how you want them to get there, and whom you want them to become along the way. At Texas, our recruitment goal is to let the player and his family know who we are so they can decide whether to join us.

Every young man we talk to has been a star athlete. We let them know that we build and coach teams, not stars. No matter what sort of team you lead, it will never come together if you don't clearly define the mission from the beginning.

But you have to listen too. Some of the best parenting advice I ever heard was from a mother who said she spent hours talking to her kids about insignificant little things when they were young so that they'd talk to her about the truly important things when they were older. Two-way lines of communication have to be maintained and kept clear even when the messages aren't that critical because there will always come a time when you need to get through in a hurry with important information.

At UT, our efforts to build a team begin with our university mission statement and its commitment to provide opportunities and support for student-athletes to reach the highest levels academically and athletically while preparing them for life after college. We accomplish this by teaching them leadership, teamwork, discipline, goal-setting, respect for self, and respect for others. We are held to that mission statement and so are our players, and the results are measurable. For the most recent eight semesters I can check, our entire baseball team has a B grade point average, which is pretty amazing when you consider the demands placed on them as athletes who play several games a week, often traveling to do so.

Putting a competitive baseball team together is perhaps one of the more challenging jobs in college athletics because, unlike in most other sports, we are competing for talent head-to-head with the high-paying professional teams. It is easy to identify the best players in the country, but much more difficult to know which recruits will choose to go to college instead of signing a major-league contract right out of high school.

Yet, year after year, Tommy and Skip bring home not only great athletes but great people. The strength of character in our players is not just a happy coincidence. Coach Harmon and Coach Johnson evaluate the skill sets of the young players and make their choices on whom to recruit based on our projected team needs offensively and defensively. But before they decide whom to recruit, they review the academic transcripts of each player. They've learned over the years that the great player who shows little commitment to academics in high school generally signs a pro contract at first op-portunity. The athlete who takes his high school studies seriously is more inclined to turn down a professional contract so that he can pursue a college degree while playing baseball instead of spending time in the minor leagues.

Like John Wooden, I prefer to form my own opinions about players rather than rely on what scouts, high school coaches, and taxi drivers may say. I always keep in mind that many players and their parents don't trust head coaches, and I discuss that up front with them. I'll note that this lack of trust often traces to their experiences with youth baseball teams where the coaches usually are the fathers of players. Quite naturally, the father coach plays his son at the "star" positions, often as the shortstop or the pitcher. The favored son usu-ally makes the local all-star team whether he deserves it or not.

When I talk to a recruit and his parents about this, they'll nod and smile, acknowledging the truth in it. So then I tell them that I stay out of recruiting until they visit campus so that their son has the opportunity to show me who he is without my having any preconceived notions or labels attached to him. I only know that Coach Harmon and Coach Johnson consider the recruit to be Longhorn material, and that's good enough for me. I trust their judgment.

The University of Texas has one of the most well-funded athletic departments in the NCAA, and our facilities are second to none, but people are often surprised to learn that few of our players are given full scholarships. The NCAA rules limit college baseball teams to just 11.7 scholarships. We take twenty-five players on the road to the championship series, so partial scholarships are the norm, and I make it a point never to know how much of a scholarship each player receives, again so that I can form my own opinions of them.

My goal is to give everyone an opportunity based on how he performs for his UT team. Waco's own Travis Tucker came to us as a walk-on out of junior college in 2006. He stood 5-9, but if you measured his heart, I'm sure it was way too big for that body. The son and cousin of major leaguers, he'd turned down a professional contract out of high school. He came to us as a sophomore and started every game at second base from day one because he committed himself totally to the team. He always gave his best and supported his teammates in every way possible. Travis beat out a player who had a longer scholarship. The other kid knew Travis was better so he transferred. Travis is a great athlete, but what sets him apart and kept him in our lineup was his personality. He had no fear of failure. He always stayed upbeat, positive, and confident. He was one of the best hitters and true leaders on our great 2009 team, which was stamped with his personality. Travis has no quit in him, and his spirit carried that team through a great season.

We asked Travis to be a student assistant coach for our 2010 season, and I have no doubt that he will be a strong head coach somewhere in the future. Travis is such a great leader that we asked him to take a more active role with the 2010 team to help their player-leaders understand the difference between being social chairmen and true field generals.

TEAM PLAYER

No single personality type fits the "team player" mold. You want a team to have a mix of personalities who blend together rather than compete against each other. Still, to be part of something greater than yourself, you must be willing to give up certain "selfish" attitudes and perspectives. I've heard of coaches and teams that demanded players consider themselves mere cogs in a machine, but I don't believe in mechanizing our teams. I don't want robots out there, I want emotionally engaged team members. I would never expect someone to stop being who he is, but I do expect each player to give up his position at the center of his own universe. Instead, I ask our players to put the team's welfare above their own ambitions.

Team members must share a mind-set if all the pieces are going to fit into a united and cohesive whole. The athlete who thinks that someone else's success takes away from his opportunities is never going to be a team player because he has a scarcity mentality. You need an abundance mentality to fit into the team concept. You have to believe that the universe has rewards enough for us all, and that when your teammates do well, it does not limit your own opportunities for success—in fact, it creates even more possibilities.

The young man who is determined to be a rugged individualist in baseball had better be prepared to shag his own fly balls and buy a pitching machine. If he can hit 'em and catch 'em too, he is one hell of a player. We try not to recruit rugged individualists, we recruit team members with specific roles in mind for them before they ever suit up in a Longhorns uniform. We try to help each player understand that when he learns to function efficiently and successfully within a team environment, he isn't doing us a favor. He is preparing himself for a successful life well beyond the Austin campus.

My job as a coach is to study the personalities and abilities of our individual players, then figure out the personality and abilities of the team. I look at the strengths and weaknesses of the team as a whole, then we find ways for our players to be successful. Once we put a team together, it isn't their job to adjust to me. It's my job to adjust to them and to find a way to win each season. The goal is to have each team focused, in sync, and playing at its peak as we enter the conference, regional, and championship tournaments.

When everyone on the team buys into a shared vision, we often find that even those players who haven't been major contributors during the regular season will be inspired to perform at their highest levels. In our first game of the 1979 College World Series, our starting right fielder, Andre David, broke his right foot when he hit a foul ball off it. That left us with a rather large hole in our offense and our defense. Andre had excelled at both.

Before I made a decision on replacing Andre, I called in a team of advisers. I'd never had to deal with sportswriters much until we made it to that College World Series. Suddenly, we were of interest to a small herd of newshounds from the *Los Angeles Times,* the *Fullerton Tribune,* the *Santa Ana Register,* and a scattering of other papers covering college baseball's biggest event. I didn't know any better so I talked to 'em all, and to my surprise they wrote down most of what came out of my mouth.

They also had no qualms about offering me coaching advice. They were especially good at making judgments based on the wisdom of hindsight. I offered them the opportunity to coach from my perspective when Andre went down. I gathered five of the scribes and gave them each a lineup card. "I know you will all offer your opinions on my decision after this game has been decided, so I'm giving you the opportunity to help me decide who to play in Andre's spot," I said.

We had a lively discussion. Our choices included a kid who was a strong hitter but not such a good fielder, and a strong fielder who was a great athlete but hadn't been hitting well or playing much. My team of advisers decided that the Titans had enough good hitters that we could afford to put in the better defensive player, Mickey Palmer. His batting average had dropped from .346 to .236 that season. Because of his hitting slump, he hadn't played in a game for a month and a half.

During batting practice before our next game, which was against Pepperdine, Mickey didn't hit a single ball out of the cage. My council of journalist advisers pretended to be too busy sharpening their pencils to notice. They paid much more attention once the game started. In his first two at bats, Mickey came up with runners on first and second so I put on the bunt sign. He beat out two bunts for base hits. Then, he doubled. Then, he tripled, and for the grand finale, he hit a home run.

Mickey Palmer came off the bench and set a record for the most hits in a single game in the College World Series. The sportswriters took all the credit, of course. That night when they came to the hotel where the team was staying, one of them, Tom Hamilton of the *Los Angeles Times,* decided to edit the marquee announcing the band in the bar. It said NOW APPEARING, FRANKIE AND THE FOUR HITS. Hamilton added PALMER HAD FIVE!

Mickey went on to have a great series in which he also made several spectacular defensive plays. He performed so well in the series that the Kansas City Royals drafted him. I decided to reward my council of advisers too. After we won that series, I ordered five extra championship rings, which I awarded to my team of media advisers. One of my best memories of that series, though, was captured in a news photograph. It showed Mickey Palmer helping the injured teammate he replaced, Andre David, hold a jersey high in the air to celebrate the victory.

SIMPLE IS AS SIMPLE DOES

Our communications from the first practice are designed to help our players understand our goals, to let each of them know that he is important to achieving them, whether he is in the lineup or on the bench. We say that in a dozen different ways. We keep our communications short and simple. Sometimes simple *is* the message.

Keith "Shiner" Shinaberry, also known as Big Easy, is a bright Austin native and free spirit who became the leader of our 2009 team even though he didn't get to pitch all that much because of a bad shoulder. An honor roll student, he found inventive ways to lead. Humor was often involved. I don't know how he did it, but he started a pregame tradition that lives on today. His teammates "fly" around the field in a V-formation—a move borrowed from the *Mighty Ducks,* a hockey movie. The "lead duck" always wore a little girl's pink backpack, for reasons unknown to me.

Before the 2009 season, I was fretting about the team. I wasn't sure how the players would respond to the distraction of my DWI arrest. Critics were predicting our downfall. In early practices the players didn't seem to like each other much. They weren't focused. I was struggling and they were wearing me out. Trying to figure out a way to pull them together, I called Shiner into the office. His teammates respected him and they liked him too. He was a natural leader. I needed him.

I let him know that this was a serious meeting by calling him Keith. Nobody ever called him Keith. The strategy worked. He entered my office like an altar boy caught sampling the church wine. He thought I was going to jump on his case, but instead I asked for his help.

"I am not sure what to do," I said. "I can't reach these guys. They just don't get it."

I talked to him about my philosophy of players doing the right thing and rewarding and encouraging each other. Shinaberry is a smart guy, but after a few minutes, I could tell that my words weren't getting through. He looked at me like a UN delegate in need of a translator. I smiled at him. He didn't smile back. He seemed confused.

"Coach, do you think you could dial it down a bit?" he said. "Just keep it simple, like you're always telling us to do."

"Keep it simple?" I said. "Keep it simple. Okay, I can do that."

We talked a little while longer about the game and how it should be played, but I stuck to the basics of my philosophy and how it was formed. Finally, I stood up, shook his hand, and said, "Well, we'll just try to keep it simple and see where it takes us."

The next team meeting I called was right before our first game of the season. I kept it simple. They won the next eleven straight games. Young men of rutting age may be the worst group of listeners on the planet, but the rule of keeping the message simple applies to all teams and groups.

ON WATCH

By now you know how I feel about fear as a motivational tool and driving force. Our players manufacture enough fears on their own, so I avoid adding to their burdens. I try to give them what they want as well as what they need. They want me to watch them. Seriously, I'm coaching to the boy inside each of them. Those kids are just like the pack of six-year-olds at the swimming pool screaming, "Watch me, watch me, watch me!" That's not to say our ballplayers are immature or needy, but they are looking for guidance, encouragement, and approval like all of us.

Sometimes the coach has to bury his negative emotions and stay positive to keep the team moving forward. When we lost the 2009 championship, I let slip a couple words of discouragement, then kicked myself and snapped into a more positive mode. Instead of focusing on the loss, I focused on what we had accomplished and on the momentum we'd built for the next season. Fortunately, the media and the fans and the players picked up on the positive message, and the results were remarkable. As I noted earlier, I've never seen such infectious enthusiasm for a Longhorns team that came in second in a national championship. That mood carried through the entire off-season and into our 2010 spring practices.

Our teams know that if we aren't moving forward, we are failing. There is no middle ground. Each game features a series of failures and recoveries and a quest for momentum. Our success depends on each player's ability to adjust and commit. Each player reacts to what I say in a unique manner. He hears the message through his own filters based on his perceptions and experience. I can tell five players the same thing and get five different reactions. So, I keep trying to reach each of them until there is a positive effect. Sometimes, that requires no little patience.

One of my Fullerton players, Matt Vejar, appeared to have a Coach Garrido block on his ear canals in his first season with us.

Matt was a good offensive player and a decent fielder, but in his first year he struggled. He didn't seem to care about the team. He didn't want to bunt. He didn't care to practice. Mostly, he didn't seem to care about anything but himself.

So, I culled him from the herd on a couple of occasions and probed for a way to reach him. Matt resisted words so I decided to draw him a picture.

"Right now, I'm trying to put together a team. I have nine round holes to fill and you are a square peg. You don't fit."

He gave me a look intended to cause internal bleeding. "You know, man, I've always been a good hitter, and if you put me in the lineup, I'll hit over .300 once I get a hundred at bats," Matt said. "That's just the way I am, and I'll always hit .300 once I've been playing regularly."

I said that might be true, but the odds of his getting 100 at bats were declining with each poor practice. "Right now, I'm concerned that you refuse to do what we ask all of our players to do. As I said, you are a square peg and I have round holes to fill. If I decide that this team really needs you because of your hitting ability, I will take a hatchet and I will chop you into a round peg and pound you into that hole."

Painting him a picture worked. He got the visual. Matt adjusted his attitude, rounded himself off nicely, and hit .300. He helped us win the 1979 College World Series and earned a place on the all-tournament team as a result. Matt was drafted by the New York Yankees. He is now an elementary-school teacher who has come to understand and appreciate my efforts to reach him and transform him into a team member.

TEAM FLOW

The beauty of a unified team was on display when the 2009 Longhorns were locked into the record-breaking 25-inning marathon game. You might expect the players not in the lineup to become distracted and bored. Yet, as that epic battle progressed, the "idle" members of our bull pen were energized. They kept coming up with creative ways to display their support and involvement. At first they were fairly subdued in their demonstrations: waving rally caps, turning their jerseys backward, hiking up their pants and pulling their socks down. Then, as the game wore on, they grew more inspired, sitting Indian-style in a horseshoe, hoping to bring good fortune. Next, they erected a tent, since the game had become an all-nighter. At one point, I think they clapped for three innings straight.

In the Tao of teamwork, the game is always on. There is no downtime for anyone wearing a Longhorns uniform. When our team is on defense, those not in the lineup are expected to be every bit as engaged as those manning the bases, the mound, and the outfield. We want them "on the rail," on their feet and mentally in the game, supporting their teammates, playing their positions in their minds and taking "mental at bats" with other hitters so they are prepared to take the field if we need them.

We demand this also because the players in the dugout and the bull pen are still connected to those on the field. They are part of the same energy force, so if they disengage by sulking on the bench or clowning around in a corner of the bull pen, they diminish the energy field. We want them up and visibly engaged, encouraging their teammates on the field and demonstrating confidence in their abilities. Everyone in a uniform should be locked into the flow of the game and lost to the world beyond the stadium.

I've heard people say there is a lot of standing around in baseball, but you don't see that in a cohesive team; not if people are doing what they are supposed to do. On defense, a sequence and a routine occur between each pitch. We have a reward system beyond someone's getting a hit, so the team rewards a batter with enthusiasm whether he gets a hit, a walk, a bunt hit, or a sacrifice;

it's all about supporting and approving of each other within the team framework.

When each player supports and encourages his teammates whether they are up or down, bonds grow strong. One season we were struggling and Kevin Costner called to cheer me up. We were talking about the importance of teammates supporting each other and lifting up those who were struggling.

"You're talking about the ride-back guys," said Kevin, who may have been making a western movie then.

"What are ride-back guys?" I asked.

"When the good guys are being chased by the bad guys and one of the good guys gets shot and falls off his horse, the ride-back guys don't abandon them. Instead, they ride back to pick up those who've fallen. They risk their own lives to bring them home."

I had some T-shirts printed up with RIDE BACK GUYS on them and handed them out whenever I saw a player filling that role. The team got the message. I've heard soldiers returning from Iraq and Afghanistan express a similar concept. They talk about how once they are over there and in the thick of it, their focus isn't on winning a war, it's about doing their best to make sure the guys on either side of them make it back home.

Trust and respect are critical ingredients to teamwork. Doing your best at all times earns you respect, and if you do that by helping the team rather than improving your own stats and your status in the draft, then the bonds of trust will form and the team will come together.

TAKING ONE FOR THE TEAM

As the late George Carlin noted, "Football has hitting, clipping, spearing, piling on, personal fouls, late hitting, and unnecessary roughness. Baseball has the sacrifice." In truth, sacrificing is not unique to baseball. The basketball player who sets a hard pick is putting his body in harm's way to free up a teammate. The linemen in the trenches who protect the quarterback and the blockers who clear the field for the running backs give up personal glory for the good of their football teams.

I'm certainly not unbiased in this, but it still seems to me that baseball has a powerful team dynamic like no other sport. In early April of the 2010 season, our Longhorns team was leading the Big 12 with a 7-2 conference record, yet when it came to hitting, we were last in the conference with a .271 team batting average that was 30 points lower than the team just above us.

That's the power of a team playing well together; all the parts fit so that even though we may be weak in one area, our overall strength puts us on top. Teamwork is not merely a concept or an ideal. It produces results you can measure on the scoreboard and in the final standings. On the field, in a game, teamwork becomes a powerful force, one that often determines who goes home a winner and who goes home shaking his head and wondering what went wrong. To sustain rallies on offense, for example, every person has to fulfill a role. Each player must concentrate on his response to the ball, trusting his teammates to fulfill their roles. The ball tells you how to react on every pitch, and that is a hard thing to do because you must react so fast.

The player must stay focused and not be overwhelmed by the situation, or by thoughts about the score, what a hit might mean, or other factors beyond his control. To do that for each pitch is difficult. He should be living in the middle of the moment so that he can react to the ball instinctively.

FOLLOW THE LEADER

Something contagious occurs in a baseball game when a team rallies. It's a bit like watching kids play follow the leader. One little guy starts leaping and running around, and pretty soon the playground is doing the "Wooly Bully" conga line. Time and again, we'll have a leadoff batter foul off five or six pitches, battling the pitcher all the way. Then, instead of swinging and striking out, he'll take one for the team and get the ump to call, "Ball four."

As that batter trots to first base on a walk, it creates a follow-the-leader momentum that is contagious. The whole tone of a game can change because we have that first batter on base. His presence there affects every aspect of the game, altering strategies on both sides. Now, the pitcher has something else to worry about, and from an offensive standpoint that is a good thing.

When that one player, that leadoff hitter, fulfills his role as a good teammate, he opens up possibilities for his teammates that did not exist until he fulfilled that role. If he takes a bad swing instead, the possibilities are much more limited. A team player sees his teammates on the field as a network of connections, all of them interlinked. Each interacts with the other mentally and physically.

GOOD TAKE

Players can and should be nurturers because they are more engaged than anyone else. They know what is truly important and what should be rewarded. Many coaches, parents, and players often err in their reward system. You can't simply offer hot dogs or blue ribbons and stars to the kids who hit home runs or pitch shutouts. Those are the glory plays that bring the cheers, but so many other elements in a game are important.

One of the sweetest encouragements I hear coming out of our dugout is "Good take!" Those words tell me that the players shouting it are fully engaged in the game because they are following it pitch by pitch even when they are not at bat. "Good take" is an encouragement to the batter for taking a strike. Why is that a good thing? Isn't a called strike without even swinging a bad thing? Not in a situation where we have a runner on third and less than two outs;

in that scenario the batter should be looking for a pitch that he can hit to the middle of the field or deep enough to score the runner—a sacrifice fly, usually. In these scenarios, then, we want the batter to be more selective. He should swing only at pitches that he can hit to midfield or deep enough to bring the runner home.

"Good take!" is a reward from teammate to teammate, a shared understanding of what is occurring in the moment; that getting a hit isn't important but scoring a run is. Teams come together when everyone not only seeks those rewards but offers them too. A team of encouragers is a team that wins because they understand that every role is important.

We do all we can to create as many nurturers and as many rewards as possible. This increases understanding of the game, it engages players in each moment, and it binds them together. The casual fan may not understand that our criteria for success and rewards are more complex than what brings them out of their seats. We are playing one pitch at a time, fighting for momentum, trying to put runners on base and advance them.

Doing what is right is another key. For example, on our teams the batter who makes contact is expected to run to be safe, always. He makes his best effort to get to first safely even if he knows that he's hit a routine ground ball that is typically an easy out. Even if he is thrown out, a unified team will offer him rewards for making his best effort and taking his best opportunity to be safe.

One of our Cal State Fullerton teams was in a regional finals game against Northeast Louisiana University, another perennial powerhouse. We were the home team so we had the last at bat. With two outs in the bottom of the ninth, one of our players hit a routine ground ball at the shortstop. He ran to be safe and the shortstop hurried the throw, pulling the first baseman four inches off the base. That play launched a rally that won the game and put us in the College World Series. That is why our teams always reward a player for doing his best to get to first, even if he is thrown out.

LONG-TERM TEAM BENEFITS

Tim Wallach was the best player on our 1979 NCAA championship team from Cal State Fullerton. Just that year, he drove in 102 runs—a school record that still stands—batting .391 with 23 home runs. Though he enjoyed a long career in the major leagues, to this day Tim says winning the College World Series was the highlight of his athletic career, not for the trophy he took home but for the friendships that endure.

The friendships on that team have held up over the years because from Wallach on down the roster, the players supported and encouraged each other. Wallach came to Cal State Fullerton from Saddleback College, a community college in Mission Viejo, California. A tall, thin kid, he was passed over five times in the major-league draft.

After he did well for us in his junior year, the California Angels offered Tim a contract, but only for $15,000. We knew he was a much better athlete than that small bonus suggested. Tim tried to get them to raise it by just $5,000, but they refused. I think the problem was that he'd been playing first base and scouts tend to think players are positioned on first base because they don't have enough speed for the outfield or strong throwing arms. That wasn't the case with Tim, and I told him that. They had assumed he was not a good athlete, but he was. Our coaches convinced him that if he played for us his senior year, his prospects for a pro contract would only improve.

Now that isn't always the case because the pros tend to try to sign graduates for less because they figure the players have fewer options once their eligibility is used up. We thought Tim could improve his value in another season. That turned out to be exactly the case. To give him a better showcase for his athletic abilities, we put Tim at third base during our fall season. We had him work on his running speed and his hitting, and he made great progress.

He began generating much more power at the plate with a better swing.

Tim Wallach made such progress that he went from being an above average college player to being regarded as the best player in America by the end of his senior year. The scouts misread the size of his heart and the strength of his spirit. He was the first Fullerton player to earn the Golden Spikes Award, and he helped us to win the College World Series. The major-league draft was held just prior to that series, and Tim was taken in the first round by the Montreal Expos, who offered him a bonus of more than $80,000.

Some college players who are drafted by major-league teams before the College World Series have been known to become self-centered and reluctant to extend themselves in that series for fear of an injury before their contracts are secured. Wallach was not that kind of guy. If anything, he stepped up his game to an even higher level. I didn't find out until years later that Tim called a meeting with the team just before the College World Series began. Always an unselfish player, he told his teammates that even though he and several other players had been offered major-league contracts, they were in Omaha to win the NCAA championship and nothing else mattered.

Tim set a CWS record of 79 putouts and helped Fullerton win its first national title, earning him further honors as the *Sporting News* National Player of the Year. A consensus first-team All-American, Tim went on to hit home runs in his first at bat in the minor leagues and in his first major-league at bat. He quickly became known as one of the best third basemen in the big leagues. He played seventeen seasons with the Expos, Dodgers, and Angels. Tim was named to the National League All-Star team five times and won three Golden Glove awards. He was also named the National League Comeback Player of the Year in 1994. In recent years he has been the manager of the Albuquerque Isotopes, the Dodgers' Triple A affiliate.

Joe Martelli was a backup catcher and a great pinch hitter on that 1979 team of underdogs that shocked the baseball world by beating Arkansas to win the CWS. He wasn't a star on the scale that Tim Wallach was, but he was a good ballplayer who contributed to our success, and he was a great teammate. Today, Joe Martelli and Tim Wallach live in the same neighborhood in Yorba Linda, California. Joe is a successful businessman with his own real estate and investment company. He and Tim may have been at different points on the athletic talent spectrum as college baseball players, but the bonds they formed as teammates are as strong today as they were in 1979.

They are not the only members of that team to remain close friends decades later. Newspaper articles have been written about that team because its members have remained so close for more than thirty years.

One of that team's star pitchers, Dave Weatherman, who went all nine innings in the championship game, considers his best friend to be Frank Ferroni, another pitcher, but who didn't get to play in the College World Series. Dave lives in Berthoud, Colorado, and Frank's home is north of San Francisco, but they still visit and talk on the phone often.

Jerald Traylor and Mark Pirruccello were both backup catchers on that team. When the season started, they were competing for the same spot and hated each other. Jerald lives in Pasadena. Mark lives in northern Minnesota. They too consider each other best friends.

That team lost their first game in the College World Series, so they had to fight their way out of the losers' bracket to get back into it. Every game they played after that was sudden death. They won that championship as a team, and what they learned about themselves and each other bonded them for life.

CHAPTER NINE

———————— ▮ ————————

The Reward Is Not on the Scoreboard

Freshmen, sophomores, juniors, seniors, it didn't matter. Everybody had something to prove as our 2009 Texas Longhorns baseball season began.

Me, most of all. I was suspended for the first four games so I had extra time to mull over my strategy. I was excited about the season, though, because I'd come uncomfortably close to being the *former* coach of the Texas Longhorns. After my DWI arrest, there was talk that our baseball team had been struggling in previous years. Some thought I should be fired or encouraged to resign. Tarring and feathering was also an option, as I recall.

The anti-Augie forces felt the arrest would negatively affect my ability to teach and motivate our players. I worried some about that too. I was curious to see how we would all respond and what sort of season we would have. Hoping to hit a higher note, I opened our first team meeting of the 2009 season by restating the rules of the road for our team:

No. 1: You know what's right, so do what's right.
No. 2: We're all seeking perfection yet we all know that we're imperfect.

No. 3:   Failure provides us with the opportunity to learn. If
you learn from your failures, you will become a more
successful athlete and a better person.

HIGHER REWARDS

Little did we suspect that the 2009 season would provide opportunities to learn and to grow beyond anything we could have imagined; not only as a baseball team and its coaches, but also as human
beings striving to make the most of our talents and our time on this
planet. The Longhorns were the fourth-ranked team in the country
coming out of the gate. Some thought that was overly generous.
We'd been shut out of the NCAA regionals for three years running.
We'd racked up 89 errors in the previous season. The media said we
had a "suspect" offense.

By most appraisals, this coach and our team had a long row to
hoe.

We had talent. Our pool of pitchers might just have been as
deep as I'd ever seen it. We'd lost a couple of our power hitters to
the major leagues, but we weren't lacking for batters with skills.
Still, most teams we faced had abundant talent. Nearly all of them
had veteran coaches too. We needed a secret ingredient.

In the previous chapter, I described the challenges of bringing individual players together as a team, what it requires of the players and
the coaches. Throughout the 2009 season, we reaped the benefits of
a team that came together in a remarkable way. These Longhorns
amazed the cynics, confounded the critics, and sent jaded sportswriters to their thesauruses in search of fresh ways to say *magical.*

I am sometimes teased and occasionally mocked when I refer
to the spiritual aspects of baseball. I will concede that in this sport
grown men chew tobacco, spit indiscriminately, and tend to make
body adjustments on camera. Yet, spirituality is such a part of our
lives that it must have a role in baseball too.

Baseball, like all sports, like business and daily life, involves a quest. Whether they are conscious of it or not, whether they would admit it or not, athletes play baseball to challenge themselves. They are seeking self-knowledge, trying to determine where they fit in. My goal is to help them in their quest, to teach them to overcome adversity, to sacrifice their individuality for the team's welfare, to focus on their strengths, to manage their fears, and to remain motivated through both victory and defeat.

Spiritual elements are part of baseball and part of our journey on this earth. I believe in a higher power. I believe God's hand is in anything I accomplish. For me that is part of spirituality, but it is also about transcending self, connecting to others, finding purpose, and contributing whatever gifts I have to something more meaningful than my own day-to-day existence.

The secret to instilling young players or anyone else with the confidence necessary to thrive is to help them find their purpose and to convince them that they have a contribution to make. The rewards flow from there. They may not be displayed on the scoreboard or noted in the record book, but after more than four decades in this game, those rewards are what I value most.

Every team we play has competitive athletes who've mastered the fundamentals of the game. Each opponent is led by experienced coaches with deep knowledge of its strategies. So what makes the difference game to game, series to series, season to season? Beyond good or bad luck—how the ball bounces and where the wind blows—I'd say the spiritual character of the players and coaches is often a determining factor. Call it team chemistry, social cohesiveness, or group dynamics, it's tough to quantify so hardheaded rationalists may dismiss the concept altogether. Yet, studies by sports psychologists have found that teams that start a season with strong bonds among the players tend to grow more cohesive as the season progresses, and they often have greater success as a result.

At its most basic levels, we may be talking about team unity, but when there is real chemistry, when the coaches and team leaders create an encouraging and supportive environment and the players truly bond, something magical happens. It's a game changer. When that attitude takes hold, the rules are off, or, as both Shakespeare and Sherlock Holmes might say, "The game is afoot!"

Coaches can nurture the spiritual elements or destroy them depending on how we lead. Command and control is a buzz killer. You can be a strong leader and coach while being a teacher and encourager too. The spiritual conditioning of our team is always on my mind. Does each player feel part of something bigger than himself? Does he have confidence and courage? Is he disciplined, focused, and aware? Do the players believe in each other? If one of them is down, do the others lift him up? When one of them excels, do they all celebrate his achievement as their own?

Those questions about the spiritual essence of the team ran through my mind as I watched our young men from the first day of practice. Their body language and social interactions told me a great deal. The coaching staff had a problem if they were throwing helmets and bats, picking at each other, and going their separate ways after practice. But if the players consulted with coaches and teammates after bad at bats, if they teased and laughed with each other in the locker room, and if they hung together off the field, we had a team that might grow into something special as the season progressed.

Strength of spirit is so important to success, in athletics and beyond. In baseball, you have to put long hours into practice to master hitting a curveball and fielding balls that come rocketing at you. You have to be strong in spirit to step up to the plate time after time and confront failure. We look at baseball and other sports champions as heroes, but few of them feel heroic because every game proves them imperfect in some way. Then again, something about the willingness to face your imperfections game after game is heroic.

TAKING IT TO CHURCH

The Longhorns baseball team hadn't made the trip to Omaha in three years, so I hoped that our hunger would make a difference—hunger and some other factors you can't measure with a math formula. I started talking early and often to our guys about the spiritual aspects of baseball and how they are every bit as important as the physical and mental sides. Winning was our goal, but to do that I hoped to tap an energy level well beyond anything Gatorade or Red Bull could provide.

The 2009 University of Texas team and their head coach were tagged as the Bad News Bears early in the season. My personal trials set us up for a shaky start. We didn't do ourselves any favors in the first week of conference play, getting swept in Kansas and later losing two and tying one at Kansas State. But by end of the regular-season schedule, these Longhorns were bad news no more. In fact, they were beyond good. They were uncanny. This team found ways to win even when there seemed to be no possible way to pull it off. Sometimes they bunted to victory, other times they powered their way with huge hits. Occasionally, they just walked.

"This Texas team isn't great. It might not even be that good," wrote one sportswriter, who nonetheless conceded, "In a game defined by averages and percentages, [the Longhorn team] has something that can't be expressed by numbers or confined to a box score."

I like to think that this team's secret lies within the sanctuary of the Church of Baseball. I take that term from one of my favorite baseball movies, *Bull Durham,* and a line delivered by the avid fan and seductress Annie Savoy, played by Susan Sarandon.

"I believe in the Church of Baseball," she says at the beginning of the movie. "I tried all the major religions and most of the minor ones. I've worshipped Buddha, Allah, Brahma, Vishnu, Siva, trees, mushrooms, and Isadora Duncan. I know things. For instance, there are 108 beads in a Catholic rosary and there are 108 stitches in a baseball. When I learned that, I gave Jesus a chance."

The Church of Baseball is not your typical bricks-and-mortar house of worship. Instead, it's a spiritual bond held together by selfless and supportive relationships. It rises up whenever individual players come together as teammates, inspiring each other, supporting each other, and doing whatever it takes to score runs and win games. If the true measure of athletic competition and a life's journey is the quality of the relationships you build, then this team won big-time. They came to love each other, and their coaches and fans loved them too.

The ultimate proof of this greeted us when our team returned to Austin after the 2009 College World Series. I can guarantee you that in the history of the University of Texas, this is the only group of Longhorns athletes—in any sport—to be given a joyous victory celebration for finishing *second* in a national championship.

Texas fans hate to lose. Due to both contract clauses and natural inclination, I am no fan of defeat either. I can assure you that the young men on that 2009 Longhorns squad wanted to win every game. Yet, if ever a team proved the reward is not on the scoreboard, it was this one.

The sportswriters and bloggers described our team as "flawed" when the season began, but they were calling it "magical" and "supernatural" by the time we reached the College World Series with a regular-season record of 42-13-1. Not much was *regular* about our regular season. We beat Oral Roberts University on a balk. We stole one game from Missouri on a throwing error and another by scoring 11 runs in one inning.

Stranger still, these Longhorns won the Big 12 Conference because a team had a plane to catch. We had to settle for a tie in a home game against Kansas State because it went into extra innings and they had to get home. That half-game victory was the deciding margin in determining the conference champ.

The Longhorns' 2009 season should have been a television reality show called *Baseball Survivors*. We clawed and scratched out victories all season long. Small ball. Long ball. Bunts. Balks. Homers. Sacrifices. Walks. Acts of nature and divine intervention. Whatever worked.

We made it to Omaha for the College World Series after an incredible play-off marked by transcendent moments. Even after we entered the championship tournament, strange and wonderful things just kept happening to a team that seemed to have tapped into something beyond its normal capacities. It was no wonder that sportswriters and fans and even coaches and players described our string of victories as if they were tricks in a magic act. I assure you that it wasn't smoke and mirrors. It was the power of a team coming together and believing that anything was possible.

GAME ONE: LIGHTING THE FIRES

On May 29, we had an ominous beginning to our first NCAA regional play-off game. Our power-hitting first baseman, Brandon Belt, was drilled with a pitch to the head. He had to be taken to the hospital. We were worried about him, naturally, and his departure put us in an unusual position. We had to replace Brandon at first base with our designated hitter, Preston Clark. That meant we had no designated hitter to bat for our pitcher, Cole Green.

The sophomore right-hander had not stepped up to the plate in a game all year. Because college pitchers rarely bat in games, Cole hadn't batted in competition since he'd played for a high school summer-league team. Still, when I told Cole that he was his own designated hitter, he stepped up in a big, yet small (ball) way.

Cole laid down a perfect sacrifice bunt and advanced the runner. We were playing at home with a crowd of seven thousand people, and they went totally bananas, cheering for him as if he'd hit a grand-slam home run. They loved that a pitcher pulled off the sacrifice bunt. Two innings later, Cole brought them to their feet again. This time he smacked a solid single, sending the Austin crowd into aftershock, another earth-rattling frenzy.

The kid fared well in his day job too. He held the Black Knights of the U.S. Military Academy at West Point to 4 hits and 1 run, striking out 6 in 7 innings. We won the game 3–1, thanks in large parts to Cole's inspirational performance and to yet another bunt, a squeeze, from Connor Rowe that scored the winning run.

Little did we suspect that our next victory would see another member of our bull pen burn through the record book.

GAME TWO: ALL-NIGHT SERVICE

This game began under the Friday-night lights but ended just before Saturday-morning cartoons. Somewhere in between, Austin Wood put on the greatest pitching performance I'd ever witnessed. Our teams are known for their mastery of small ball, but in this regional game the Longhorns proved they could play long ball—all night long. The game went 25 innings, setting a record as the longest college game ever played.

Our opponent was Boston College. Our starting pitcher, Chance Ruffin, kept us in the game into the seventh inning, which is normally considered a good day's work. At that point, the score was 2–2 and Boston had a runner on second. We sent our senior closer, Austin Wood, out to the mound as the relief pitcher.

Austin grew up in Kingwood, Texas, and helped his high school baseball team win a state title. As a high school senior, he went 14–2. He was mature and had become a team leader by accepting the difficult role of a short-relief pitcher. He unselfishly committed to helping the team any way he could.

In this must-win game for us, Austin stayed mostly with three pitches, using pinpoint control. He didn't give up a single run or even a hit for an incredible 12⅓ innings. A 9-inning no-hitter is considered a rare feat. He did it for more than 12 innings.

Austin threw more pitches than anyone else had ever thrown in a game—169—and he struck out 14 batters, retiring the side in order 9 times. His performance is even more amazing when you consider that Austin pitched 2 innings the day before in our victory over Army.

Normally, you don't let your relief pitcher throw more than 60 pitches in a game, but he was on a roll. When he approached 120 pitches, I conferred with our pitching coach, Skip Johnson, about making a change. Just then, Austin walked by, heard what was being discussed, and said flatly, "Don't you even think about taking me out of this game!"

We monitor our pitchers carefully, well aware that sometimes we have to step in if they are growing weary or in danger of injuring themselves. Coaches have to know their players, and we knew that Austin was no grandstander. He is pragmatic and levelheaded. We also knew that he doesn't throw many breaking balls, which is where most pitchers run into arm trouble if they pitch too many innings. We consulted with our trainer before we made a decision.

Once again, this was a ballplayer who was in the moment, playing with pure, childlike joy. Who were we to rob him of the opportunity to make history? His father, Jimmy, was in the stands and felt the same way. "I could tell he was having the time of his life. So I wasn't worried about it. That was one of those once-in-a-lifetime things, and he was loving it," Jimmy later told a reporter.

Austin was in a zone. He wanted to claim this game as his own, and I felt he had earned that right. We were the visiting team, so if he'd allowed just one run, we would have lost the game. Still, I felt it was Austin's game to win or lose.

He pitched a perfect game until Boston College finally put a bat on the ball with a two-out single in the nineteenth inning. We made it out of that inning without a run scoring. In the next inning, Austin showed signs of wearing down, so we sent in relief.

We'd just seen the most incredible pitching performance of my coaching career, but as Austin Wood left the mound, there were more firsts. Members of the Boston team lined up outside their dugout and gave Austin a standing ovation as he walked off the mound. A few of them even did the "I am not worthy" bow.

The epic battle continued. We finally broke the tie with Travis Tucker driving in the winning run. It was his twelfth at bat and the twenty-fifth inning. We won 3–2, finally calling it a night at 1:05 a.m. Saturday. That wild game became part of baseball history. A few weeks later, the Longhorns' equipment manager, Vinny Alcazar, received a phone call from Cooperstown, New York. Vinny listened to the caller, thanked him, then hung up and called Austin Wood and Travis Tucker. He informed them that the National Baseball Hall of Fame was planning an exhibit on the longest college game ever played. The museum requested Austin's size-7 Longhorns baseball cap and Travis's white eXo Louisville Slugger baseball bat, nicknamed White Thunder.

"Congratulations," Vinny told them, "your equipment is headed to the Hall of Fame!"

GAME THREE: GOING TO THE MOUNTAINTOP

Later on May 31, the same day we'd finished the record-breaking marathon, we wearily suited up for another NCAA regional play-off game. Again, we took on Army, the Black Knights whom we'd beaten two days earlier. The winner of this game would move on to the superregionals. The loser would simply go home.

We were still a little groggy after our 25-inning all-nighter, so I didn't know what to expect. For most of the game, it looked as if the Bad News Bears were back in Longhorn uniforms. Twice we had the bases loaded, and twice we failed to score a single run. Our best pitcher had a rare meltdown and we had to pull him in the fourth inning.

This Longhorns team was not known for its hitting, but we were so far behind that bunting wasn't an option. Prayer seemed like our only appropriate alternative. Army seized the lead with 2 home runs in the eighth inning. By the bottom of the ninth, it looked as if there were no way we could win. We were down by 4 runs, 10–6. Just as it appeared that the baseball gods had stopped smiling on us and our season was about to end, the Church of Baseball threw open its doors, cranked up the choir, and welcomed in the 'Horns.

Our first batter walked. Next came a single. We put in Tant Shepherd as a pinch hitter, and he nailed another single. Longhorn bodies were on every base, awaiting deliverance. A sacrifice fly drove in a run, making it 10–7.

We still had two men on base when Travis Tucker walked to reload the bases. Then freshman shortstop Brandon Loy took his place at the plate. Brandon, whose father, Darren, played on the UT baseball team that won the 1983 College World Series, swung for the fences and hit his target. He smacked a double high off the center-field wall that cleared the bases and tied the score 10–10.

The clouds parted. A ray of sunlight lit the field. The Longhorns reloaded the bases and up came Preston Clark, whose middle name might have been Hard Luck up to that moment. He was the only player on this team with a 2005 national championship ring, but he hadn't played or even made the trip to Omaha for that series. Academic problems had kept him home in Austin. Injuries had plagued him this season. He'd had eight surgeries. Because of a bad shoulder, he could no longer play catcher, so we'd used him as a designated hitter and as an all-purpose fielder.

Preston was always ready, willing, and able. He was so versatile that during his career at Texas he played third base, first base, designated hitter, and catcher. Though he'd hit just one home run all year, Preston unleashed four years of frustration with a massive cut at the first pitch thrown to him, propelling it over the left-field fence for a grand slam that won the game.

Thanks to that victory the Longhorns were headed for the NCAA superregionals. Given our string of mythical feats, I joked that maybe our true destination was Mount Olympus.

"There's something spiritual about baseball," I told a postgame press conference. "It's like Mother Nature, and you don't mess with it. We've experienced it two nights in a row, and they help a team reach that level of invincibility that allows them to win a national championship. If we hold on to this confidence, all things are attainable."

There was no earthly reason we kept winning games the way we won them. This team was playing for its own reward and reaping the benefits along the way. They played wherever I put 'em. They cheered each other on. They laughed like loons. They proclaimed in public that they loved each other.

Baseball isn't always about baseball. It's about the alchemy of turning players into a team, metal into gold. Spiritual chemistry bonded this group into something bigger than us all. They'd become believers.

GAME FOUR: BUNTING BONANZA

Our next opponents, the Horned Frogs of Texas Christian, unleashed 3 home runs for 4 runs to open the first game of our 3-game superregional series. In response to that onslaught, we pulled out the book of small ball and followed it chapter and verse.

We set the NCAA record for most sacrifice bunts in a single game. Every time we put a runner on base we bunted, and bunted, and bunted some more. Then, just so no one could call us boring, we rolled out the heavy artillery in the form of a five-foot-ten-inch senior named Mike Torres, who'd only hit 2 homers all season. He doubled his home-run numbers in that game. But before he stepped up to the plate, Mike checked with his coaches one more time to make sure he wasn't supposed to bunt. Can you blame him? We'd been grinding it out one base at a time and driving the TCU infielders insane, especially with two sacrifice squeezes that scored runners from third. But we sensed that Mike was in a groove, and groove it he did. He hit a solo homer in the third, and then retraced its path with another in the seventh that scored three more runs, setting up a 10–4 win.

Before the Torres twin homers, our Longhorns team was ranked 210th in the nation in home runs—the lowest ranking of any team still in contention for the NCAA championship. We were labeled "offensively challenged" in the media after we finished the regular season with a team batting average of just .289, which put us second to last in the Big 12. So, obviously, there was no way the small-ballers of UT could win games with power hitting, right? I sure didn't think so, but then, what did I know?

GAME FIVE: THE MAGIC MEN

Texas Christian gave us a taste of our own medicine in our next game, hitting 2 home runs to beat us 3–2 and sending our two teams into a final, deciding June 8 game in our 3-game superregional series. In the first inning that game, our "suspect" offense broke out of jail. Mike Torres singled. We advanced him into scoring position with a sacrifice bunt, and he didn't linger. Brandon Belt, who'd recovered quickly after being hit by a pitch in our first play-off game, smashed a line-drive triple off the center-field wall.

Brandon didn't hang out on base long either. Designated hitter Russell Moldenhauer brought him home on a fielder's choice. Then, Kevin Keyes hit his seventh homer of the season over the Horned Frogs bull pen in left field. We weren't supposed to do things like that according to the experts. We benefited also from a pair of power doubles in the fourth inning by Kevin Keyes and catcher Cameron Rupp that added 2 runs and gave us the victory 5–2.

Great defense didn't hurt. We had 3 double plays and a strong 6 innings by our fearless freshman pitcher Taylor Jungmann. As a result, the Texas Longhorns were headed to the College World Series for the first time in four long seasons.

The University of Texas had won college baseball's national title 6 times in 32 previous trips to the CWS. I'd taken them to the top twice, in 2002 and 2005. But everyone agreed we were packing something special for Omaha this time. Not one of our players had ever competed in the College World Series, but we were having too much fun to worry about that. As I told the sportswriters, I knew where all the best restaurants were in Omaha, and the rest would take care of itself. We'd come so far in spirit; everything that awaited us in Nebraska was dessert.

Kirk Bohls of Austin's *American-Statesman* newspaper captured our karma:

"Texas? It's short on offensive talent but long on pitching and even longer on magic. The Longhorns have embraced their supernatural side and conjured up some of the most improbable wins in school history."

GAME SIX: WALKING TO WIN

The unofficial motto of our campus hometown is Help Keep Austin Weird. The 2009 Longhorns baseball team was stocked with good citizens who obviously took that request seriously, especially in this game against the University of Southern Mississippi.

For 9⅔ innings, we experienced new depths of awfulness and ineptitude against a scrappy Cinderella team out of Hattiesburg. We surrendered the lead three times. We suffered major breakdowns in pitching and defense, including the first catchers-interference call in the College World Series in twenty-eight years.

Things finally began to look better in the sixth inning when we took a 3–2 lead thanks to an unlikely hero, Russell Moldenhauer. With a 0-2 count against a Conference USA Pitcher of the Year, Moldenhauer clobbered his first home run of the year. He'd spent most of the year on the bench due to injuries and a batting slump, but I'd started Russell as our cleanup hitter on this game. I'd been watching him in batting practice and I had a hunch he was about to break out of Slump City.

In nearly every College World Series, one player comes out of the shadows of the regular season and shines in Omaha. Moldenhauer looked like that guy to me. He'd had a disappointing regular season, but Russell was an honor student and had a great attitude. Instead of hanging his head, he'd schooled himself on every aspect of his game. He'd been reading classic books on hitting and the mental aspects of baseball. He also studied videos of major-league players with the best swings.

When I benched him early in the season, Russell didn't sulk. Instead, he volunteered to keep records of each pitch thrown by opposing pitchers, thinking it might improve his hitting.

I love ballplayers with that spirit, and I try to reward them at every opportunity. But I wasn't just doing Russell a favor. His hard work and good attitude were paying off. He was crushing the ball with confidence in batting practice.

By the end of this series, they were calling him Molden-homer. Russell knocked out 4 home runs in the College World Series and awakened the giant within. Veteran sportswriter Rick Cleveland of Jackson, Mississippi, described my Moldenhauer lineup move as "mystic." I'd prefer to think of it as simply a case in which a young man's great attitude and hard work paid off in runs batted in.

Even with Russell's bat unleashed, Southern Miss was not going down without a fight in this game. This team was averaging 10 runs a game. They kept rallying and tied the score again in the top of the ninth, 6–6.

But then, they let us walk away with it.

With one out in the bottom of the ninth, Travis Tucker was hit by a pitch, putting him on first. Our next batter, Brandon Belt, drew a walk, which resulted in Southern Miss's yanking their pitcher. USM's reliever struck out Tant Shepherd for the second out, but then walked Kyle Lusson, which brought shortstop Brandon Loy to bat with the bases loaded.

This looked like a "moment" in the making. Brandon's mother presented Brandon with his first bat and ball at the age of two. Rumor was the kid slept with them. His batting average in high school was .517.

Surely Brandon must have felt he was born and bred for this moment. I sensed it. So I called a meeting before he could dig in at home plate. The Southern Miss pitchers had been having control problems all day, and the guy on the mound looked to be coming down with the same virus. They'd walked 8 runners in the game. We hadn't had a hit this inning, but they'd loaded the bases for us with walks and wild pitches.

I gave Brandon my most encouraging and inspiring expression, looked him in the eyes, and told him firmly, "Don't swing. You're going to take."

Brandon was a good soldier. He nodded and stepped up to the plate, making sure to crowd it so the strike zone seemed even smaller. The next four pitches were balls. Brandon walked and we scored without firing a shot, winning 7–6.

The folks in Omaha hadn't seen nothin' yet.

GAME SEVEN: BETTER LATE THAN NEVER

"Where does the delightful madness stop? Does it have to stop?" asked Austin sportswriter Kirk Bohls after our out-of-body, out-of-mind College World Series game with Arizona State.

I had no answer for him. This Longhorn team not only defied explanations, they defied natural law.

"They're finding ways to win that's nothing short of miraculous," I said.

For once, nobody accused me of overstatement.

We went into the Arizona State game as underdogs even though we were the top-seeded team in the tournament. But that wasn't any stranger than what occurred in the game itself:

- Before we came to Omaha, our freshman pitcher Taylor Jungmann had not served as a relief pitcher for three months. But in this game and for the second straight time, he held a powerful-hitting team scoreless during his time on the mound.
- Our sophomore catcher, Cameron Rupp, had gone 28 games without hitting a home run at the beginning of this season. He hit 2 in this game.
- A Longhorns team that was infamous for its lack of hitting and reliance on small ball transformed into a crew of sluggers. They had 14 hits against Mike Leake, the Pac-10 Pitcher of the Year who had a 16-1 record and a contract with the Cincinnati Reds in his back pocket.

Did I mention that we were losing 0–6 in the fourth inning?

At that point I called a team meeting in the dugout. It was time to go to church once again. I reminded our players of all the incredible comebacks we'd staged during the season and so far in this tournament.

"Don't worry about being down 0–6. Just think about how good it will feel to come back and win this game," I told them.

It must have felt good. They knocked ASU's star pitcher and first-round draft pick off the mound, hitting him harder than he'd been clubbed all season. Cameron Rupp hit a three-run homer to cut ASU's lead in half. Then Preston Clark and Connor Rowe hit back-to-back singles. Travis Tucker bunted in another run. Brandon Belt drove in two more with a single.

Tie game.

In the next inning, Cameron Rupp did to the relief pitcher pretty much what he'd done to the starter. He smashed the first pitch over the same section of the right-field wall, giving us the lead. We added three more runs in the eighth to seal the deal.

Down 0–6 after four innings against one of the best pitchers in college baseball?

No problem!

GAME EIGHT: RUPP-ROWE COMBO

Three days later, we drew Arizona State for the game that would determine whether we went into the championship finals. We were tied at 2–2 through 5 innings in yet another barn burner.

Luckily, we had no shortage of supermen ready to step up.

Austin Wood had come in as a relief pitcher, and he'd already struck out 6 batters when he faced ASU's Kole Calhoun, who was on a roll with 9 hits and 11 runs batted in during the series. One man was on base.

Our pitching coach, Skip Johnson, conferred with Austin and suggested that he walk Calhoun. Austin must have reminded him that he had a baseball cap headed for the Hall of Fame because they scratched that idea.

"I laughed at him," Wood said later. "I like challenges."

Austin and Kole battled to a 2-2 count, then squared off.

Calhoun must have been expecting a fastball, but if so, he's still waiting for it. Wood threw him a beautiful slow-motion, 79-mile-per-hour changeup low and away.

Swing and a miss.

Two outs.

The next batter did better. He nailed a fastball for a triple and scored a run, giving ASU the lead. We got out of the inning when Travis Tucker snagged a line drive, so we came up to bat in the bottom of the ninth needing one run for a tie and two to win.

Austin Wood felt bad about giving up that run, but his teammates gathered around and promised to win the game for him. They held a meeting in the dugout and reminded each other of all the games they'd won with rallies in the final inning.

We liked big finishes so we decided to give 'em another one.

Our first batter struck out, but Cameron Rupp stepped up with enough confidence for ten teams. I turned to Austin in the dugout and said, "Here comes a fastball. Let's see what he can do with it."

The umpires and media reported that Cameron knocked the fastball more than 408 feet, over the center-field wall. It was gone so fast I think the force of his swing may simply have turned the ball into cosmic dust.

Cameron savored the moment, trotting around the bases before scoring the tying run. Business as usual.

Preston Clark may have been a bit too pumped up following that display. He swung for the Rockies but popped it up to the catcher.

Two outs.

Connor Rowe stepped into the batter's box. At 5-10, 170 pounds, Rowe is built more like a cross-country runner. But he packs a lot of muscle on his wiry frame, and he unleashed it at just the right time. The first pitch was a changeup and Connor hit it into the first row of the left-field seats for his seventh homer of the season.

Walk-off homer. Game over. We were in the championship finals.

Connor dashed around the bases doing a whirling-dervish dance, then dove into a Longhorn pile that was half group hug and half mosh pit. Somewhere in the madness, Austin Wood had his nose bloodied by an inadvertent elbow shot thrown by an umpire scrambling to avoid the stampede. You could hardly blame the ump, this was a runaway team.

THE FINALS

The second win over Arizona State put our Longhorns in the best-of-three final against Louisiana State University to determine the national championship. The first game had all the usual drama but not our typical climactic conclusion.

Once again, the tall Texans dispatched the bad guys, kissed the prettiest girls, and rode out of town on the best horses.

Russell Moldenhauer continued his spectacular ascension from Slump City with 2 of our 5 solo home runs in the game. We had a 6–4 lead going into the ninth. I felt good about that since we'd won all 39 games in which we had a last-inning lead in the regular season. But later in the game, we had more pitch problems than an *American Idol* loser.

LSU tied the score in the ninth.

The U.S. cavalry apparently did not get my text messages calling for help. We never scored again. LSU singled in the winning run in the eleventh, and we finished the game without a flourish, going three up and three down with two strikeouts and a ground-out.

We did better in the next game; not great, but better—and with a much better result. Led by a terrific display of fielding by our third baseman, Mike Torres, we ground out a 4–3 win over the Tigers.

Still, cracks kept appearing in our defense. We'd had the fourth-best fielding percentage in the country coming into the CWS, but we'd been bumbling and stumbling in Omaha. We had 6 errors in 3 games even though we were also making some spectacular plays and pulling out victories.

Our magical run was about to end.

The final game was not our finest hour. We'd hope to go back to church, but instead we were taken to school by the No. 1–ranked Tigers of LSU. One of their players who hadn't even made the lineup in our previous game drove in 3 runs. Kevin Keyes hit a big two-run homer, but twice we failed to score with the bases loaded.

I knew our season's supply of mojo was maxed out when our official CWS superhero, Russell Moldenhauer, blasted another shot into left center only to have the LSU fielder run it down as if it had been hit by a mere mortal.

We lost.

They won.

LSU took home the trophy. We left the field with runner-up regrets.

I tried to be philosophical but I'm not sure my heart was in it.

"There are worse sports than baseball," I told one writer. "Sports like gunfighting and gladiator sports; those are sports where you can only lose once. Those are sports I am glad we weren't playing tonight."

I characterized our loss of the championship series not as an end but as a beginning. Cynics may say that's a loser plastering lipstick on a pig, but I believed it and so did our team.

Coming back time after time, confounding our critics and cheering the cynics, we found something out there. We learned about ourselves and each other. Our experiences bonded us for life in ways that will only become apparent with the passing of time.

Longhorns will be boring their grandchildren to tears for years to come with tales of their 2009 odyssey. The journey took me from the depths of my DWI arrest to the heights of a thrilling run at the national championship with a team that never stopped surprising themselves or the coaches and everyone in the stands, press boxes, and watching on TV.

What a long, strange trip it had been . . . but then something even stranger and more wonderful happened to cap off a wondrous season.

By the time our plane of losers had left Omaha and landed in Austin, the Longhorns were heroes again. We were stunned to receive a water-cannon salute from the fire trucks at the Bergstrom International Airport, and even more shocked to find a big crowd gathered in hundred-degree heat at our home field on campus.

They cheered us as if we were champions, and even more amazing, they kept cheering for days, weeks, and months to come. All over Austin and across the state, the focus wasn't on what we'd lost at the very end. Instead, they talked about what we'd accomplished along the way.

It was simply phenomenal.

In a hard-nosed state known for accepting only winners, we were widely and warmly embraced. With so much enthusiasm and so many congratulations for a fine season, we sometimes had to remind ourselves that we had not claimed the ultimate trophy. Why did we get this reception?

The reward is not always on the scoreboard. What is won is not nearly as important as who we become. In the larger accounting, we came out ahead. I believe our 2009 team inspired people with its contagious spirit. These Longhorns never quit. They defied the odds. They never lost faith in each other. And they always pushed themselves to be their best.

I think the people of Texas, home of the Alamo and the battle of San Jac, admire that sort of heroic spirit. Texans appreciate selflessness and unity in the face of adversity. These young men became part of something greater than themselves. They will be remembered as a captivating Longhorns team, beloved by the University of Texas, the city of Austin, and the Lone Star State.

The unprecedented celebration of our 2009 nonchampionship season was not the result of collective amnesia, nor was it some form of mass hysteria; it was perhaps the greatest public display I've ever witnessed of a gospel truth. One taken from the Church of Baseball.

The Longhorns' assistant athletic director, Bill Little, cited this in reference to the movie *The Bad News Bears* upon our return to Austin. He noted that the popular sandlot baseball movie was widely loved not because the bad news kids won in the end—they lost. Instead, people loved the team in the movie "because of who they became, and the fact that they took us all along for the ride. They were totally human, and absolutely fun."

The spirit of the 2009 Longhorns fit that description to a Big *T*.

CHAPTER TEN

Five Things I Think
I Know about Baseball

Every day, baseball teaches me something new—about how it should be played, about the people who play it, and about myself. So, I don't pretend to know much for sure. As I mentioned earlier, I'm still living on a learner's permit. That said, I will admit to five things I'm fairly certain are true about the sport I've devoted my life to studying and teaching.

So, here they are. Hopefully, I will keep growing and this list will expand; but then again, the sixth thing I know for certain about baseball is that just when you think you know something, this game will make a fool out of you.

I have proof of that. I was coaching at Cal State Fullerton in 1978 when George McQuarn, our basketball coach, stopped me in a hallway one day to introduce me to one of his recruits, a kid out of Long Beach. He wasn't a big guy and he seemed a little heavyset for a basketball player. Coach McQuarn explained that he was recruiting this kid for the basketball team but that he wanted to play baseball too.

He claimed he was an outfielder, but back then we played fall ball and the team was usually set by the time basketball season was over. I told him I'd give him a chance, but I said he might have a hard time making the team if he came out late in the season. The recruit decided to go to San Diego State, where they allowed him to play both basketball and baseball.

That recruit set all sorts of records in baseball and basketball at San Diego State. He also had the distinction of being drafted by both the San Diego Padres baseball team and the San Diego Clippers basketball team—on the same day. He decided to play baseball—I knew he couldn't possibly do both!

Still, he did okay in the major leagues. After winning his seventh batting title in the major leagues, the former recruit Tony Gwynn told a *Los Angeles Times* reporter that Coach Augie Garrido had discouraged him from playing at Cal State Fullerton. Despite the distraction of having played college basketball, Tony played twenty seasons for the Padres and made the all-star team fifteen times. He was inducted into the Baseball Hall of Fame as one of the best hitters in the history of the game.

Tony is now the baseball coach at his alma mater, where the stadium is named after him. Unfortunately for me, our teams often play each other. He never forgets to remind me that I knew better than to accept a player who thought he could play two sports. Tony is not the only one to rub it in. Several years ago, I heard that Coach McQuarn had undergone a triple bypass, so I called him at the hospital to see how he was doing.

"Oh, I'm fine, Augie," he said. "By the way, have you seen what Tony Gwynn is hitting this season?"

So, with the Tony Gwynn caveat, here's what I *think* I know about baseball.

I. BASEBALL IS NOT A GAME THAT BUILDS CHARACTER, IT REVEALS CHARACTER

In 1979, our Cal State Fullerton team made its second trip to the NCAA Division I championship and the College World Series. We quickly lost our first game 6–1 to Mississippi State. Luckily it was a double-elimination tournament back then, but it was do-or-die from there on out. Since our only previous trip to the CWS in 1975 had quickly ended with losses in the first two games, I knew our players would be sweating it.

"This is going exactly our way," I assured them. "We have them right where we want them. From here on out, everyone we play will feel just like you do now, and they will be playing not to lose. We'll be playing to win."

That Titan team won our next four games, which put us in the championship final for the first time in Fullerton's history. Someone dubbed this team the Junkyard Dogs because they were fierce mutts who hadn't, for the most part, been recruited by the bigger schools. We were deep, talented, and stocked with players eager to prove that they were every bit as good as the guys from the power-house schools.

They'd already given notice. We'd been ranked as the third-best team in the country going into the College World Series.

Our opponent in the championship final was Arkansas. At that time, the Razorbacks had never won an NCAA championship in a team sport—any sport. So they were hungry. We were both considered big-hitting, big-scoring teams—we'd scored 46 times in the previous 5 games, they'd scored 34—but we'd beaten them once already.

We'd also beaten Pepperdine, the other upstart small school, to get to this final game, though only after one of our top pitchers, Dave Weatherman, was knocked off the mound in the first inning. Ironically, Dave had been recruited by Pepperdine but turned them down because the coach who recruited him talked so much about his plans for beating Fullerton that Dave figured he might as well play for us. I guess Pepperdine took their revenge.

Though he was a good pitcher, Dave really struggled in the first inning. Even so, his record was 14-2 going into the tournament. Pepperdine jumped all over him right away with a two-run homer followed by another run. We had to take him out before we fell too deep into a hole. Dave didn't argue with our decision to pull him, but he did go down into the visitors' locker room and wreak a little havoc. While he was venting, his teammates were saving the game. By the time he came back out into the light, we had the lead.

After the final out, we took just a minute to congratulate ourselves, then we began preparing for the final against Arkansas the next day. I'd heard it was supposed to be a stormy day, so when someone in the press asked me whom I was going to start on the mound, I shrugged and said I was going with the weather, man, either the one on TV or the one on our team.

I just figured Dave hadn't pitched all that much in that first inning against Pepperdine so he was as rested as anybody else we had. Plus, I knew Dave felt he had something to prove. He also had the confidence and the determination to go back out and give us a good game. I'd been telling those Fullerton players that at times in their lives they'd want something so badly they'd be willing to do anything to get it—whether it was a girl or a game or a dream job. The determining factor, I told them, would be whether they were prepared to meet that challenge. I'd watched Dave Weatherman work his ass off in practice and games all year. I figured he was prepared.

I walked past him in the dugout after the Pepperdine game and told him, "Get some sleep tonight. You are on the mound tomorrow."

He thought at first I was joking. Years later, he said he'd wondered if I'd somehow missed his first-inning implosion. I hadn't. I simply thought he could get the job done for us and I wanted to give him that opportunity. The skies were ominous the next day, threatening a storm that never came. It was cold and windy, but the gales were blowing in, which boded well for pitchers and bad for batters.

Dave had his usual first-inning jitters. He went to 3-0 on the first batter, then 3-1, before the Razorback did him a favor and grounded out. Dave settled down then, despite battling a sore arm. For the first four innings, whenever the Titans came in to bat, Dave hustled down to the showers where our pitching coach and trainer worked on his arm, shooting hot water on his shoulders and massaging his arm to keep it loose and reduce the soreness.

In the top of the fifth, the Razorbacks scored a runner from second when a batter hit a shot right at Dave and he couldn't get to it. He was so ticked off at himself that he refused to go for his rubdown that inning. Instead, he stayed in the dugout, which turned out to be a good thing because his teammates rallied to bail him out while he cheered them on. We tied the score. Then we punched out another run in the bottom of the sixth, and Dave really kicked in. He shut down Arkansas's batters in the final three innings to give us our first NCAA championship.

If you asked him the next day about the last half of the game, Dave couldn't have told you much, and he still can't, because as the game went on, he became locked in his own world. His teammates recall that they tried to talk to him in the dugout, but our pitcher was so focused he didn't hear a word they said.

"They didn't call it 'being in the zone' back then, but whatever it was, I was in it," he told me recently.

Dave signed with the Oakland A's and played a couple years in the minors before joining the coaching staff of his former Fullerton pitching coach Bill Kernen at California State University, Northridge. Then Dave ran a baseball school for several years as a side job while working his way up the corporate ladder. He now manages an American Honda Corporation data center in Longmont, Colorado.

Dave Weatherman agrees with his old coach that baseball reveals character. He didn't consciously recognize what he'd taken from his playing days until several years had passed.

"You feel like a winner coming out of that baseball program, and I've come to understand the value of that over the years," he said. "A while back, one of my own former players told me a story that reminded me of something I learned about myself while playing at Fullerton. This player, Denny, had taken over his late father's business, and he was determined to do whatever it took to not only keep it from failing but to build upon what his father had done. He believed that he could make it work if he put everything he had into it and refused to give up.

"In sharing that with me, Denny reminded me that since college I'd lived with that same mind-set. I can remember thinking at various times that I was in a rough spot but feeling I would figure it out somehow and land on my feet. Even if it meant longer hours and even days of extra work, I always trusted things would be okay. I learned to have that sort of confidence while playing baseball at Cal State Fullerton, where we worked our tails off to be prepared and then trusted that the outcome would be positive. I learned to manage my fears and to control those things I could. That's one of the many positive things I took away from the game. My expectation is always that by working hard I can make good things happen, that I will figure it out eventually."

Baseball continues to teach Dave, as he was reminded when he heard Huston Street talking about his Longhorn experiences in the documentary *Inning by Inning* put together by my friend Rick Linklater. Huston said he'd learned "that pressure is a choice and I've carried that with me. The whole idea is that everything is a choice. You have to choose what you focus on. . . . In the game if you can focus on the right things, then the results will take care of themselves."

Dave said that Huston's words resonated with him. "Most people go through life thinking they have no control, and that is incorrect," Dave said. "When you feel yourself growing angry or going somewhere you don't want to go emotionally, you can consciously self-correct, which is huge. I've tried to use this in my personal life, and I have shared this philosophy with my staff, family, and friends. Just knowing that they have a choice can make a difference for many people."

2. THE FUN IS IN THE FUNDAMENTALS

The temptation for many athletes is to overthink the game, making baseball more complex than it should be. But when a player tries to do too much, he sets himself up for failure. I tell our guys that baseball is a game designed for twelve-year-olds and that's the spirit they should play with. No matter how old you are, go out and play your game as if you were twelve-year-olds. Have fun with it.

To have fun playing baseball, you have to put aside all the distractions and expectations and simply play the game just the way you played it when you were a kid. Back then, you just went out and swung the bat and threw the ball and let the score take care of itself. As you become more experienced and get better coaching, you hopefully master some of the more advanced fundamentals, such as those Kevin Lusson demonstrated in our 11-inning game with Texas A&M in the 2010 season.

One of the many fundamentals taught by college coaches but rarely shown on highlight films or applauded by fans is the *high-quality at bat*. This isn't just about getting a hit or putting a man on base, it's also to make a pitcher throw as many pitches as possible, forcing him to work harder than he wants to work. We make it a goal in each at bat to wear down the opposing pitcher as much as possible, to frustrate him and to force him into making mental and physical mistakes.

Kevin, whose older brother Kyle also plays for the Longhorns, had the best at bat by any player in the season during that close game with our longtime rivals at Texas A&M. His fundamentals were so strong that he set a benchmark for his teammates. We coach players to run up the count on pitchers whenever possible, especially early in the game so they will tire and make mistakes.

The pitcher is the most influential player on the field. Some say he has 80 percent of the power to control the game, and I agree that it's way up there. So anything we can do to steal away some of his influence, we will do.

If we can force the pitcher to throw 30 pitches in an inning, then even if we haven't scored a run, we feel that we've made some progress. Kevin Lusson obviously paid attention in this class. With one man on base, Kevin locked into a battle with one of the best college pitchers in the country, Barret Loux, who was ranked fourth in the nation for strikeouts. Kevin stood in there like a warrior and made the 6-5, 220-pound pitching machine, who was drafted out of high school by the Detroit Tigers, throw pitch after pitch to him.

Time after time, Lusson fouled off the good ones and let the bad throws go by. Kevin made the Aggies' star throw 12 pitches to him. He made a statement and then added a punctuation mark by slamming the final pitch over the fence for a two-run homer.

We won that extra-inning game by one run, so Kevin's 12-pitch at bat was critical. More important, he provided a demonstration of great fundamental baseball that inspired his teammates and made his coach happy. Kevin was in the zone, focused only on the ball coming at him. The Aggies pitcher didn't want to walk him so he kept laying them in there, and Kevin fouled them off until he forced Loux to throw him a home-run ball.

All of our players know how to do that, but staying locked in and making it happen is a major feat, especially when the player is struggling. That is where the real challenge is. Kevin is a great athlete, a former high school quarterback, who battles with his own expectations of perfection. But in that at bat, he found the fun in a fundamental. He wasn't trying to meet anyone's expectations. He was beyond trying. He was playing. Kevin was simply locked in on seeing the ball and reacting to it in the moment. That is where the spiritual stuff takes place, in that zone. He wasn't trying to get a hit or drive in a run. He was keeping it simple, playing with courage, trusting his swing, and allowing his instincts to take over.

Our coaching mantra to players is that the key to hitting is not to focus on batting averages; it's about quality at bats. Kevin Lusson demonstrated the power of that fundamental fact. He took on one of the best strike-throwers in college baseball pitch by pitch and beat him.

If you understand and love baseball, you have to love moments like that. You won't see highlight films of a player standing in there and fouling off pitch after pitch, but coaches should reward that sort of play because it will win ball games. Our offensive system rewards people not just for the usual glory plays but also for making productive outs, for advancing and scoring runners, for putting down bunts, taking walks, and even taking strikes that aren't located in the right place for the hit we need.

The hero myth is so dominant in our society that it takes real courage to stay with the fundamentals. The player who hits a pop fly with a full count and the bases loaded is a hero wannabe who has failed because he was trying when he should have been playing. Kevin Lusson proved during that 12-pitch at bat that he has the courage and the character to be a great hitter if he releases everything else and just plays the way he is capable of playing.

To find the fun in fundamentals, you have to let the child in you run free because baseball is a game. It's not work. It's play. The hitter has to be aggressive and competitive and intense but also relaxed and trusting of his skills. The key is in finding that balance. Baseball will beat up on you if you have not developed routines and processes in practice.

Fun for the player comes as a result of giving his best effort and being caught up in the flow of the game with all of his energy and talents fully engaged. The fundamentals are the details that each player must master to be in control of his game and confident in his role on the team. They include the critical aspects of offense and defense, the mental focus, and teamwork skills.

Often, the young players who come to us out of high school don't have a team mind-set, nor do they have much understanding of the mental aspects of the game. Coaches, scouts, and other serious students of baseball talk more and more of their concerns about the "Trophy Generation" of young athletes who've grown up being rewarded for showing up. They are awarded ribbons, trophies, or gold stars for every at bat or just for the heroic glory plays such as home runs and no-hitters. The Trophy Generation has been nurtured by the proliferation of pay-for-play organizations. These young men often lack the gunslinger instincts necessary to win at our level of play.

We want our players to be aggressive competitors because the cruelties of baseball can easily defeat those who are not driven to do whatever it takes to win. Earlier in my career, the pay-for-play system was not in place and the players we recruited were often from the sort of backgrounds that required them to be fiercely competitive, tough-minded, and team-oriented.

They knew they had to be team players if they wanted to be in the game and in position to win. We spent more time developing their physical skills; probably 90 percent of our practices went into those, and 10 percent went into the mental game. Now it's about a 50-50 split because today's athletes come to us with more physical skills but less understanding of the importance of teamwork and mental conditioning. We tell each player early and often that he controls his role on the team and the level of his performance. It's all about mastering the fundamentals to the point that you don't have to try, you just play. This requires self-awareness, knowing when to be mindful of what you are doing and when to just go out with confidence and play for fun. That is the whole journey of mastery, being consistently good and sometimes even great.

3. GIVING UP CONTROL GIVES YOU CONTROL

By his own description, John Bryant was a "very high-strung, perfectionist type player" in his days as a Cal State Fullerton Titan. He didn't handle losing or failure well, and as a result he was always trying to control things he could not control. John was a handful for the coaching staff at Fullerton. He was rebellious and outspoken. Early in the 1984 season, he tended to throw hats and bats and say words that grandmothers and preachers found offensive. Patience and self-control were not in his skill set. He broke not just bats but team rules.

If this were a movie review, I'd be required to give you a "spoiler alert" now because I'm about to give away the ending. Today, John Bryant is the longtime associate baseball coach at Santa Ana College, and a high school special-education teacher who works with learning-disabled kids. He is still married to his college sweetheart and is a good father to their daughter and two sons. Although John would be the first to tell you that he still works at releasing the bad and focusing on the good, obviously he learned patience and self-control somewhere. We both like to think it was on the Titan baseball team during that 1984 season. The record book tends to support our shared theory.

Normally a strong hitter, John went through a deep slump early that season. It wasn't because he lacked athletic talent. He had tons of that. His attitude and his approach to the game and to his life were major issues. As he told me recently, "If I had been my own coach, I would have kicked me off the team." If you are thinking that the young John Bryant was a lot like the young Augie Garrido, I wouldn't disagree. My own father once commented that I could never have played for myself, and he was right. I wouldn't have put up with me either.

Our coaches worked with John, and his teammates encouraged and supported him too. We also had Ken Ravizza help him find ways to release his anger and frustrations so his athletic talents didn't go to waste. We asked John to take an index card and write down a goal for each game. We also gave him routines and processes for focusing. He learned to take it step by step and to give up trying to control anything other than himself. This method is applicable for just about any pursuit. If you are struggling with a task that is within your capabilities, break it down into manageable increments or smaller bites.

To help batters focus, for example, Ken instructs them to "control the controllables" by creating a pre-at-bat routine that begins with putting on the batting helment. "Make the act of putting on your helmet the start of your at bat by thinking of it as putting on your 'hitting head.'" The sports psychology consultant notes that the same process can be used by anyone in their work, such as when putting on a tie or an identification card before going to the office. The idea is to have a conscious process for focusing your mind on your mission while blocking out negative thoughts and distractions.

Early in the season, John Bryant put our tools to the test. He came to bat with the bases loaded in the ninth inning. His goal for the game was to remain in control of his emotions and to let the ball tell him what to do instead of being distracted by other things. You could see him fighting to do that as he stepped to the plate. The first pitch came down the middle. Bryant swung and missed. In the past, he might have exploded in anger and lost it. Instead, he stepped out of the box, took a deep breath, then stepped back in for the next pitch. John took a ball and then fouled off a couple pitches. He ran his at bat up to a full count, but when the next pitch came, he swung and missed again, striking out.

He was upset with himself, even devastated, but John didn't throw his helmet or his bat. He took deep breaths and released the stress. He was disappointed. He felt he'd failed, but this time John was determined to learn from his failure rather than being overcome with anger. He was learning to let go of those things beyond his control and that he could choose his response to circumstances and emotions.

I waved John over after that at bat and called over his teammates to make a point to them all. I wanted him and everyone else to understand that he may have struck out, but he had not failed. He had worked the process skillfully.

"That was the best at bat I've ever seen you take," I said. "You worked that pitcher. The game didn't treat you well, but you did what you needed to do."

I told him to stick with the processes we'd given him. "If you follow the process, you can live with the results no matter what they are because you know you did your best," I said. "It's a matter of following the process consistently so that it becomes instinctive."

John's struggles didn't end that day. He did pull out of his slump, though, and he learned to clear his mind, to focus on each pitch, and to take good swings. He also finally had his eyes checked and learned that he needed glasses, which improved his overall vision. All of this helped him become a much better power hitter. He would record 6 triples for the season, which proved that he belonged in the lineup.

Still, John had issues to deal with. Later in the season I had to suspend him and our home-run leader, Bob Caffrey, for breaking curfew on a road trip. An overnight stay after a game turned into a raucous party at a hotel.

Bryant and Caffrey went AWOL during the party and missed curfew by a country mile, so I took their uniforms and locked them away for two weeks while they did hard time on "Dawn Patrol." All season, I'd fought to keep this team on track. I'd wielded carrots, sticks, smoke, mirrors, and duct tape. I even rearranged my entire infield. There was no lack of talent but it was like leading a band of anarchists, infidels, and insurgents. I had to impose order because these lunatics wanted to run the asylum. Bryant and Caffrey found themselves serving as examples, and it wasn't fun.

They had to rise with the sun each morning and run four miles with several select teammates who were also in my doghouse. Then I assigned the delinquent duo to every dirty and undesirable job I could legally force them to do, short of hand-washing their teammates' dirty cars. They shagged balls in the outfield, caught in the bull pen, swept the dugout, cleaned gum off the bleachers, and fetched water for the other players. I let them know that if they didn't do all of those things with the right attitude, their uniforms would stay in storage.

It was a good thing Bryant and Caffrey took me seriously. They were back on the team by the time we entered the regional championships. We played San Diego State in the final game on Memorial Day, and it was 115 degrees on the field. The seats in the stands were like barbecue grills—so hot that the fans couldn't sit on them and had to find places in the shade.

We blew a 7–0 lead and the game went into extra innings. Caffrey and Bryant completed their penance in the bottom of the eleventh when Caffrey got on and Bryant brought him home from second base with a single to win the regionals and put us back in the College World Series.

The delinquent duo had turned into the dynamic duo, and they weren't done yet.

I've written earlier about that 1984 CWS in which we lost the first game but fought our way back to the championship final against the University of Texas. Eddie Delzer was the hero on the mound for that game, but he wasn't the only hero. Caffrey and Bryant responded to adversity about as well as you could ask of two young athletes.

In the championship game, Texas scored in the first inning. In the second, John Bryant made it to first after being hit by a pitch. He then stole second and scored on a ground single to tie the game. We remained deadlocked until the fourth inning, when Caffrey singled to get on. Then John comes up again and smashes a triple to score his partner in crime. Bryant then marched home for the victory on a sacrifice fly.

My season-long "project" player scored two of our runs and knocked in the third to lead us to the NCAA championship by a 3–1 score. It was a huge victory for the team, and a big step to a better life for John Bryant, who learned the power of controlling what you can and letting go of the rest.

"I went through a difficult time, but the support I received from my coaches and my teammates helped me through it," John said recently. "Even today when I have difficult circumstances, I draw upon that experience and the counseling they gave me. I still remind myself to let go of those things I can't control, and to take on big challenges by setting small goals and working on them one step at a time."

4. BASEBALL IS NOT A NINE-INNING GAME; IT IS NINE ONE-INNING GAMES

In the 2009 College World Series, our Texas Longhorns had to beat Arizona State twice to advance into the championship series. We won the first game, and in the second, we demonstrated the importance of approaching baseball not as a nine-inning game but as nine one-inning games.

Arizona State scored their first run in the third inning.

The Longhorns responded with a solo home run to tie the game.

Arizona recaptured the lead in the fourth inning by a 2–1 margin.

We came back in the fifth and tied it again.

The score remained deadlocked until the top of the ninth. The Sun Devils' best hitter, Jason Kipnis, rapped a single and made it to second on an error.

Our pitcher Austin Wood struck out the next two batters, but then the next Arizona State player blasted a shot to right field for a triple, scoring Kipnis and giving the Sun Devils what could have been the winning run. We didn't let them score again, but we went into the bottom of the ninth down 3–2.

I told our players that Mother Momentum was sitting in the wrong dugout at that point. "She's all dressed up for the party and just waiting. Why don't you go over there and ask her to dance?"

The battle for Mother Momentum's affections is the real game within the game of baseball, and it is why I preach that baseball should be approached as nine one-inning games. We want our players to view every inning as a battle for competitive advantage. If you can put runners on base and points on the scoreboard while keeping Mother Momentum on your side, victory is yours.

We had one out before ol' Mama Mo glanced our way in that game. Our catcher, Cameron Rupp, was batting and he'd taken the count to 3-1. Everyone in the stadium knew that the pitcher wasn't about to walk him and put the winning run on base. A fastball was called for. A fastball he threw. And a fastball Cameron clobbered over the center-field wall and maybe over the wide Missouri River into Iowa.

Tie game 3–3.

With that blast, Mother Momentum sashayed over and took a seat in the Longhorn dugout, casting a smile upon outfielder Connor Rowe. Before the game, I'd told an ESPN reporter that Connor was batting ninth in our lineup because he always seemed to find a way to get on base, giving the top of the order a chance to bring him home. Then I added a storm warning about Connor: "He's got some lightning in his body. When he hits it, it can go far."

I love it when our players make me look like I know something.

With two outs and the score tied in the bottom of the ninth, lightning struck. Connor put the pitch over the left-field wall. We won the ninth inning, the game, and a ride to the championship series with Mother Momentum in the driver's seat.

• • •

I've collected a few paintings over the years, but few of them are sports-related. I think the only way to capture the game of baseball would be to do in the style of Chuck Close, the artist and photographer. He takes thousands of small scenes or "pixels" and puts them together to create a larger image. Baseball games are determined pitch by pitch. We coach it as nine one-inning games rather than a nine-inning game because we want our players focused moment to moment, not on the end results.

There are no early-round knockouts in baseball. You might score 20 runs but they might respond with 22. That happens more often than you might think, which is why I love an early lead. Nothing helps a pitcher's curveball like a 5-run head start. Everybody plays better when there is room to breathe. If you are behind or otherwise trying to change the momentum, you can easily fall into the trap of trying too hard. You can come from behind, of course, and I'm thankful that we've done it many times, but it's much easier on my blood pressure if the other team is chasing us.

The danger of approaching baseball as a nine-inning game is that your players won't pay attention to the details of the game as they occur. Instead, they will be looking ahead. College-age males share certain quirky characteristics, and procrastination runs high on the list. Their first priority is to do it later, whatever it is. They'll gladly save their vital energies for a final push. Thus, the coach's insistence on an inning-by-inning strategy.

You get 3 outs every inning; 27 outs in a regular game. When you break it down like that, you gain perspective on how important every pitch and every at bat is. Playing inning by inning, fighting to put bodies on bases and then moving them into scoring position, is a strategy that has worked for us. It puts the focus on the here and now and on the right goals and rewards. With that strategy in mind, our players learn to select pitches they can place in strategic spots to move runners safely home. Productive outs and quality at bats also become important. Small ball is critical to this strategy too. It's all about claiming ground and scoring runs, in any way and every way possible.

Baseball is a series of battles over ninety-foot stretches, the distance between the bases. Every ninety feet gained is critical. So any opportunity to claim one of the four bases is worth seizing. The base runner's job is to keep advancing while also doing everything he can to distract the pitcher and throw off the timing of the defense.

We want our base runners to be speedy but also smart. They need to have a plan and to visualize what they intend to do before stepping off the bag. Once they are off the bag, they need to be focused on the pitcher and trusting of their ability to carry out the plan.

Small steps lead to big things. First base first. Second base second. If your strategy relies on doing the big, flashy things such as belting home runs, great pitching will beat you every time. But with our small-ball strategies, we can kill our opponent with a thousand cuts. If we get in a groove and start cranking out big hits, it's icing on the cake.

5. TO WIN YOU MUST PRACTICE LIKE YOU PLAY AND PLAY LIKE YOU PRACTICE

Our 2010 Longhorns team had a Pflugerville slugger, Kevin Keyes, from that Austin suburb. Kevin is a big, strong outfielder who turned down a contract with the Texas Rangers to play for us. He is one of our best power hitters and always a threat, but early in the 2010 season, the stats showed Kevin's batting average dropped in certain key game situations.

We keep batting statistics for all sorts of scenarios and Kevin's showed that with the bases empty he was batting very, very well— .418 average. That dropped significantly, though, at certain critical moments. With runners on base—including with the bases loaded—Kevin's batting average dropped anywhere from .167 to .067.

After viewing those stats, I called Kevin in during a practice and told him that based on the numbers when he was at bat with runners on base, those Longhorns might as well be running in circles between him and the pitcher because they are all he was seeing.

"You sure aren't seeing the ball—or hitting it when you could bring in the most runs," I said.

This is not an unusual problem for college baseball players, who often get overexcited at the plate when runners are on base. I've worked with Ken Ravizza on teaching our players to practice like they play and to play like they practice, meaning that we want them to maintain a consistent level of performance—a high one—in both practices and games. This also means that in games we want our players to have a process to rely upon in challenging times so they can find focus, return to their routines, and tune out the distractions of fans as well as the expectations of what might happen if they get a hit or fail to get a hit.

It is not enough to simply tell our players to approach the game pitch by pitch. We have to give them the tools and the skills to do that, especially when the pressure is intense. It's just human nature to want to be the hero with runners on base in a big game. For most of their lives, young men who play baseball are rewarded for getting big hits in those situations. So, they focus on the reward rather than their batting routines and the processes. As a result, their heart rates increase, their adrenaline flows, and they don't follow the processes that they've mastered to become good hitters.

Kevin Keyes is not deaf, blind, or dumb. When he is standing in a baseball stadium with eight thousand fans screaming and runners are on base, he gets pumped up. As I noted earlier, we give him and our other players routines to help them calm and focus themselves, but if in games they don't use those routines that they've practiced, they sometimes get lost, fall to the pressure of the situation, and fail.

I reminded Kevin that he needed to react to the ball and let it tell him when to swing instead of thinking about scoring runners.

"Stick with your routines and the process," I said. "The results will take care of themselves."

Just a couple days after our little talk, Kevin Keyes did exactly that. We were in the third inning against the University of Kansas. The score was tied 1–1 and there were two outs. The bases were loaded when Kevin came up to bat. He'd already hit a double in the game and set up our first score.

The Jayhawks pitcher was wary of Kevin's power. He tried to tempt Kevin, but instead of swinging away as usual, Kevin played the way he'd practiced, letting the ball tell him what to do. Kevin battled the pitcher, running the count run up to 3-2. The next pitch was outside, and rather than try to be the home-run hero, Kevin took it for a walk.

Since the bases were already loaded, that walk scored a run, putting us in the lead while leaving the bases loaded, which turned out to be a good thing. The next batter, Kevin Lusson (see No. 2, earlier), rang up his first grand-slam home run of the season.

Then, four innings later, the baseball gods rewarded Kevin Keyes for his patience at the plate. He hit a two-run homer sealing our win with a 10–4 score. Grand-slam home runs are exciting, but for me, the best moment of that game was Kevin Keyes's playing like he practiced, having the confidence and self-control to take the walk that set up the grand slam.

Staying in control of the mental and physical aspects of baseball is a huge challenge. In the weeks that followed, Kevin would again strike out with the bases loaded because he's human and baseball is a tough game. Yet, he made some excellent progress after our talk, knocking out a series of big hits with runners on base, including 3 homers in one two-day stretch.

Kevin Keyes won't become a stronger hitter in games. He'll have to do that in practice. Baseball games, like wars, are won and lost before the battle ever begins. They are won in training or practice, when skills are learned, refined, and mastered. Every major college program today has a teacher-coach at the helm, and they all run practices that are highly organized with competitive segments that mimic game conditions. It hasn't always been that way. Before I played for Pete Beiden at Fresno State, most of the practices I'd seen consisted of someone dumping bats and balls out of a bag and then telling us to take some hacks and shag some balls. Back then, most coaches were more like managers. They didn't teach the intricacies of the physical game, and they sure didn't offer help with the mental aspects of baseball.

Coach Beiden was one of the first coaches I'd seen run highly organized and disciplined practices, and his successes inspired others to do the same. He was also much more of a teacher and a strategist than most, and his methods became a model. Like many other of his former players who went on to become coaches, I used Pete's practice methods and added my own touches. I borrowed individual and team development drills from football and basketball coaching to hone physical skills, and Ken Ravizza helped me develop and refine the mental skills to play the game, which began at Cal State Fullerton and continues to this day.

My coaching staff helps each player develop routines and processes for focusing the body and mind during games, then we practice those over and over in game conditions by having scrimmages and other competitive drills during practice. Freshman and other new players are often surprised at the pace of our practices. There is not much time for lounging around or socializing because we want them to bring an A-game mentality to both games and practices. If we maintain that mentality and play at a high level on the practice field and on the stadium diamond, then the hope is we will be at least good all of the time and even great some of the time.

I can bore people to death with my philosophies and schedules on practice, but I've also been known to make things interesting by providing watermelons to the team that wins our scrimmages, or burning stuffed chimpanzees at the stake on the pitcher's mound to "get the monkey off our backs" when we haven't been playing well and can't get over it.

Some of my former Cal State Fullerton players are particularly fond of the practice in which I threatened to shoot the university's fencing coach, Les Bleamaster, who'd fenced in the Olympics. Coach Bleamaster often gave fencing demonstrations on campus and around the area, so he was well-known and respected before I decided to make him my (ahem) foil one day at a Titans practice.

I blew the whistle, and my top, that day because our players weren't putting out much effort in practice or in games. So, in a sense, they were practicing like they played and playing like they practiced, but not at a high level; they were loafing on the practice field and on the ball diamond.

"You are not focused and you are not doing your best," I lamented.

Then, searching for a way to grab their attention, I said, "You all know the fencing coach here. He's a former Olympic competitor, a great swordsman. But do you know that if he challenged me to a duel, I would win? Yes, I would win because if he came at me with his sword, I'd pull out a gun and I'd shoot that son of bitch. I wouldn't have a chance against him if all I had was another sword. I'd have to find another way to beat him. That's what this team needs to realize. We can't beat anybody right now unless we find a different way to do it because their fundamentals are better than ours. We need a different way to win. I'm trying to teach you how to practice to win. I'm giving you that different way, but so far, you won't take it! I've got the guns for you, but you are all holding on to your swords and you're going to get cut to pieces!"

That speech probably won't be filed in the Baseball Coaches

Hall of Fame, but it worked in that moment. My point then, and now, is that your work ethic isn't something you can flip on and off. If you haven't paid the price by working hard in practice and mastering the necessary skills, you won't be able to call upon them when you need them in a game. That is why we demand our players do their best in practice.

> When [Augie] let loose, you felt like you let him down, like you let your best friend down or your dad down. You genuinely felt like "I disappointed this person," and the players use that as a motivational tool to turn it around. It was like we have to turn this around. It's not that we have to do it for ourselves, personally, or for Texas baseball; "I have to do this for Coach Garrido."
>
> BUCK CODY
> *University of Texas*
> *San Francisco Giants*
> *Real estate marketing associate*

My practice ploy worked for the Titans of Fullerton that year. They went on to win the College World Series. A few years later, I tried a different strategy to motivate my new charges at the University of Texas in Austin. It didn't go so well.

The baseball program had been through some tough years, and I felt we needed to make a fresh start, so I came up with the idea of challenging the Longhorns baseball team members—none of whom had been my recruits—by giving them practice uniforms that lacked any of the usual team symbols or words. I told them that if they wanted Texas *T*'s on their uniforms, they'd have to earn them. "You don't get them until you earn them," I announced.

Okay, so I hadn't really thought out my Texas challenge. There I was, the new coach brought in to replace a beloved and legendary predecessor, who'd been there twenty-nine years, immediately telling all these players who'd grown up in Texas and who'd been playing for Texas that they had to convince me—the Californian—that they deserved the right to wear the word *Texas* and the Texas *T* on their uniforms.

Let's just say the reviews on my effort to start anew were decidedly mixed. A common response was "Who the hell does he think he is?"

We had a couple bad years after that, then, gratefully, we had some good ones. Needless to say, I don't make our Longhorns earn their *T*'s anymore. I do still believe in the importance of maintaining a high level of performance in practices as well as games. I have more fun in games and I think our players do too because we prepare so well in our practices.

Baseball players are ultimately athlete-performers in much the same way that ballet dancers, figure skaters, gymnasts, and divers are, and for them to ensure their success they have to find joy in mastering their performances. They do that first by practicing and mastering the skills sets and the mental sets. When they find the fun in the process rather than playing for the reward, that is when the joy and the artistry come out.

I began to think of baseball players as performance athletes while my daughter Lisa was taking ballet lessons as a little girl. Watching her practice the five basic foot positions, doing the exercises, and later performing helped me figure out how to teach footwork and body positioning to my players. I actually modeled my methods for teaching the double play on those the ballet instructor used to teach my daughter. The idea is to take the basic steps and movements and to learn them step by step, building muscle memory, then to talk about body positioning and angles, as well as rhythm and timing.

My appreciation for the complexities and physical demands

of ballet grew when I took my daughter to see the movie *White Nights,* starring Mikhail Baryshnikov, who is probably the greatest athlete I've ever seen. In a dance scene in that movie, he is on his knees on the floor and leaps up from that position to standing on his toes. He is in a class all by himself, but Baryshnikov offers an example of the discipline and practice it takes to be the best at what you do. As I tell my players, to become the best, you have to devote your entire lifestyle to it, from what you eat to when you sleep and whom you hang out with.

It's not so well-known that I've performed in a ballet myself, twice. Austin's ballet troupe performs *The Nutcracker* each holiday season. My daughter worked her way up from a mouse to a primary dancer over the years, but I've done two tours as Mother Ginger. Each year they invite a local "celebrity" to perform as Mother Ginger, who makes a brief appearance wearing a giant hoop skirt that conceals a group of children dancers. You only spend about three minutes onstage, but when you're in drag, with giant boobs, a huge wig, and a hoop skirt, it seems like a long time. Being supremely confident in my manhood I had no problem with it, but it helped that the list of others who've donned the Mother Ginger outfit includes Lance Armstrong, Michael Dell, Thomas "Hollywood" Henderson, and Kinky Friedman.

I've used ballet training in my coaching as well as aerobics and yoga. One of the biggest challenges many of our incoming players have is mastering the footwork in fielding, hitting, and pitching. We've incorporated drills from both ballet and gymnastics to help them. The mental challenges of other sports and athletic arts also reflect those in baseball. That really hit me when I saw Olympic ice-skater Brian Boitano being interviewed after his amazing performance in the 1988 Winter Olympics in Calgary. The commentator said it had been a spectacular display and asked if Boitano thought he'd won the gold. Boitano replied that he didn't know what the judges would say but he felt he'd given his best effort, so if someone else won, it was because that person was a better skater. Later, after he'd been awarded the gold for what is widely considered one of the best Olympic performances in history, Boitano offered this, which reflects the same inner struggle that our athletes go through during competition:

"The magic of it was that I came here only expecting to hopefully skate as well as I could. I didn't care so much about the medals. . . . I wanted to prove to myself that under extreme pressure I could hold it together and do it, and that's what I did. As I stepped on the ice, it was hard because there was a voice talking, saying, 'This is it. This is the Olympics!' But there was another voice that said, 'This is like any other competition. You know how to do it. You've done it millions of times.' So it was like a fight, a tug-of-war. I just said to myself, 'Take one thing at a time. You know how to do everything. It can't go wrong if you just do everything that you tell yourself to do.' It was a fight. It was an exhausting fight, pressure at its ultimate, and I'm more proud of myself for getting through it with the best all-around competition I've ever skated in my life than anything else."

Boitano won his gold medal because he practiced like he played, and he played like he practiced.

The biggest thing that [Augie] taught me was that if you are going to do something, don't do it half-ass. Do your best at whatever you do. He also got me to believe that I could do whatever I put my mind to if I made it a priority and put all I had into it.

JOE MARTELLI
Cal State Fullerton
Real estate and investment firm

∎

CHAPTER ELEVEN

Be Your Own Best Friend

Our 1992 team at Cal State Fullerton was loaded with major-league talent including Phil Nevin, whom I mentioned earlier, and also our catcher, Jason Moler, another leader on that team. Jason was a high school football star and played catcher like a linebacker. In fact, the NCAA created what we call the "Jason Moler rule," which prohibits the catcher from blocking home plate if he doesn't have the ball. Jason tended to dare runners to go through him.

In the 1992 College World Series, Pepperdine was rallying and a runner was coming around third to score. The throw from the outfield hadn't come in yet, but Jason blocked the plate, and when the player tried to get to it, Jason flipped him in the air and over home. Our pitcher, Dan Naulty, backed up the play at home. While Jason was catapulting the runner over the plate, Dan fielded the throw and tagged the runner out before he could touch the base, securing the third out and taking us out of the inning. We still lost the game, unfortunately, and the NCAA decided that Jason's big play at home might have been a little too much like football on the baseball diamond.

It was a tough loss, but many of those 1992 Titan team members used that heartbreaking College World Series championship game as motivation to become successful after college. They never wanted that feeling of coming up short again. Jason is one of those who learned valuable lessons from the experience, he says.

Here's his take on what he took away from his college career, which was full of drama, excitement, and character-revealing moments.

I grew up in Yorba Linda, just eight miles from the campus of Cal State University Fullerton. I'd head over to the Titans' ball field to watch Augie Garrido coach whenever I didn't have practice or a game in high school. I knew early on that he was the guy I wanted to play for in college. I liked the way Coach Garrido taught the game. He demanded that his players respect it. He was "old school" and that was the way he expected his teams to play.

I was a football player too and I loved that hard-nosed mentality in a baseball coach. I especially enjoyed watching Augie argue with the umpires on behalf of his players. He had the same philosophy as my dad—extremely tough but always there for us. My dad was an assistant principal, "the hammer," who enforced the school's rules. I didn't always like what my dad had to say, but I did know that he wanted the best for me. I saw that Augie was the same way, and I sensed that he would be good for me as a coach. He's reportedly mellowed a lot, but in those days you couldn't play for Augie unless you had a thick skin. Still, you always knew he had your back if something happened to you.

Though I wasn't drafted by the major leagues out of high school, I was recruited by many of the big schools, including Stanford and Arizona. I'd already decided I wanted to play for Augie at Fullerton, but during my senior year in high school, he took the head coaching job at the University of Illinois.

I followed him to the central-Illinois prairie and flatlands. When we were snowed out on May 6, I knew I was in trouble. Actually, my real trouble was off the field. I'd been raised in a strict household by two teachers who kept the reins tight. My first taste of freedom led me to the bars in campus town, where I quickly found trouble. I was injured and it affected my performance on the field.

Coach Garrido called me into his office.

"What happened?"

"I was drunk. I was an idiot. I got hurt."

"Well, there will be consequences. But I respect the fact that you didn't lie to me. Tell me the truth and I will always back you; lie to me, I'm done with you."

I wasn't the most mature kid but I understood that I needed someone like Augie to keep me in line. Without him I would probably have partied my way right out of baseball. Augie made me pay for my mistakes, but I never lied to him and he was true to his word. He was like a second father to me. The two people I did not want to disappoint were my father and my coach.

Augie was also an incredible teacher. I'd played for one of the top high school baseball coaches in the country so my fundamentals were sound, but Coach Garrido is philosophical and taught more on the mental aspects of the game. I played two years at the University of Illinois, but when Coach Garrido went back to Fullerton, I decided to follow him again. I'd been a third baseman and a pitcher at the U of I, but Augie felt my best chances to make it in the major leagues was as a catcher, so I moved behind the plate my senior year.

I had a good summer in a semipro league in Alaska, and while I was playing in the NBC tournament in Wichita, I was contacted by representatives of the Montreal Expos, the Dodgers, and the Chicago Cubs. I told Coach Garrido about the major-league interest, and he was on the next flight to Wichita. He said he would not normally advise against taking a professional contract because the income opportunities were life-changing. In my case, however, he thought another year of college would only enhance my opportunities.

"You've only been catching for a few months, and look at all the interest you've generated," he said. "If you come back and catch for us next season, I promise you three things will happen. One, you'll be drafted higher and make more money. Two, you will make the Olympic team. Three, we will win a national championship."

Two of those three promises came to pass: I was drafted higher and received twice as much money as I'd been offered after my junior year. I made the Olympic baseball team, but an injury kept me from playing in Barcelona. Unfortunately, we lost the NCAA championship by one run. Augie didn't lose that game, we did. He'd kept his word and proved that he was looking out for my interests.

When he'd recruited me, Coach Garrido promised my parents that I would earn a college degree, and he made sure I did that. During my final season with the Philadelphia Phillies organization, Augie offered me an assistant coaching position in Austin. I decided to retire and start my coaching career. After a couple of years, I figured out that I liked playing more than I liked coaching. I pursued a career in business and sales because it is as close to athletic competition as anything I'd found. As a sales manager, at one time I had hundreds of people working for me, but it was tough to have an impact on so many employees day to day. Now I have a team of thirty, which allows me to coach and teach them, much as Augie did for us. I learned a million things from Augie. The guy had such a powerful impact on my life. I can trace much of what I do each day to his principles and teachings.

One thing I was slow to learn were Augie's lessons on always being your own best friend, meaning to not condemn yourself for mistakes but to be self-forgiving. I wish I'd done more of that. I had extremely high expectations of myself and was harder and less forgiving of myself than anyone else could ever be.

Looking back on it now, I think I would have had a much better career had I been more encouraging and less critical of myself.

I wasn't smart enough at the time to figure that out, but I promise you, now I attempt to teach it to anyone who will listen.

There is rarely a day I don't use something Augie taught me in either my business or in my personal life. Dealing with failure and learning from it, self-motivation, focusing on the process, taking it step by step—all those skills Coach Garrido taught us are a big part of business and life. I've even been known to say to my new hires, "Tell me the truth I will always have your back; lie to me and I'm done with you."

Does that sound familiar?

Jason is now forty years old and vice president of development at Voyager HospiceCare in Austin, where he and his wife, Shannon, have a beautiful place in the country. He is the father of four-year-old twin girls, and he is the sort of young man whom coaches are grateful for having known. I can't say that he needed all that much guidance from me because Jason has wonderful parents who had far more influence on him than I did.

His story reminds me that over the years I've observed a part of human nature that psychologists and philosophers have long talked about. This is that we carry inside us the child we were born to be, what existential philosophers call the authentic self. As we grow up, we often stray from that authentic person because hurts, disappointments, failures, and other things beyond our control lead us to develop protective behaviors out of self-preservation. Instead of retaining the authentic qualities of that child inside us, we become a parent to him or her, and all too often we are hard on that poor kid.

When we build protective walls around the true self, we also tend to shut off access to the person we really want to become. My own battle with insecurities led to my becoming fear-driven, oversensitive to criticism and slights, and unable to forge trusting relationships. Now, as for many people, using fears as motivation worked for me up to a point. As I noted earlier, I was a successful coach, but in my late thirties I realized my relationships were not working and I was headed for a meltdown.

I had become my own worst enemy instead of my own best friend. I had to self-correct and it wasn't easy, but I believe I would never have experienced the success that I've had since, especially in my personal relationships, but in my coaching as well. Like many of my players, I tried to self-parent and I was hard on and unforgiving of myself, and that carried over into my treatment of those around me.

Whatever you do, I encourage you to find a way to do it with joy and passion. Finally, if you screw up or come up short, do for yourself what you would do for your best friend. Don't criticize or condemn; instead, be the encourager. Learn from your mistakes and tell yourself, "You'll get 'em next time."

Let me leave you with that final thought: Forgiveness is a great gift you can give to yourself. Stop beating yourself up, be a self-supporter. I just went through this with one of our players on our 2010 team. This talented young man is a perfectionist and his own biggest critic. He becomes embarrassed if he doesn't perform up to his own expectations, and that tends to make him tense and prone to more mistakes.

The only thing that keeps him from being consistently excellent on the field is that he is so unforgiving of himself.

"You need to ease up on that kid inside you," I told him. "Encourage him. Make him laugh. Remind him of the great things he's done and tell him to go out and play with those images in mind."

This player does listen and takes things to heart, and he is learning to be his own best friend, more and more. I'm going to make sure he does it for as long as he is within my circle of influence, because I believe it's an important step toward fulfilling his destiny.

The same holds for you. Coach yourself to be kind to yourself so that you can become whom you really want to be. Know that it's possible to do whatever it is you do out of passion and joy. Share that, be a friend to yourself and to those around you, and always remember to enjoy the ride.

Now, go out there and have fun with it!

Your coach,
Augie Garrido

Coach Garrido is one of those guys you have to break in with, but once you do, you are in for life. It's the real deal.

DUSTIN MAJEWSKI
University of Texas
Toronto Blue Jays

Acknowledgments

I'd like to thank all of the extraordinary players, coaches, teachers, administrators, family, and friends who have empowered me to look into my heart in all of my endeavors, especially this book. You've helped me identify my true purpose in life and you've given me the confidence and courage to recognize it. I love you all.

Thanks also to my publishing team, including my literary agents Jan Miller Rich and Nena Madonia; my editor at Touchstone/Simon & Schuster, Zachary Schisgal; and to Wes Smith, my easy-going fast-typing collaborator who helped me wrangle my diverse thoughts and experiences into a well-honed message.

Thanks as well to Kevin Costner for providing the Introduction, not to mention his friendship and support, which never ceases to amaze me or to give me strength.